Home Front:
Viet Nam and Families at War

by
Willard D. Gray

Order this book online at www.trafford.com
or email orders@trafford.com

Most Trafford titles are also available at major online book retailers.

Printed in Victoria, BC, Canada.

ISBN: 978-1-4269-2207-7 (sc)
ISBN: 978-1-4269-2208-4 (hc)

Library of Congress Control Number: 2009940360

*Our mission is to efficiently provide the world's finest, most comprehensive book publishing
service, enabling every author to experience success. To find out how to publish your book, your
way, and have it available worldwide, visit us online at www.trafford.com*

Trafford rev. 3/15/10

 www.trafford.com

North America & international
toll-free: 1 888 232 4444 (USA & Canada)
phone: 250 383 6864 ♦ fax: 812 355 4082

Note to the reader: Thanks to the encouragement of a handful of American vets, I have chosen to use the traditional spelling of Viet Nam, which was coined in the seventeenth century by the Vietnamese emperor Gia Long and means roughly "people of south China." As American vet and photographer-author Ted Englemann has pointed out, to combine the two words is ethnocentric at best, culturally insensitive at worst. Imagine, Englemann writes, referring to the Big Apple as "Newyork."

Contents

Acknowledgements

I would indeed be remiss if I did not recognize a few loyal individuals who stood shoulder to shoulder with my family during a traumatic time in our lives and those who were willing to come forward as the social situation grew worse. Especially:

The late Beauford Wilson, a lifelong friend and neighbor.

The late John "Shorty" Lanear, lifelong friend and welder.

The late Pearl Dunahee, oil field teamster and neighbor.

Gene Dunahee, childhood neighbor and friend.

Acquired during our troubled days:

Dan Yount, owner and publisher of my childhood city newspaper.

Judy Gassman, perceptive and knowledgeable journalist employed by my childhood paper.

Donald Bridwell and his late brother, Leonard "Jay."

William "Bill" Dallas Blacker and his late wife, Fern.

Harold Royer, 97 years old, and Julie, his late wife of 64 years.

Tom O'Brien, a newly arrived farmer in my childhood region, together with his sons Larry and Jim, and their wives Teresa and Lisa.

Billie R. Brian, independent oil producer and promoter.

Joe and Pat Funk, former in-laws of my youngest son.

And

William Greenleaf and Matt Kite, inspired writers.

Stan Novak, artist for cover.

Dedication

This book is dedicated to my late daughter, Mary Catherine Gray Jones, who toiled selflessly on her brother's behalf, only to pay a heavy price for such devotion. She hoped to erase the stigma he brought home with him from the battlefields of Viet Nam, but never lived to see the day.

It is also dedicated to my wife of over sixty-one years, Mary Antoinette Hanaka Gray, whose sacrifice is unequaled: first as a nurse serving her country in World War II, and second, as a mother looking after her children during my many years of absence while I served in the regular Army. For her efforts, she earned the scorn of many in her community and estrangement from—and division within—her own family.

I would be remiss if I did not recognize a small but loyal following of friends and neighbors who understood and supported us in our troubling time. They stood by us when no one else would.

Finally, I recognize the sacrifices made by every victim of war. So many of my fellow veterans left the best of their lives on the battlefield and have been trying ever since to repair the wounds sustained while serving their country. My prayers go to them and their families. May each of them one day learn to forgive their tormentors—and themselves.

Preface

The casket is resting atop the burial vault when Mary and I arrive at the little cemetery. A few floral wreaths and a half-dozen potted plants have been placed around the casket, and the cover is adorned with a large floral spray which reads *Mother*. A dozen folding chairs huddle around the casket under a canvas canopy that has been erected to shield us from the afternoon sun.

The casket is closed, with Marianne Seibert resting inside. I have known Marianne for many years, and I know she was, indeed, a loving, caring mother. She was also a poet, teacher, and artist. And she was my good friend.

Only a few mourners have come to pay their respects. Besides her husband Stanley, there are daughters Diane and Barbara, their husbands and children, and four of Marianne's closest friends. The family wanted to keep the service small, and I know Marianne would have approved.

The cemetery occupies the top of a low hill surrounded by checkerboard fields of corn and beans. It is very peaceful and quiet on this warm Saturday afternoon. As the minister begins speaking in low tones, I lift my eyes and look out over the fields and think about the poem Marianne wrote a month before she died. I have read it so many times I know it word for word:

If I should die, know this of me—
There is a little of my home,
Of Germany, in this land, but I am free.
Her flowers, her valleys where I used to roam,
Her woods, her rivers I so loved,
The dust so shaped by family and friends
Under a German sky, a German sun,
Has made a small part of this land her own.
And if my son died under a foreign sky,
So can I . . . so can I . . .

With death approaching, Marianne's thoughts were on the hills, valleys, rivers, and forests of the Cologne region of Germany, where she grew up.

She was sentimentally attracted to a part of the earth and memories that would accompany her to her final days in another land.

But the poem ends, as so many things began and ended for Marianne, with thoughts of her son Michael:

And if my son died under a foreign sky,
So can I . . .so can I . . .

I feel sure that as she closed her eyes for the last time, she was thinking of Michael. Marianne has surrendered to death, but she never surrendered her hope that Michael might yet come home, that he had not died in that fiery helicopter crash in Viet Nam as the Army insisted.

The brief service is over. The small tape player begins playing a German song, and my eyes return to the casket. I will miss Marianne, but I know she is at peace now, after enduring so much. Stanley, hunched in grief, comforted by his daughters, will have to continue somehow without her.

As will Mary and I. For many years we shared a bond with the Seiberts. They spent decades trying to learn the truth about what happened to their son, while Mary and I tried to cope with what happened to ours. I remember the last time I saw Tommy, his face grimly set, his eyes narrow and dark, his hair falling in a lank wave across his sweaty forehead. Tommy returned from Viet Nam alive, but only as a shadow of the young man who had gone there. He scorned his family, and my efforts to have his less-than-honorable discharge upgraded.

Mary and I have shared that bond of loss and grief with the Seiberts. And we aren't alone. There is Penny Hayes, whom I have known for several years. Penny married Viet Nam veteran Ken Hayes, and paid dearly for Ken's involvement in the war even though she didn't even know him at the time.

"I need to forget the bad parts of the past," Penny told me after Ken's death. "I need to forget what it was like to wake up with a gun pointed at my head, or to be held with that neck hold Ken learned from Army training, to have someone beside me think I am the enemy."

It wasn't Stanley and Marianne Seibert who started the war in Viet Nam, or Penny Hayes, or my family. It was a flawed U.S. foreign policy which ultimately failed. But the policymakers have not been called upon to pay the price for their mistakes.

How many other families have paid that awful price? How many are still paying? How many have been devastated by what happened to their sons and brothers and husbands in Viet Nam? And for what? How many Amercian families have been betrayed by the very government that sent their young men to fight and die in distant jungles?

Anger rises up inside me, accompanied by a deep abiding bitterness at that sense of betrayal. I turn to face the afternoon sun, looking out over the cultivated fields, trying to hold onto the peaceful setting. Perspiration runs down my neck, under my collar. I can taste it in the corners of my mouth.

In 1970, more than eight out of ten Americans believed what they were told by Washington about Viet Nam. Only 18% knew it was outright lies and propaganda. In the farm country of southeastern Illinois, it was anathema to question the U.S. involvement in Viet Nam. The Grays and the Seiberts were the only purveyors of variant views regarding the U.S. government's propaganda. In their lonely search for enlightenment about Michael, the Seiberts were reviled by relatives and neighbors. Mary and I also faced hatred and recriminations by local citizens.

Our daughter paid, too: she lost a once-loving brother. Mary Catherine was uniquely able to adapt to circumstances and surroundings throughout her short life. With a degree in art from Rutgers University, Mary became a co-founder of the Rutgers' Art Review and was a week-end escort at the Metropolitan Museum of Fine Art in New York. Before a two-year bout with a brain tumor took her from us in 1993, she begged me not to tell Tommy of her illness or impending death. My daughter once told me, "I will never have children. I wouldn't want them to go through the trauma that we have had to bear."

Most of the mourners have gone now from the hilltop cemetery, and I can see that Mary is ready to go. My eyes return to the closed casket, and my thoughts return to Marianne Seibert. Many years ago she asked me to help her write a book about what happened to our families, and the betrayal of a government that was supposed to protect us. I was involved in too many projects and didn't feel that I had the time to devote to such a book. Now I regret the decision.

Maybe it's time, I think as Mary and I turn to walk slowly toward our car. How many families have endured the same kinds of grief and loss that we've had to endure? Many books have been written about the horrors of war that were faced by America's young soldiers in Viet Nam, but I have not found a single book about the horrors that awaited their families when those men came home.

Can I find those families who are still grieving silently, today, three decades later? Will they talk to me? Thousands of soldiers returned home with Post-Traumatic Stress Disorder, a complex and sometimes volatile condition which was not even recognized by the U.S. government as a disability until 1982. What about the families of soldiers listed as missing in action? Politicians milked the MIA issue long after it had any credibility. Viet Nam veterans returned home to a hostile America, where they were jeered and spat upon. How did this affect their families? How did a man return home to his wife and children after viewing and participating in the carnage of modern war? What was it like for parents whose sons never came home? What was the effect of a less-than-honorable discharge, which barred a man from over 40% of American jobs? What about the families of men who were severely wounded, or exposed to Agent Orange?

I glance at Mary who walks beside me, looking down, quiet in her grief.

I will write the book. It is a silent promise to Marianne Seibert. *I have to let people see what has happened. I have to make them understand.*

PART I:
TWO DIFFERENT ERAS – TWO CONTRASTING OUTLOOKS

On April 17, 2002, two American F-16 fighter jets piloted by Illinois Air National Guardsmen were screaming over rugged Afghanistan when the pilots detected antiaircraft fire from the ground below. Despite being told to hold their fire by AWACS controllers circling overhead, they let loose a 500-pound laser-guided bomb, killing four Canadian soldiers and wounding eight others. The Canadians had been conducting antitank exercises with live ammo. And, though the U.S. military had been notified of the training mission well ahead of time, the pilots may have been left out of the loop.

As details of the friendly fire incident began to emerge, the American public learned about "go pills" and their wide use in the U.S. military. Before flying the ill-fated mission, the two pilots had been ordered by their superiors to take amphetamines and had dutifully complied. Had the mission ended as most usually did – without tragedy for the Americans and their allies – the pilots would have been ordered afterward to take the edge off with a few sleep-inducing "no-go pills." In this case, they were given antidepressants after they touched down. [1]

Just moments earlier, the pilots' range of emotions that would typically be experienced during battle – fear, resolve, and euphoria – had been synthetically squeezed by Dexedrine, a dextro amphetamine known to induce, among other symptoms, paranoia. [2]

When the smoke finally cleared, the somewhat muted criticism in the States paled in comparison to the furor north of the border. Canadian citizens, especially family members of the victims, were shocked by the seeming incompetence of the American pilots, not to mention the dangerous practice of putting jacked-up fighter pilots in the cockpits of thirty-million-dollar killing machines.

Those of us who lived through Viet Nam, however, weren't so shocked. Parents, spouses, siblings, children – and of course the Viet Nam vets themselves – already knew well the volatile art of mixing drugs with war. It was an old practice, dating back at least to America's guerilla war in the Philippines at the dawn of the 20th century. Back then, soldiers used opium.

In Viet Nam, men and women in the American military had more options at their disposal, including speed, heroin, hash, and plain old marijuana, as ubiquitous as cheap canned beer. Combat medics like my son were encouraged to take uppers in the field – whatever it took to remain active and alert. And combat medics like my son were kicked out of the service when they blurred the line between professional and recreational drug abuse. Somehow, only the military higher-ups, with the tacit understanding of the Defense Department and members of Congress, missed the absurdity. That, or they simply saw no reason to blanch at their own hypocrisy.

Drugs, as PBS commentator Bill Moyers pointed out after the tragedy in Afghanistan, are the hidden weapons of modern warfare. "Their use in Viet Nam was so rampant," Moyers stated flatly, "many soldiers came home addicted . . . But when those addicted came home, they were largely on their own; our government, whether Democrat or Republican, considered waging a war on drugs more important than helping addicted people recover." [3]

In 1968, after the Tet Offensive had disabused many of the notion of a quick war, as many as 1,000 American soldiers were being arrested every week for possession of marijuana. In one case study involving Major General John Cushman's GIs in the Mekong Delta, heroin use ran as high as twenty percent. By 1973, it had peaked at thirty-four percent across the board in Viet Nam. While Americans were contributing roughly $88 million to the Viet Namese drug market, over a thousand U.S. soldiers were sent packing each month, returning stateside as drug addicts and the owners of less-than-honorable and dishonorable discharges. [4]

Once home, they were left to their own devices. No debriefing. No drug counseling. Just the certain knowledge that their blemished records would forever haunt them.

Not everyone who served in Viet Nam abused drugs, of course. The majority never touched the stuff, professionally or recreationally. And most soldiers, whether they were using drugs or not, comported themselves with honor and dignity while selflessly fighting a dubious war, many losing their lives in the proud service of their country. Those who survived came home changed. And they found a changed world awaiting them.

Surely the mishap in Afghanistan would have been incomprehensible to them before their tour in the bush. Now, some three decades later, it seems a predictable outcome to the fifty- and sixty-somethings whose idealism took a direct hit in Viet Nam. "For in much wisdom is much vexation," says the Preacher in Ecclesiastes, "and he who increases knowledge increases sorrow."

Nothing educates quicker than war, its lessons dispensed in stark and brutal fashion. What Viet Nam and every war since has brought home to soldiers and their families is that we stand to lose more than our lives in battle. If we're not careful, we lose hope. We lose moral clarity and the courage to insist on the truth, however discomfiting. We lose ourselves.

\#

Is there any way to make right the wrongs that Viet Nam dealt to the men and women who fought there, and for their families who also pay the price?

Unfortunately, the answer is no. But an amnesty for those who were given less-than-honorable discharges would go a long way toward helping.

Barry Lynn, executive director of Americans United for Separation of Church and State, and a former lobbyist for the United Church of Christ, testified in front of Congress several times in the mid-1970s. He had studied the issue extensively, even helping some Viet Nam vets upgrade their discharge status. He went public with his findings in *The Nation* on December 24, 1977.

There were, Lynn testified, more than 450,000 Viet Nam vets who had been sent home between 1964 and 1973 with something less than a fully honorable discharge. According to Lynn, the U.S. military had issued 32,000 dishonorable (for felonies) or bad conduct discharges and 425,000 undesirable or general discharges "with no hearing in most cases and with minimal due process protections even when hearings were held [no verbatim transcripts, no confrontation with hostile witnesses]. The discharges were rarely given for serious crimes, but usually for absence, disobedience, political activism, and trivial noncriminal misdemeanors related to an unwillingness to adjust to military life."

There have been some 30 amnesties issued by the presidents and Congress through the 1940s. The last amnesty was issued on December 24, 1952, by President Truman for, "All persons convicted for having deserted between Aug 1945 and June 25, 1950." On December 8, 1863, President Lincoln issued the following, "Full pardon to all implicated in or participating in the existing rebellion with exception and subject to oath."

As part of my efforts to secure amnesties for Viet Nam veterans, I met personally with Barry Lynn in New York City in the early 1970s, along with Louise Ransom. She and her husband Robert lost their son Michael to Friendly Fire..

FOOTNOTES:

1) "U.S. pilots took drugs prior to Canadian deaths, court told," *Irish Examiner*, January 15, 2003.

2) "Military looks to drugs for battle readiness," by Brad Knickerbocker, *The Christian Science Monitor*, August 9, 2002.

3) NOW: with Bill Moyers (PBS), Jan. 24, 2003.

4) "Higher and Higher: American Drug Use in Viet Nam," by Peter Brush, *Viet Nam Magazine*, December 2002.

Chapter 1: MIA
The Seibert Family

At the Viet Nam Veterans Memorial Wall in Washington, D.C., visitors who stop at panel 20W, line 119, will come across the name of Michael Robert Seibert. It doesn't say how or when he died in Viet Nam, simply that he was one of over 58,000 men and women who never returned from the war. His fate, though dimly seen, is right there, etched in stone.

A cursory search on the Internet tells us a little more about Michael. He was from Parkersburg, Illinois, and served with the 1st Cavalry Division. His tour of duty began on January 23, 1969, and ended seven months later on August 9, when he was killed near Tay Ninh, South Viet Nam, by hostile fire, his helicopter incinerated as it crashed to the earth. His body was eventually recovered. He was twenty years old.

Michael's DD Form 214, issued from Army Headquarters by the Office of the Adjutant General on October 2, 1969, is more succinct: killed in action.

End of story.

#

Back in Illinois, the sun is rising on the flat horizon, the early morning light turning everything – including the cornfields surrounding the Seibert family home – into gold. The year is 1969. It's Saturday morning in late August, and Michael's two sisters, Diane, 14, and Barbara, 11, are watching Bugs Bunny on TV.

The closest town is Parkersburg – just a crossroads, really – seven miles away. Population 200. This is prairie country, where support for the American war machine is, for all practical purposes, universal, where dissent means ostracism. Summers here burn hot and humid. Lean, sun-baked muscles glisten in the early-morning sun as men bale hay, repair fences, and dig irrigation ditches. The locals stick together – like the stubborn, blue-white clay they plow.

As Diane and Barbara watch TV, the family dog barks outside. A solemn young man has parked his car in the driveway. He walks to the north porch door and knocks. Diane gets up and is the first to greet the visitor on the porch.

"Good morning," the man says. "I'm with the United States Army."

By now, Diane's mother, Marianne, has stepped outside to join them on the porch.

"I have some news about Michael," the soldier says, hesitating, "It was his wish that this news be told to the whole family."

Marianne's eyes widen. "My son!" she shrieks. "My son!"

"I'm sorry, ma'am," the soldier says as he tries to calm her. "I can't say anything more until your husband is present. Do you know where he is?"

He looks at the two girls, and they shake their heads, dumbfounded. He looks back at their mother, who's clearly distraught.

"Where is my son?" she wails. "Tell me he is all right!"

The soldier finally relents.

"Michael was a gunner on a helicopter," he says. "His helicopter was shot down at tree level by the Vietcong in a heavy gunfight. He's missing in action."

Marianne collapses. She sobs to her oldest daughter, "Go get your father!"

Diane doesn't know where to begin to look for her father Stanley, but she follows the Army rep to his car and they leave together. They sit silently in the car, listening to the engine hum, as Diane directs the soldier to her grandparents' house. Diane's father isn't there; he and her grandfather left earlier in the morning. While at the house, Diane tells her step-grandmother what has happened, and Grandma Eleanor gets on the phone to spread the news.

They go next to Uncle Russell's house. Again, Diane's father isn't there. But she talks to Aunt Virginia, who also reaches for the phone when they leave.

By this time, the soldier's patience is wearing thin.

"I have to return to base," he says after they arrive back at the Seibert house. "I'm sorry. This is part of my job I hate."

Desperate now, Diane runs up the lane to Ora Tucker's house, over a half mile away. Her father isn't there, either. She sprints back from the neighbor's house, her lungs aching and her heart pounding in her ears.

Then it dawns on her where her father is.

She jumps on her bay mare and rides bareback to a field nearby where, sure enough, her father and grandfather are baling hay.

"Michael's been shot down!" she screams.

Both men stand still. They say nothing.

Diane turns her horse around and charges home. She finds her mother in her parents' bedroom lying across the bed, wailing, cursing, pulling at her hair. Barbara had been alone with her but didn't know how to comfort her mother.

Still hysterical, Marianne grabs a suitcase, throws it on the bed, and starts filling it with clothes. She looks up to see Stanley in the bedroom doorway. His face is pale, expressionless.

"We have to find him!" Marianne shrieks. "We have to get hold of the Red Cross now! We can't waste time! We have to find him!"

Stanley feels the walls closing in on him. His world is coming apart. Marianne's anguish suddenly focuses on him.

"I'm going to divorce you," she says. "I'm leaving you right now."

The two then go at it, arguing fiercely.

Finally, Diane screams, "If you get a divorce, I won't live with either one of you. I'll run away!"

Barbara, meanwhile, has run off to another room to hide.

#

Three decades have passed since that fateful day, but the question on everyone's lips back then – What happened to Michael? – remains unanswered.

Michael's father, now in his mid-70s, admits that his memory has faded. Piecing together the puzzle of Michael's death is made more difficult because many who played crucial roles in those turbulent times have either passed on or moved away.

Still, fragments remain. As do doubts. A cloud hangs over Michael's death that hasn't faded with memory.

"I was told by one person that the two pilots were high on dope the day they were shot down," Stanley recalls. "Michael was a gunner on that mission. Supposedly they spotted one bag of rice in a paddy, and that's what they went down to destroy.

"Then they sent an award back for him being responsible for destroying a large enemy hospital complex. I didn't know that we were supposed to destroy hospitals. When I questioned this officer, he said he turned it in to make it sound good. In reality, it was a little tin shack in the jungle, probably a bicycle repair shop."

Stanley pauses, trying to make sense of it all.

"Michael was last seen alive at a fire base called Charlie. My opinion is that he had something on one of the officers in charge, that he was killed by our own forces before the helicopter even crashed. The guy who ordered the mission was transferred to parts unknown.

"Supposedly, Michael was shot down, but they refused to go in for ten days on a rescue mission. When they got there, the weapon that Michael was supposed to be carrying was found leaning against a tree. Three guys were burned together and fused as corpses. They sent back his charred dog tags. They looked touched up to me. We don't know what they got [of his remains]. We were mandated to bury what was left of him in El Paso, Texas, because the parents of the other two were senior officers and wanted them buried there."

Certain memories are like landmines, triggering explosions of anger.

"Michael had been saving his money and was supposed to go to Australia for R&R. He had about eight or nine hundred dollars. It was never found. You weren't allowed to take anything with you on the flight. Them bastards stole it. We got his passport back. And about ten cents worth of [South] Viet Namese money."

Marianne, meanwhile, was absolutely certain that Michael had been captured and was now a prisoner of war. She carried that belief with her to her grave.

"Can you blame her?" Stanley asks. "They did not provide any proof of his death. We didn't see any remains. They wouldn't open the coffin. They wouldn't bring his body home. They segregated us from the other families at the funeral and kept us under guard. They shadowed us everywhere we went. Kept between us and the other two families. We tried to contact one of the families, but they wouldn't talk to us."

Diane feels especially bitter about the circumstances of Michael's burial.

"My mother wanted to bring what was left of him home, but we were denied that. The circumstances of his burial were one more final insult to our family. It felt as if he were insignificant, buried in a common grave like a pauper. Buried far from home where we could not grieve normally. No closure, a terrible grief that never surrenders, even today. I wonder how many families had to go through that experience."

Michael was a prodigious letter writer while he served in Viet Nam, penning notes to his family and friends at least twice a week. Diane remembers the last letter he sent home.

"It was written in red," she says. "The tone of his letter was not normal for him, and the content was brief. It read something like, 'I've become one of the glory seekers.' Somehow in that letter he let us know he was to go on a suicide mission. The reason for this unexpected mission was alluded to in a previous letter, where he said he had gotten into some trouble on the base. Something about discovering some drugs. He reported it to his CO. After reporting it to the commanding officer, he was reprimanded to this suicide mission."

The staff sergeant who first visited the Seiberts showed up on their porch on August 23, 1969, though Michael's helicopter went down two weeks prior on August 9. Michael wasn't confirmed dead for eight more agonizing weeks, during which time the Seiberts waited anxiously for news of their son.

Delays, changes in status, a convoluted trickle of conflicting information, the cold bureaucracy of the U.S. Army – all conspired to make the official story of Michael's death (once it had been delivered) seem incomplete at best, unbelievable at worst.

\#

Michael Robert Seibert was born on November 15, 1948, in Olney, Illinois. His first two years were spent in Olney before the family moved to the two-story farmhouse about fifteen miles from Olney.

He grew up on the farm, learning how to care for animals, operate machinery, and tend to crops. He had his own dog, and his own pony.

"He done pretty good here," Stanley recalls. "He was just a kid and going to school. But when he could, he helped."

Once, when Stanley dislocated his back, Michael took over for his father.

"He wasn't very big," Stanley says. "All of a sudden, he's getting the tractor out and the cultivator out, and he's cultivating the corn."

According to Diane, Michael was a pretty lean kid, but he had six-pack abs, which he developed by lifting large steel cans of whole milk.

"He had to drive the dairy route," Diane says. "He would receive the milk in large containers, lift them onto the truck, and deliver them to Prairie Farms Dairy."

Michael loved anything with a motor, especially if it left skid marks on the pavement. He drove a red 1963 Pontiac Tempest convertible, plus a Honda motorcycle of equal vintage. The Tempest still sits in Diane's garage, where she and her husband, Walter Haner, himself a combat veteran of Viet Nam, look after it. The motorcycle is at Barbara's, in the care of her and her husband, Randy Cunningham.

Everyone knew it was likely that Michael would be drafted to Viet Nam. And no one feared it more than his mother, Marianne.

"When my brother was about to get drafted," Diane recalls, "my mother urged him to get out of the country. Go to Germany and live with relatives. Or go to Canada and make a life for himself. But Michael was attached to his home and family and friends and did not want to leave. My God, he was barely eighteen. To be confronted with such issues as moving, death, war, draft dodging, communism, and patriotism had to be more than he could manage. I think Michael just threw his hands up to fate with the secret hope that he would return and maybe even make us proud."

Born December 12, 1922, near Cologne, Germany, Marianne experienced the horrors of war firsthand when her village was flattened by Allied bombers during World War II. Food shortages, blackouts, night raids. She never forgot her baptism by fire.

"She told us about walking through burning cities," Diane says, "past dead bodies. She told us what napalm was and how it looked when it fell from the sky. When it fell on the asphalt, the streets turned into rivers of fire. When people tried to run from the bombing, they stepped into the streets and went up in flames."

Marianne met Stanley, five years her junior, a year after the war ended at the 7th Army headquarters, where they both worked. Stanley was inducted in 1945, with only the war in the Pacific still raging. After undergoing infantry training, he was put into the financing department.

"They didn't ask me," he quips. "They told me."

He got into payroll and accounting, completing a sixteen-week course in three weeks. After taking a short furlough, he was put on a ship and sent to Europe, where he went from payroll to accounting. He served two years before taking his discharge oversees. From there, he went to work as a civilian for the War Department in northern Germany.

"I stayed there on account of her," says Stanley, who had met Marianne, a secretary, a year earlier. "Plus, I could make more money over there – twice as much as in the States. She said, 'Come back tomorrow as soon as you get your papers.'"

He did just that. And the two fell in love. It took six months for the paperwork to go through so they could get married. Then, navigating their way through a Byzantine maze of red tape, they got married. Twice. First on May 13, 1947, in Germany by the mayor of Bremen, and again twelve days later by an American chaplain on the Army base nearby. After that, Marianne had thirty days to leave the country or lose her American citizenship.

"For a while, she was stateless," Stanley says. "She couldn't be in either country. We had to get out of Germany. She just took the clothes she could wear and one dollar. They wouldn't let her take anything with her. She was taking a big risk, too. We ended up being married fifty-three years before she passed away [in June 2000]."

The young couple returned to Stanley's stomping grounds in rural Illinois, eventually buying some land and the farmhouse near Parkersburg. The Seiberts, a well-traveled and well-educated couple, were putting down roots in America's conservative heartland, where outsiders, especially foreigners, were rarely accepted.

That same year, 1947, George Kennan of the State Department, using the pseudonym X, wrote an article for *Foreign Affairs* in which he laid out the concept of "containment." Korea, Viet Nam, Saigon – soon such hitherto exotic and far-flung locations would become part of the American lexicon. And young men like Michael Seibert, born a year later at Richland County Memorial Hospital, would meet their destinies in the jungles of Viet Nam.

#

Despite developing a hernia from the repetitive motion of lifting milk canisters day after day on his dairy route, Michael passed his U.S. Army physical and was drafted on August 19, 1968. He was going to junior college at the time. He traded his textbooks for a rifle at Fort Polk in Louisiana, where he attended boot camp. He was then trained as a helicopter mechanic and crew chief at Fort Eustis, Virginia.

Before heading for Viet Nam, he spent two weeks at home with his family, friends, and neighbors. He waxed and polished his Tempest and Honda and carefully placed them in storage at his parents' home, where he assumed he would return in a year.

Upon arrival in Viet Nam, he was given a new job: procuring. He also did repairs and kept records of all the helicopters.

"He said in one of his letters that he had to borrow, beg, and steal to repair anything," Stanley recalls.

As for the war, Michael quickly learned that the American effort was futile – and perhaps unjust. In one letter to his father, he wrote, "I don't know why we're fighting these people. We should be helping them."

Although he had been assured by higher-ups that his job would remain the same, Michael's duties eventually changed. An officer put him on the flight line, and he flew twenty-eight missions in three days.

Michael was flying with the famed air cavalry (9th Cavalry/1st Division, Troop A), "an aggressive, proactive unit very much in the image of the old horse cavalry," according to John Jewett, a combat helicopter pilot who served with the First Aviation Brigade from August 1968 to August 1969.

Like Michael, John flew out of Tay Ninh. He says that Michael's fateful mission on August 9, 1969, took him directly into an area that, at the time, was one of the worst combat zones in Viet Nam. The air cavalry was fighting well-armed and highly disciplined NVA regulars, not Vietcong freelancers.

Michael was flying a hunter/killer mission. He was a gunner on an LOH-6 with nothing to hide behind. The LOH-6 was a small, highly maneuverable helicopter staffed by a three-man crew, including a pilot and an observer. Michael's helicopter was the hunter. Its job: find the enemy. He and his crew were shadowed by the killer, a Cobra gun ship which was there to provide fire support in the event that contact was made.

They flew north of NuiBai Din, or Black Virgin Mountain, a prominent peak between Landing Zones Beverly and Katum and a stone's throw from the Cambodian border, right into the teeth of an NVA stronghold, complete with reinforced concrete bunkers.

"Being in that low helicopter," John explains, "that was the most dangerous aviation job in Viet Nam. Michael's job took great courage – sitting in the opened side of a Huey with nothing to hide behind except his gun."

What happened next is still a mystery to the Seibert family. The official report reads that Michael's helicopter was hit by ground fire and exploded. But the Seiberts didn't speak with any witnesses until later. And they were never given Michael's body. No part of his nails, teeth, or hair was identified in the autopsy. His remains, along with those of the pilot and observer, were buried in one casket.

All the Seiberts got were his charred dog tags and a medical chart showing the three men's burnt remains. When Stanley gave the chart to the family doctor for inspection, he sent them on to a forensic expert in New York City who, upon studying them, insisted the remains were hardly identifiable and that one body looked to be Asian, not Caucasian.

There was a ten-day delay between when Michael was shot down and when his body was finally recovered. Apparently, the area had to be secured by ground troops first. But that, too, added to the mystery. And what of Michael's gun, found leaning against a tree?

"A dink would never leave a functioning weapon," John maintains. "They would take it and sell it. No one would leave a weapon leaning against a tree."

The suspicion that Michael may have known something he wasn't supposed to know, or that someone in his unit had it out for him, also didn't add up.

"That's not something that would happen in an aviation unit," John explains. "If you've got a loser, they don't fly. They get rid of you. No one wants to be in a helicopter with you."

Indeed, the hunter and the killer were dependent on each other every step of the way. Loyalty to your unit and your fellow soldier was strong among the air cavalry; special pains were taken – including sustaining new casualties – to recover the bodies of fallen comrades.

So why the mystery? Why did the Seiberts have to find out how Michael died in bits and pieces from different sources? Why was Michael's death – or disappearance – shrouded in secrecy and indifference?

John offers one explanation: red tape.

Army bureaucracy can turn a simple thing – like informing a family that their loved one has been lost to the war – into a convoluted mess, replacing finality with an open wound.

"We had a case once in our unit where we all saw someone get hit in the body as their aircraft went up," John says, "and we all made statements. I don't know how they messed it up, but the Army had him listed as MIA for years."

#

Back in Illinois, before Diane and her family knew that Michael was missing or, worse yet, killed in action, the Seiberts simply tried to carry on as best they could.

"Life was difficult for us while Michael was in Viet Nam," Diane says. "We concentrated on the farm work, with me helping Dad any way I could. I was eager to help him and take on those same physically demanding tasks Michael would have done. And my father did utilize my help much of the time."

Diane helped out with barn chores, machinery repairs, and moving machinery from field to field. She also helped with the garden.

"My mother wrote to my brother every day and sent him newspaper clippings," she says. "She prepared care packages for him, things he liked but might be missing. We sent a message about once a week. My mother was a very organized individual and kept the house in perfect order. We had a special calendar in the study. Each day we marked how many days until Michael would come home.

"We talked about the war a lot. We were always listening to Walter Cronkite. We occasionally would pull in a foreign newscast on the radio. We had a short-wave radio in the house with a wire antenna, and I would tune in to Radio Free Europe to listen to the other side of the news."

Adds Diane: "We thought about Michael all the time, trying to avoid the thought that there was a possibility he might not come home. Prior to his leaving for Viet Nam, I had a terrible dream that something would happen to him. I told the dream to my mother, who told me to tell Michael so he might be convinced to go to Canada. In my dream, I saw him in a crashed helicopter with his insides coming out. Michael just thought that was a stupid dream, but it frightened me.

"I have learned over the years that I have some psychic ability. Things come to me as a picture in my head. I don't know why. But most of my premonitions come true, and my premonitions are warnings of doom and gloom. I have since learned to take them seriously. If I have a dream or premonition about someone, I tell them about it now. They may or may not think I'm crazy, but just telling and forewarning them perhaps alters the outcome. I don't know for sure."

When the news began to filter in that Michael was indeed either dead or missing, hard facts were hard to come by.

"The Army wouldn't answer our letters or phone calls," Stanley says. "They don't have to notify you for three days. That gives them a chance to get their stories straight."

When news did trickle in, it often simply added doubt to the situation. At one point, the Seiberts had been informed of two different crash sites. When Marianne asked too many questions, she was threatened by an Army liaison, who assured her that she and her family could be investigated.

For what?

Finally, the Army requested that the Seiberts come to a meeting at O'Hare Airport in Chicago, where several families of MIA soldiers were to be briefed. Stanley woke up at 3:00 a.m. and did his chores. Then the family hit the road for Chicago. They arrived hungry and exhausted.

"Once we got there," Stanley recalls, "they acted real funny, like we weren't supposed to be there. They made a bunch of phone calls and shuttled us around and finally one official gets off the phone and says, 'You're not supposed to be here. Didn't they tell you? Your son's been declared KIA.'

"I drove 350 miles there just to find that out."

On the way home, insult was added to injury when Stanley got caught in a speed trap and was issued a $50 speeding ticket.

Months later, the Seiberts managed to track down someone from Michael's unit in a trailer court near Fort Rucker in Alabama. The captain tried to avoid the Seiberts at first. When cornered, he maintained that he saw Michael's helicopter go down and that he hovered for ten minutes to look for survivors. But his testimony made no one feel any better. The seeds of doubt had already been sown.

"Dad worked at his farming with an obsession," Diane says. "After all, his main helper, Michael, had been taken away. His only son. I think Father believed that Michael would come back. When Dad did express his feelings during those years, it was in fits of anger or rage. Mom and Dad fought often."

Though Michael's status had been officially changed to KIA, the Seiberts felt no finality, only doubt. They sought help from the Red Cross, the American Legion, Veterans of Foreign Wars, even Walter Cronkite. To no avail.

In 1970, they flew to Paris to meet with the Viet Namese peace negotiators. Marianne brought photos of Michael, along with detailed descriptions written in German and English. Upon arrival, the Seiberts were sent straight to the

American embassy. From there, they took a taxi to the peace talks and waited for the peace delegation to arrive.

"We were shoved aside by the entourage," Diane says, "and the beautiful Viet Namese woman would not talk to us or look at Michael's picture or take the envelope of information my mother had so desperately and lovingly prepared. My mother was devastated. She collapsed on the street in Paris. Several local French officers came to her aid and were sympathetic. They told us where the compound was located where the Viet Namese delegation was staying. We took a taxi there. We were eerily and coldly greeted by the people in this brick enclosed compound. They opened the gate. We walked in. The guardhouse in the compound had a huge picture of Ho Chi Minh hanging inside, and as I looked around, I could see Viet Namese faces peering at us from all the windows. I suspect we had machine guns pointed at us. We offered the picture of Michael, all the documentation we had, and offered all the money we had on us. They refused it all."

The trip, like every inquiry before it, was a bust. The Seiberts were left to cope on their own, with only my family to give them support. There was even public criticism that the Seiberts had tried to communicate with communists.

Frustrated and nearly hopeless, Marianne did what any mother would do: she resorted to desperate measures. She consulted a world-renowned psychic, Ann Gehman. But as had been the case elsewhere, her attempt at closure failed. Gehman could not pick up on Michael's "vibe," or soul.

"That reinforced our belief that his cross, supposedly recovered in the crash, was merely recovered from his belongings," Diane says. "We believed the U.S. military made less than a minuscule effort to obtain his remains in the jungle after so many days, and perhaps there was not much to recover. But they could have at least been truthful about it."

Stanley received help from a handful of neighbors who got together and harvested his crops for him in one day. The Army sent a $250 check to cover burial expenses. The proceeds from Michael's life insurance policy were split between Diane and Barbara to go toward college and other future expenses.

But, for the most part, the community that had encouraged Michael to make good on his patriotic duty turned its back on his family when he didn't come home.

Stanley and Marianne, both opposed to the war, had made their opinions known. And the family paid for it. Hate mail. Anonymous phone calls. Condemnation from teachers and preachers. Ostracism from the local church. America's xenophobic heartland managed to turn dissent into deceit, castigating the Seiberts with the trite and ugly rhetoric of knee-jerk patriotism.

Better dead than red. America: love it or leave it.

"We got four threatening letters, not signed, telling us to get out of the community," Stanley remembers. "They told my wife to go back to Germany. We probably should have.

"We weren't supposed to ask questions. We weren't supposed to stir up stuff."

Diane and Barbara suffered, too. They were verbally and physically abused in high school.

Marianne, meanwhile, entered a deep depression. And, predictably, some locals were unsympathetic.

"She was pretty much laid up," Stanley says. "Could hardly cook or eat. One teacher from the school told her to get over it. People who never experienced what we experienced just couldn't understand."

"The house was always dark," Diane recalls. "My mother was bedridden at the time and heavily sedated for weeks that turned into months. She had to take sedatives of one type or another the rest of her life. For two years, I didn't know if I would come home and find that my mother had committed suicide. It was a real fear."

Gradually, the fear disappeared, replaced instead by numbness. The Seiberts rebuilt their shattered lives and forged close ties with a few devoted families nearby who, like them, had lost someone – or something – to the Viet Nam War. Diane and Barbara both grew up, got married, became parents themselves, and pursued careers.

For twenty years, Marianne kept Michael's bedroom exactly as it was the day he left. Today, his 1963 red convertible Tempest and his Honda motorcycle, both waxed and polished, await his return. And the war that ended three decades ago continues to take casualties on the home front.

"We ain't done with this yet," Stanley says.

Some neighbors still hold a grudge against the Seiberts for protesting the war. Others have never expressed their condolences for the family's loss.

Alan Yonaka, who went to the same high school as Michael and grew up about five miles away, is still mystified by his former schoolmate's death. An Army engineer who drove a bulldozer in Viet Nam, Alan met up with Michael at a firebase just days before Michael was shot down. It was a chance encounter, and, though they barely knew each other back home, both men were amazed to have come so far only to cross paths in Viet Nam.

"I don't remember much about it or what we said," recalls Alan, who was on his way to Hawaii for some R&R and a visit with his wife and young son. "But when I came back from R&R, they told me he'd been killed. I said there was no way he could have been killed; he was a helicopter dispatcher. They claim he was an observer or a gunner or something on a helicopter. No one would tell me anything."

In fact, Alan's wife heard the news of Michael's death before he did. When the couple met in Hawaii, she told him Michael had been shot down.

"To this day, I don't know what happened to him," he explains. "I can't believe he would have volunteered to go into a hot zone. Those gunners were flying into some nasty stuff. I guess he was tired of being a company clerk or dispatcher or whatever he was doing and volunteered to go. Maybe he was just sick and tired of doing what he was doing."

Alan never sensed the ostracism the Seibert family endured; nor did he notice their vilification by some in the community. He was too busy starting up his own business, Yonaka Bulldozing Services. But he shares their pain to this day.

"After I got back," he says, "I told Stanley everything I knew and that I wished I knew more. But I just didn't know any more. I feel bad for Stanley and his family. They didn't have any closure. There's still this doubt. It just torments you from now on. I wish I would have known more."

As for Mr. and Mrs. Seibert, they rode the waves of anger and isolation for decades before Marianne passed away in June 2000, still believing her son was alive somewhere in Viet Nam.

"We had our ups and downs," Stanley says. "But we managed."

#

On March 29, 1973, the last American troops left Viet Nam. Three days later, Hanoi released 591 American POW's as part of "Operation Homecoming." The war was finally over.

For some families on the home front, of course, the struggle was just beginning. Over 2,500 soldiers remained unaccounted for. A handful came back alive. Others were officially deemed killed in action, though their bodies were never recovered; witnesses – fellow officers, pilots, and grunts – attested to their deaths. The remains of still others were eventually recovered, identified, and returned to their families.

Acronyms like MIA, KIA, and BNR (Body Not Recovered) were used to describe the collective fate of the missing soldiers, whose names became political fodder for activists, congressmen, and con artists alike. Says Stanley Karnow in his sweeping history, *Viet Nam: A History*:

> *". . . numbers of U.S. politicians, presidents included, deliberately inflamed the issue for their own aims. They also refused to state openly what most of them believed privately – that no live Americans were being held in Viet Nam. Their duplicity spawned a cottage industry in spurious 'sightings.' Understandably reluctant to give up hope, many families of the missing men trusted lobbies that perpetuated the cruel hoax – and, in the process, duped the public. Surveys further showed that the majority of Americans – veterans among them – believed that Hanoi was detaining U.S. captives against their will."*

Indeed, countless vets, advocacy groups, and politicians passionately maintain to this day that both the U.S. government and its communist counterpart in Hanoi have yet to come clean on the MIA issue. They insist that Viet Nam still holds American prisoners – and remains – hostage.

Yet the number of soldiers missing in action from Viet Nam amounts to a fraction – less than four percent – of American losses. In both World War II and Korea, missing in action reports totaled fourteen percent of the casualties. Factor in the remote terrain where many Americans lost their lives in Viet Nam, plus the rapid decay of corpses in the jungle and the decades that have passed since the war, and it would seem logical that not all remains will be found, whether American citizens are being lied to or not. Such a feat would be impossible, as the Viet Namese, searching for their own missing, have found.

When the Clinton Administration formally recognized Viet Nam on July 11, 1995, the U.S. government drew one step closer to perhaps resolving the issue once and for all. Many are hopeful that closer relations between the two countries will open the door to any discoveries of remaining GI's, dead or alive.

In the end, the body count has done little to tell the stories of the men and women lost to the war. Nor has it told the stories of their families who, left to their own devices, tried to get on with the business of grieving despite the hovering clouds of uncertainty.

Michael Robert Seibert is listed on the wall. Panel 20W. Line 119. Killed in action August 9, 1969. His fate is right there, etched in stone.

Chapter 2: Casualties of War
Three Families

Monica

"I remember when I would go to my aunt's house, I could see her tilting her head back in a full-hearted laugh," Monica recalls. "She would just be laughing hysterically. After Hobie's death, none of us were ever the same. My aunt would laugh still, but it was a short, brief laugh. She never did get that hearty, robust laugh back."

Monica Stanton-Gibson, a school bus driver and mother of six in Williamsburg, Virginia, was only seven years old when she lost her cousin to the Viet Nam War. George Hobert Noe, or Hobie as everyone in his family called him, arrived in Viet Nam on May 8, 1969, a fresh-faced 20-year-old kid from Cawood, Kentucky. He was in-country all of eighteen days before an errant grenade ended his short life.

"He always had us laughing," Monica says of her cousin. "He had a big, huge toothy grin and big, huge Dumbo ears. He was always acting like Barney Fife and Gomer Pyle. You couldn't be around him without laughing yourself to death."

When Hobie was drafted into the U.S. Army, Monica's father, John Stanton, was already in Viet Nam as a staff sergeant with the supply department. He had been in the Army for years, and well before April 17, 1962, when Monica was born at Fort Belvoir, Virginia.

As is the case with most military families, the Stantons moved frequently. Monica's brother and two sisters, all younger, were born while John was stationed in Japan. By the time Viet Nam came along, the family was living in Cawood, a small town in rural Kentucky, where much of the extended family resided. Monica's grandmother lived nearby, along with her uncle, who raised chickens and pigs. Hobie's family lived at the top of a hill, which was home to a profusion of flowers Aunt Gertrude perennially fussed over.

When John went to Viet Nam, the Stantons moved in with Grandma Stanton. And life in Cawood passed slowly and assuredly as the extended family exchanged visits and whiled away the days. That is, until Hobie dropped a bombshell on the eve of his departure to Viet Nam.

"I'm not sure if he was home on leave at the time," Monica says, "but I do remember him coming home and having a short time there. And I remember him telling his mother that he would not be back."

Aunt Gertrude told her son not to talk that way, and he acquiesced, but not before insisting she fathom the full weight of his words.

If Hobie could intuit his future, so could his cousin. When the phone rang a few weeks later at Grandma Stanton's house, Monica already knew the news.

"She had gone to her bedroom," Monica explains. "She had a phone in there. She had not even picked it up before I started screaming at the top of my lungs, 'Don't pick up the phone! Hobie's dead!' I just knew. How, I don't know."

Sure enough, after she picked up, Grandma Stanton's face became ashen with the news that Hobie had been killed in Viet Nam. It wasn't the last time Monica would have a premonition involving Hobie and the war.

Officially, Hobie had been killed by a hostile grenade. The truth, though, slowly found its way to the surface. Hobie's family learned that an American soldier, frozen in fear one night, had dropped his hand grenade and Hobie had thrown himself onto it in the bottom of their foxhole, dying a hero's death.

Decades later, after a little digging on the Internet, they found out that this story, too, was only partially grounded in reality. The American soldier in question was, in fact, in a foxhole *behind* Hobie and unaware that any friendly forces could be in front of him. Somehow, he had gotten turned around in the pitch-black darkness. The soldier panicked when he heard movement and lobbed a grenade into Hobie's foxhole, killing Hobie and injuring four others.

The story was corroborated by two soldiers there that night, both of whom responded to an Internet posting by Monica's sister Sandy in 2002. Of the two versions, which differed in detail, the family found Ray Schelble's the most convincing.

Schelble, who was in the perimeter position next to Hobie's the night he died, says the men had just reinforced Alpha Company of the 1st Battalion, 46th Infantry, which had been badly hit. The new guys were scared out of their boots. The old hands were exhausted and demoralized. Everybody was jumpy.

"George and I came out to the field just as the company was picking up the dead bodies they had had to leave behind when they were attacked," he explains. "They had been lying there for a week or two. When I got off the chopper my first day, the heat was like stepping into a furnace, and the stench from the rotting bodies was unbelievable. There was damaged GI equipment strewn everywhere over a wide area. The guys in Alpha Company ripped up their equipment and left it when they finally had to run. It didn't take long to realize that most of us in the company were brand new, and the few experienced guys were extremely spooked, and justifiably so.

George was a victim of a series of unfortunate circumstances. It was nothing he did. It could have been any of us, and we all knew it. He was just in the wrong place at the wrong time.

"To this day, I still feel very sorry for the guy who made the mistake – a mistake any of us could have made. After what he'd been through before George and I got out to the field, and then to have this happen . . . . He was a great guy and a class act. It had a deep impact on him then, and I'm sure it still does."

For Monica, knowing *how* Hobie died helped. But she still wanted to know *why*.

"The thing that has really plagued me," Monica says, "and the thing that has made me really angry with God is: my cousin was killed for what? His whole death seemed totally worthless."

She felt that way until Ray Schelble shared with her part of a letter he sent home from Viet Nam just weeks after Hobie was killed.

"I'm sending you a copy of an old newsletter we get, and I'd appreciate it if you could hold onto it for me," Ray had written to his parents. "All of the guys you see killed were killed just about a week and a half before I got here except the one I've got underlined. He was a buddy of mine who was killed when one of our men got mixed up and threw a grenade into the next foxhole. It was real ugly, but I think it helped tighten up the company since we are just about all new to the bush. It wasn't worth it, though."

Hobie didn't have to die that night. He *shouldn't* have died that night. But it's the sliver of hope – and meaning – that Monica clings to. His death, needless and tragic, rallied his company and perhaps even saved lives down the road. And he's inspiring people still.

"I had every intention of going to the Wall just one time," says Monica, who made the two-and-a-half-hour drive to the Viet Nam Veterans Memorial in Washington, D.C. in August

2001. "But there's just this draw to go back. Just the design of it and everything – I just felt like I was on the side where I was living, and he was on the other side with the dead. Just touching his name on the wall and kissing his name – I felt like he was doing that back to me, saying, 'Hey, Cous.' There's something there that just says, 'Come back.' I've only been there once. I will be back."

Adds Monica, "I haven't really researched why we were there or what we were there for, and honestly couldn't tell you what we were there for. My focus has been on how our soldiers were treated when they came home. They went there to fight for their country, and they came back to people that were spitting on them and harassing them, hollering, 'baby killer!' at them. If I was a veteran, I would be looking at those people and saying, 'I lost a limb for this?' I would be very angry at my country. If you look at the numbers, so many of them were eighteen to twenty, and it just makes you sick."

Monica has a 20-year-old son in the infantry and an 18-year-old son who would be eligible for the draft, should it be reinstated. She knows full well that she could be following in her Aunt Gertrude's footsteps.

"The next time you're looking at your freedoms, think about it," she says. "How dare I sit back and say, 'freedom, freedom, but not at the expense of my children's lives.' There may come a day when I'm in the same position my aunt was, and it will be my child that is that sacrifice."

During the Viet Nam War, Army policy was this: when an American soldier was killed, someone from his hometown would be asked to escort the body home. When John Stanton generously agreed to do so, he had no idea the fallen soldier was his nephew.

Monica had her second premonition in as many weeks when a hearse pulled off the road next to her grandmother's house. Between the road and the driveway was a rickety old one-way bridge which, until then, had always inspired fear in

Monica. Her family was just leaving and pulled to a stop on the bridge.

"I jumped out of the car onto the bridge and screamed, 'It's Daddy! It's Daddy!'"

The kids hadn't been told their father would be escorting Hobie home, but Monica somehow intuited it.

These days, Monica is the only one in her extended family who can talk about the war. Her mother has never opened a letter from Hobie she received after he was shipped home in a body bag. And she lost an uncle to suicide not long after he returned from the war a shell of his former self.

"It's over," her father tells her of Viet Nam. "It's done with. Leave it buried, and go on with your life."

If only it were that simple. The family has never been the same. Aunt Gertrude, who has since passed away, never did learn to laugh again. The source of the family's pain remains unspoken. Hence Monica's quest.

"I do know that part of the reason why I have been so headstrong to get Hobie's story out is because of the feeling, you know, that no one in my family wants to talk about it anymore," she says. "It leaves you wondering, 'Am I crazy for mourning this person or trying to remember him all these years?' When you read things on these web sites or visit the Wall, it helps you feel like you're not crazy or stupid or hanging onto the grieving just because you feel this way. They were very special individuals, and you don't want people to ever forget.

"I don't want anyone to forget."

#

Jeannine

Her memory is like the earth beneath her feet. Dark, rich, deep – it has as much to say about the future as it does the past. But it can't break up on its own. It has to be cultivated.

It has to be reached into. It has to be penetrated with spade, pick, or plow, its musty underside folded and furrowed into something new. This, or nothing will grow in it.

"When I dream about him," she says, recalling the love of her life, "we're both seventeen again."

Seventeen, and a limitless world in front of them. Seventeen, and a weightless future that never comes. Seventeen, and everything that ever mattered is now. While just over the horizon boys become men, and men become ghosts, and ghosts become memories in one bloody instant, she and he drink from the giddy anxiety of first love.

"When I started reading some of the books on Viet Nam," she says years later, "I read some of the nurses' stories. I had walked around maybe twenty years, and it hit me: how can anyone compete with a ghost? Later, I read that line in one of the books, and I thought, 'Oh, my God. There are other people out there who have experienced the same thing?'"

Yes. But precious few.

Jeannine Vehrencamp, a legal secretary in Vancouver, Washington, was born on August 16, 1948, in Los Angeles, California. Her family moved around a bit before settling in Wrightwood, a little resort town two-and-a-half hours northeast of LA.

"My mom doesn't have good memories of the place," says Jeannine, who was the middle child of three girls, "but I think it was the perfect place to raise kids. You had the pine trees, streets with no sidewalks, a little country store. Everybody knew everybody. You didn't have to worry about locking your door. We grew up in a very rustic cabin that was built around 1910. We did a lot of bike riding around town. We collected Coke bottles to turn them in to the store in exchange for ice cream on hot, sunny days."

It was on such a day in the summer of 1965 that she met Jimmie Duayne Cintron, a blue-eyed John Travolta look-alike who wore black Levi's and a black T-shirt in the sweltering heat of Kernville, California. An old Western town situated in the desert mountains northeast of Bakersfield, Kernville was and still is an outdoor enthusiast's paradise. At 2,650 feet and with a population hovering near 1,500, it makes a natural jumping-off point for visits to Kern River, the Sequoia National Forest, and a handful of remote lakes and gulches.

Jimmie was seventeen. Jeannine was just about. He was from Acampo (near Stockton) but was spending the summer with his grandparents in Kernville and working at the town grocery store. She and her family were visiting her older sister and brother-in-law. Jimmie and Jeannine met on July 21st on what amounted to a blind date at the river.

"She didn't say she had invited someone," Jeannine says of her older sister Cheryl. "But these two guys showed up in their white Mustang."

One of said guys was Jimmie, who hit it off instantly with Jeannine. The feeling was mutual. They met on a Wednesday and spent the rest of the week together.

"We went to the movies the following night," Jeannine remembers. "Any time he had off we spent together. Then we went back to the river. Saturday we went to a dance. On Sunday, the day I was leaving, he took me to lunch on his lunch break. I remember walking down the street in the hot sun. Every time I think back on him, I don't remember conversations. I just remember how I felt."

Jeannine has managed to piece together the puzzle of her first and only true love by going through the letters, one by one, Jimmie sent to her so many years ago. Herself a victim of Post-Traumatic Stress Disorder, she had to go back before she could go forward. The most important summer of her life had been buried in the recesses of her psyche, a dimly understood, vaguely felt ache with no name.

After spending five days together in July, Jimmie and Jeannine wouldn't see each other again until the following month, when he came to Wrightwood for a weekend visit.

The visit was too short, and the two professed as much in the torrent of letters and long-distance phone calls that followed.

Then history, as indifferent as it is relentless, cut in, interrupting the dance between the two hopelessly-in-love teenagers. In October, Jeannine received a letter from Jimmie that would have far-reaching consequences. After having casually pondered his options in a previous letter, he informed Jeannine that he had quit school to join the Marines. The two were planning on being married. But the following spring, everything changed.

"He went into the Marines in March of 1966," Jeannine recalls. "And up to this point he had been in contact with his CO at the depot. His CO told him how hard it was going to be if he got married. He had to sign a letter saying he would not get married until after boot camp. We were still planning on getting married. I was hoping to get married right after I graduated. In May, he wrote a letter to say he was ending it."

Adds Jeannine, "He always said he never wanted to hurt me. He wanted to do what was best for me. He didn't want to see me waiting around for four years. I think he really agonized over what to do. I called him, and we talked about it. We continued writing. I thought everything was okay. Then around July he went into advanced infantry training at Camp Pendleton in San Diego. His letters were a little different. When I read them now, I can tell. He still said he loved me, but . . . when I was seventeen, I wanted to believe it was all okay."

Perhaps Jimmie, having endured boot camp and advanced infantry training in Pendleton, had a sinking suspicion that the ordeal had just begun. He was trapped, as it were, within forces he could no longer control, riding the irrevocable wave of his own destiny.

He graduated in July, and the letters dried up. Jeannine, unaware of where he had gone or how she could reach him, didn't hear from him until October, when she got a letter from Okinawa.

"He wrote to explain he had made a very big mistake in not seeing me, and he knew it," she says. "He apologized for what he did. I wrote back, and I said, 'I'm here, and I'm yours. I'll wait.'"

Jeannine asked when they could see each other again, but Jimmie gently rebuffed the naive question. He was in Okinawa, and Viet Nam loomed. He turned eighteen on December 31, 1966. A day later he wrote Jeannine to let her know he would be shipping out for Viet Nam in just over two weeks.

In Viet Nam, Jimmie, who served with Key-low Company, Third Battalion, First Marines, First Platoon, kept his fellow soldiers abreast of his love affair with Jeannine. One buddy even wrote a letter to Jeannine. Only seventeen at the time, she didn't understand how the soldier had found her address or how he even knew her. Jimmie explained everything in his next letter, saying the marine was a good friend and had told Jimmie he'd be a fool not to marry Jeannine. But things still seemed strange. Jimmie kept sending mixed signals, telling his sweetheart he loved her in one letter while suggesting she prepare to move on in others. When Jeannine went to a show with another boy and then told Jimmie about it in her next letter, she got an angry letter back from another of Jimmie's buddies.

"I thought, 'What's going on?'" Jeannine recalls. "'Why am I getting these letters from these guys?' I know now he was just sharing, and his buddy was just trying to protect him. It was very hard. For the first time, I allowed myself to feel angry. And I wrote the letter."

Was the marriage off? Had she said goodbye to Jimmie forever? Jeannine still can't talk about the letter.

"A couple weeks later, my sister came down from Kernville to visit. She needed to go back up briefly, and I drove her that day. Sitting there where he used to work and thinking about him, I could see his face in front of me. I thought, 'My God, if I never see his face again, I couldn't stand it.'

"I get back to Wrightwood, and we sit down for dinner. My daddy says he has something he needs to show me and takes me upstairs."

He showed her a news clipping. Jimmie was dead.

"I remember looking at that," she says. "I couldn't fathom it. Before I could write another letter, he was killed. I never got the chance. To add to the devastation, I got a scrawled note with three words from one of his buddies that said, 'You killed him.' I took it to heart and carried that guilt and pain around for thirty years."

Jimmie was cut down by small arms fire in Quang Nam, South Viet Nam, on April 22, 1967. While riding on top of a tank, he was hit and killed instantly. His death was considered ironic by his fellow marines, for he was sitting on the middle tank, usually considered the safest ride, of a three-tank column. The lead tank often had to contend with booby traps, while the last one typically fell victim to snipers.

Days, then weeks, then months went by for Jeannine back in Wrightwood. But the fog wouldn't lift.

"I cried," she says. "Especially at night, when I was alone in my bedroom. I remember looking out my window up at the stars, thinking, 'I'll never see him again.' And it just wouldn't compute. Forever, it would not compute."

Fifteen years, countless parties, and a string of abusive relationships later, she bottomed out. The year was 1982. Jeannine, who had been masking her pain with alcohol, marijuana, cocaine, and prescription drugs, finally joined a twelve-step program. This, though, was just the beginning. It would be another fifteen years before she could face Viet Nam and Jimmie's death.

"At that point," she says, "I was just making a living and figuring out what I wanted to do. I still had his letters at my parents' house. One year my parents were coming up to visit me [in Vancouver], and I asked them to bring that box of letters back up with them. After that, every once in a while I'd read one of those letters and just sob. In 1997 I was looking at the thirtieth anniversary of his death, and I was going to be forty-nine. I remember thinking, 'How did I get here? What happened? Why am I still single? Why don't I have kids?' Every time I got to Jimmie, I hit a wall. And I couldn't remember. I realized I had to understand what happened.

"I got out his letters, and I started with the first one, and I read them. Reading the letters, I had more questions. So I thought I needed to go to the library and check out some books. I found a section on Viet Nam. The first day I walked out with five or six books. Personal stories, nurses' stories, hospital stories – everything I could get my hands on. I was like a sponge. I just read. That October, my neighbors had me pick up their paper while they were away for the weekend. I picked it up that Saturday night, and one section was on the Viet Nam Veterans Memorial Traveling Wall, which was coming to Vancouver in a year. I put it on my refrigerator and thought, 'I have to go to that.' Three weeks went by, and every time I walked by the refrigerator, I looked at it. Eventually, I decided I had to volunteer there. I tracked down the coordinators and put my name on the volunteer list."

Recovering for Jeannine meant recovering her memory. She was working the swing shift at Hewlett Packard at the time, and she would use her lunch break to go online and do research. She visited sites dedicated to the war and traded e-mails with Viet Nam vets. Chuck McAllister, a vet who ran a site dedicated to Jimmie's former outfit, told her about PTSD and suggested she see a counselor.

She also got in touch with another vet, Tommy Schomber, who was there the night Jimmie died and even tried to save him. By the time Jeannine contacted him, Tommy was plagued by his own demons and took his own life shortly after. But before he died, he gave Jeannine a precious gift, satisfying her thirst for redemption and relieving her of the guilt she had been carrying for so long. He made sure she knew she wasn't responsible for Jimmie's death. Perhaps just as importantly, he simply talked with her about the young man they both had loved.

"He told me Jimmie was the kind of guy you could depend on," Jeannine says. "If Jimmie was on watch, Tommy would look up from the foxhole, and Jimmie would look down and say, 'Don't worry. I got it.' He said Jimmie was the kind of guy who could size up the situation quickly and that he had a dry sense of humor. They'd all be standing at attention, and he'd say something quietly, and all their lips would be twitching.

"That night after I spoke with him, the dream I had been having for thirty years changed. He gave me Jimmie back. I had always dreamed of trying to find Jimmie in a crowd. I would go from person to person, asking if he was there. The answer was always, 'He was just here.' But I could never find him. After talking with Tommy, my dream has been of Jimmie holding me. The contentment and serenity I feel is absolutely wonderful."

The healing process eventually took Jeannine to Jimmie's hometown, Acampo, where she reunited with his family after thirty years.

"I was terrified," she recalls. "There were a lot of people there. It was overwhelming. But everybody just talking made me feel right at home. I was sitting there, and part of me was thinking, 'This is what I could have had. This could have been my life.' I was doing okay until Jimmie's younger half-brother, Melvin, put his hand on my shoulder. I just lost it. Just the contact . . . ."

Jeannine went with Art, another of Jimmie's three half-brothers, to visit Jimmie's grave at a mausoleum in Sacramento. The two traded stories and reminisced between silent moments. The next day they visited California's memorial wall dedicated to its Viet Nam veterans. The names were listed alphabetically, starting with hometown and then last name. Jimmie's name was first on the wall.

Visiting his family and grave, volunteering at the traveling wall, corresponding with vets – all helped Jeannine claw her way out of a decades-long funk. But the process is an ongoing one, and one that waxes and wanes in intensity.

"When we were being downsized by HP," she recalls, "they provided classes for us to help with the transition. I met a gentleman at one, and I could tell he was a Viet Nam vet. I told him I had started this healing process to get closure, and he said, 'I don't think you'll ever have closure. I think what you'll do is learn to incorporate it into your life.' I don't ever want to forget Jimmie. He was a special person, and I want to hold his memory. I also want to recognize and honor him."

For Jeannine, that means coming to grips with who Jimmie was and the role he played in her life. He wasn't just a highschool crush. He was the man she was meant to spend the rest of her life with. He was her soul mate. After he died, she tried to forget. It was easier, at least up front, to lose herself in an abusive relationship or a mind-numbing drug than to remember the life that was stolen from her.

Reliving her past meant finally experiencing the full range of pain she had anaesthetized herself from while a 17-year-old girl still reeling in shock. It meant looking back at her youth and feeling like she was watching someone else – not her – find and then lose a love that would never be realized. It meant rediscovering the moments that made her sick with nostalgia – the way the air felt on her skin on a warm summer night, the way the night sky practically exploded with stars, the way a simple melody from a car radio could transport her to a life she lost.

"I'm driving home that night," she says, recalling the day she decided to reclaim her memories, "and the streets are bare. I'm going through traffic lights. It was quiet. And I found myself just sobbing. And I said out loud, 'Jimmie, as long as I'm alive, you will not be forgotten.' In that instant, *Down in the Boondocks* came on the radio."

She's back at the river with Jimmie, and it's time to go home. The sun has long since disappeared. She decides to play a joke on her sister and hide with her new boyfriend in the pitch-black darkness. She grabs the 17-year-old boy's hand and whispers in his ear the melody to Billy Joe Royal's hit single, *Down in the Boondocks*.

They had a song. They had the future all sussed out. They had everything that ever mattered.

#

Micki

Somewhere . . . a life she never lived. Somehow . . . a nostalgic sensation she never lost. Somebody . . . a familiar presence she never knew.

When Micki Spillyards holds a faded photo of her father, she holds onto the unknowable.

"I feel like I've definitely missed out on a lot of who I am," she says. "I look a lot like him. It's unbelievable how much I look like him."

Born Michelle LeeAnn Bechard on June 29, 1969, Micki was conceived in West Germany, where her father, Raymond Joseph Bechard, was stationed with the U.S. Army. She was delivered nine months later at Fort Carson, Colorado where her mother, Cecile GeorgeAnne, had retreated from a troubled marriage.

But Raymond, who had long since left for a second tour in Viet Nam, never made it home to meet his daughter. He was killed three and a half months before she was born.

Three decades later, Micki is in her thirties: a wife, a mother, and a successful web designer. She knows where she's going, knows who she is. Yet something gnaws at her.

She can't shake loose the feeling that something is missing, that something has been left undone.

"Everything that has to do with my father has been locked up in my parents' attic for years and years and years," she says. "Last time I remember seeing a picture of him was when I was a senior in high school. Just recently, I realized, man, I wanna find this information out."

So she went online. The search began.

Thus far, Micki hasn't found out much that she didn't already know. She hasn't met any of her father's old Army buddies. No one has come forward to recount the last days of his life. But simply reopening her past has allowed Micki to rediscover her roots, to reflect on the circuitous path she followed to the present. More than anything, she has realized that the story of her childhood – and how she came into this world – makes even the most melodramatic made-for-television mini-series look, well, boring.

Raymond Bechard was born on November 3, 1943 in the Canadian province of Quebec. His parents moved him and his brother to Augusta, Maine, when they were teenagers. But their French-Canadian roots followed them. Their mother, in fact, never learned to read or write in English. Raymond was known for cutting loose in French whenever he lost his temper.

Raymond joined the Army in 1963, a 19-year-old boy ready to see the world. He got all that he bargained for and more when he served a year in Viet Nam in 1967. A gunshot wound to the hand, inflicted by a sniper, earned him a Purple Heart. When his tour was up, he continued his service stateside at Fort Carson, an Army base near Colorado Springs, Colorado.

Not long after returning home, he met Nancy Lou Castle – or Lou, as everyone called her – at a bar. She was serving drinks, and he was instantly smitten. He asked her out on a date only to find out that she was married and that she and her husband Patrick owned the bar together. Undeterred,

Raymond bought the couple a drink. After all, he didn't know anyone in town and was just hoping for some good company. As it happened, the three became fast friends, with Raymond even living with the Castles for a few months.

Lou, meanwhile, introduced Raymond to her sister, Cecile Gwartney. The two started dating, and she became pregnant.

"I think he felt obligated to marry her," says Micki, who wonders if Raymond was secretly in love with Nancy. "He moved her out to Maine to live with his mother. She miscarried the baby. But they had already gotten married. Then she came to live with him in Germany. Rumor has it that she wasn't really pregnant, that she kind of trapped him."

Cecile and Raymond's marriage, only a few months old, began to fray after the couple moved to an Army base in West Germany. She returned home to Colorado Springs as a result, and he signed up for another tour in Viet Nam shortly thereafter. He had only been in Viet Nam a few weeks when his estranged wife wrote to tell him she was pregnant and that she had actually conceived in Germany. Then, on March 9, 1969, with his wife five-and-a-half months pregnant, Raymond was killed by small arms fire in Kontum, South Viet Nam. He died while trying to come to the aid of a fellow soldier who had been wounded, and he was posthumously awarded another Purple Heart, plus the Silver Star, for his gallantry.

Had that been the only tragedy in Cecile's life, she no doubt would have found a way to pick up the pieces and start afresh with her new daughter. Instead, Raymond's death marked the beginning of a series of calamities.

"Shortly after giving birth to me, she got involved with another man in the Army and got married," Micki says. "She got pregnant again. She had the baby prematurely, and it died. He cleaned out their bank account and all the money she had gotten from my father's death and took off. She didn't have any money and moved back with her parents.

"I was with my grandparents, with my aunt and uncle, with my other aunt and uncle. She was not very stable. When I was about four, she met another man who was a Viet Nam vet, and they got engaged. The story, as I understand it, is that they were talking about the Viet Nam War, and she said something about baby killers. She swears that she wasn't saying that *he* was a baby killer. But he took it the wrong way and drove himself off of Pike's Peak and killed himself. So she pretty much lost it at that point, and that's when I went to live with my aunt and uncle."

Lou, after divorcing Patrick, had since tied the knot with her highschool sweetheart, Dan Ward. The two officially adopted Micki when she was seven, but Micki insists her first seven years weren't as precarious as they could have been.

"My aunt was like *the* motherly person of the entire group," she says. "My grandparents on my mom's side lived in the same house from the time my parents were teenagers, and my aunt and uncle lived just two houses down from there. A lot of time was spent with my aunt or my grandparents, so that allowed a lot of stability for me."

Moving in permanently with her aunt and uncle, meanwhile, wasn't exactly a seamless transition.

"They're very loving with each other, very stable, very conservative churchgoers, Republican," Micki says. "I was raised in an Assembly of God home. They believe in speaking in tongues, the laying on of hands. They've mellowed out quite a bit in their old age, thank God, but they're very different than what my mom is like.

"But I was very fortunate. I don't know what I would have done if they hadn't been so selfless and taken me into their home when they were first wed. And they had two children from her first marriage already. It was completely and totally selfless."

When she was twelve, Micki moved with her new family from Security, a small suburb of Colorado Springs, to Bastrop,

Texas, where her uncle worked in the oil fields. Dan's work led to another relocation when Micki was a sophomore in high school. This time, the family moved to nearby Bryan, Texas.

"Only a year and a half later," Micki explains, "the oil industry went bust, and we moved to Tucson, Arizona, in the summer between my junior and senior years in high school. My birth mother had moved to California with her husband in the early eighties, and then to Tucson. This was the first time we had lived that close to each other in over eight years.

"I was very upset with my parents for moving us yet again, and really rebelled against them. I began hanging out with a rough crowd and shunning the church scene that my parents were in. In December of that year, when my parents told me that we were moving back to Bastrop over the Christmas break, I freaked out and refused to go. I used the whole you're-not-my-parents-therefore-you-can't-tell-me-what-to-do line and moved out of their house and in with my real mother so I could finish out my senior year in Tucson."

Adds Micki, "I really rebelled for some time. But I came around. And I spent numerous hours mending the relationship with my adoptive parents. I also had to mend the relationship with Mom. There was some resentment there because she wasn't strong enough to take care of me. I wouldn't listen to her when it came time for me to have a baby because I thought, 'You don't even know how to be a parent.'"

Although Micki moved out on her own shortly after graduation, she continued to live in Tucson and remained close to her birth mother. After a few months at community college, she dropped out and landed a job at a bar. When she was twenty-two, she went back to school, earning a degree at the Arts Center in Tucson. She got married, had a son, Sean, and worked as a production artist for a short stint before her alma mater recruited her to teach.

When her first marriage failed, she left Tucson for Texas. Her mother had long since moved to Las Vegas. And there was nothing for her in the desert.

These days, she's back in Bastrop, where she and her second husband John share five acres with her adoptive parents. Sean, an athletic kid with a wry sense of humor, is eleven years old and ready to start junior high. Everyone has survived the growing pains, and Micki feels blessed to be on good terms with her mother and her adoptive parents. But her past still beckons.

"It's been very different living a life without knowing my blood father or his family," she explains. "I have an amazing dad who filled that void, and I wouldn't change my life for the world. But my curiosity about my father has always been something that has driven me. I have tried to find things out about my father, but I'm continually facing the hurt feelings of the man who raised me. It's weird."

When she first moved in with them, her aunt and uncle gave Micki her father's medals, plus a stein that contained all of the money – some of it still stained with blood – he had on him when he was killed in Viet Nam. She lost many of the items, and the remaining ones found their way into a box in the attic, courtesy of her aunt. She'd like to see them again, but she can't bring up the medals with her adoptive father. At least not yet.

In fact, the more she explores her relationship with her former aunt and uncle turned parents, the more she realizes how truly complicated the situation is.

"To tell you the truth," she says, "I believe it's more my adoptive mother who really has the issue with me pursuing information about my real father. Maybe it is so painful for her that she uses my adoptive father's feelings as an excuse to keep me from opening that wound. It sounds weird, but the more I think about it, the more I think that is the issue."

What of her mother, who suffered a nervous breakdown after Raymond was killed and whose life seemed destined for tragedy?

"I'm still in contact with her," Micki says of her mother, who has been married to the same man for the last twenty-five years. "But she's not living a very happy life. She fights depression. She's addicted to pain pills. I just don't think she could get a break."

Micki still calls her mother "Mom." But Aunt Nancy Lou is also "Mom." And Uncle Dan will always be the only father she knew.

As for her birth father, the mystery remains.

"What did his friends think of him?" she wonders. "What was his sense of humor like? There really isn't one thing I am most curious about. It's *everything* that I'm curious about."

She's been told that her father was a dead ringer for Jack Webb, a la *Dragnet,* that he regularly had everyone in stitches with his Pepe Le Pew imitation, and that he drove a Ford Mustang – what Micki's cousins would later call his "horsy car."

"My aunt has shared more stories with me than even my mother has about my father," she says. "She paints him as someone with a fantastic sense of humor, handsome, and as a gentleman. My mother, on the other hand, says that he was an alcoholic and that they were not very happy and that he had a bad temper."

The closest Micki ever got to his world was during a visit to Augusta, Maine, three decades ago.

"Once, and only once, I met his mother," she recalls. "I had this yellow blanket that I used to carry with me everywhere, and I called it my 'neengee.' My mother had no idea why I called it that. While we were with my grandmother and she heard that, she dropped the cup she was holding and turned white. My mother asked her what was wrong, and she proceeded to tell the story of how my father had called a blanket that he had carried around with him that exact same thing. Now how in the world had I thought up that same thing?"

She shares the same blood, even if she never knew him. How many others out there lost a father to Viet Nam before they even had a chance to meet him?

"Funny," she says, "but I have never met anyone else whose father was killed before they could meet him. I would love to find others like that because I am sure they are out there, and I would be very curious to see how it has affected them.

"It's so hard to add an emotion to what I feel about my father. I don't feel like I have a void in my life, but I do have a great sense of curiosity about him and his family and what of them is in me. I believe that genetics have a lot to do with who you are as a person, and yet I know nothing about the genetics of that part of me."

Living with that sort of conundrum has given Micki a certain sense of self-reliance, an independent streak that can't be quelled.

"I really don't have any kind of mentor or hero," she says. "I've chosen my own path, had many trials, found myself down and out a couple of times, but have always picked myself back up and kept on going. I am forever striving to find what I consider to be 'happiness,' and sometimes I feel like I am cursed to suffer like my mother did. Other times I know that I have had it pretty damn good, all things considered."

Nevertheless, a war she never fought changed her life forever.

"Only recently have I even started to watch movies on Viet Nam," she says. "I really don't know very much about it at all. I was very shielded from anything pertaining to the war while growing up, and I feel like that was a little unfair of my parents. I believe that it was an unnecessary war, and I find it mortifying that people actually spat on the soldiers when they came back.

"I want to find out more and would love to find someone who was there with my father. I would give anything to know him through the eyes of someone who isn't trying to protect me or shield me, to hear someone share with me stories about him."

Chapter 3: Homecoming
The Webb Family

What did the American soldier bring to Viet Nam? Who was he before he held a gun in his hands?

He exhales slowly, cautiously. The war is over, he assures himself. He's all strapped in, counting the hours between now and his return to the world. The stultifying heat, the fetid odor of rotting vegetation, the sun-scorched corner of hell he has called home for the last 365 days shrinks as the plane lifts. The monotonous jungle beneath him gives way to an ocean that stretches beyond the pale blue horizon. It's big enough, he thinks, deep enough to drown the memories. The smell of death, the almost comically disfigured bodies, the look in a buddy's eyes that says he knows his number's up – everything from the bush will be jettisoned, deep-sixed in the ocean 30,000 feet beneath him. It's big enough. Deep enough.

Does it matter what he brought to Viet Nam? Does it matter who he was before he joined the war? He's headed home. *Home.*

#

"The first thing I saw when I got off the plane at Travis Air Force Base [in Oakland, California] was a young lady in a miniskirt," Steven B. Webb says, recalling the day he came home from Viet Nam in March 1970. "I didn't even know what a miniskirt was. I thought, 'Holy cow! What happened to the world while I was gone?'"

Steve's mild amusement turned into profound shock a few days later in nearby Burbank.

"We went to a big parade," he says of his Marine unit. "We were in our dress outfits. There were protestors there. One girl told me I was a baby killer and that all of us should have died in Viet Nam. I tried to be nice and explain to her that 1968 was the Year of the Monkey in Viet Nam. Some of the Viet Namese believed that the only way a child born that year could go to heaven was to die for a loyal cause. That's why a lot of the Viet Namese women would bundle up their kids with dynamite, take them up to American GI's, and then blow them up. I tried to explain it to her, but she wouldn't listen. I just walked away."

Several months later, Steve's older brother came home from the same war. His was an anonymous homecoming. Dale Lee Webb arrived at LA International Airport and quietly boarded another plane, this one bound for Billings, Montana.

Like his homecoming, Dale's experiences in Viet Nam, though by no means combat-free, had been relatively quiet compared to Steve's. Although he had taken a few hairy helicopter rides into hot LZ's, sometimes even firing a machine gun during the descent, most of Dale's time in Viet Nam was spent shuffling papers, making reports, and helping to keep the Marine bureaucracy running efficiently. Steve, on the other hand, had passed his days in the bush with an M-16 in his hands and twenty-one bandoleers wrapped around his chest. For him, Viet Nam was a tension-filled endurance test, an ordeal as psychologically exhausting as it had been physically demanding.

Today, one brother has held the same job for over a decade and has managed to keep Viet Nam in the past. The other struggles with Post-Traumatic Stress Disorder and eschews personal and professional commitments at all costs. But if there is a relationship between their experiences in Viet Nam and how they have coped since, the link is a mysterious one.

Steve, despite his grueling marathon in Viet Nam, emerged comparatively unscathed. Dale, who caught only brief glimpses of the war on the ground, is still struggling to put it behind him.

"I don't think Viet Nam changed either one of them," Marian Webb says of her two oldest sons. "Dale is the same now as he was when he was just a tiny little kid."

Is he?

"He writes yucky poems," Marian concedes. "Usually about dying."

#

Belfry, Montana. This is rugged country. Farm country. Wild West country. Summer is a simmering cauldron, winter a seething icebox. The Beartooth Mountains loom in the southwest. The Wyoming state line runs east to west just beyond the southern horizon. Billings is only an hour or so drive to the north.

Dale and Steve grew up here in this sparsely populated town that sits at 3,000 feet. So did their younger brothers, John and Ed, as well as their sister, Sharon, the youngest of the five siblings. They were raised on a 280-acre farm which their parents, Elmer and Marian Webb, leased for a decade before eventually buying in 1960.

"Looking back, it was probably the best thing that ever happened to me," Steve says of growing up on the farm. "I'd love to be back on one now. At the time, we thought it was boring – and an awful lot of hard work. You learn responsibility at a young age. You know – driving tractors and farm equipment when you're ten years old. We had a lot of chores. We milked thirteen cows every night and every morning. We did everything from hoeing the garden to cutting and stacking hay to pulling calves when they were born.

"We'd separate the cream from the milk. We had an old separator you'd turn by hand, and the speed would make the cream rise to the top and float off and be separated. We'd save the cream in five-gallon cans and sell it to a creamery in a town nearby. Mom would get her butter and sometimes ice cream, and they'd give her a check, which she'd use to buy groceries."

Adds Steve, whose family butchered cows and pigs once a year, "We were considered poor dirt farmers, but in the summertime we'd have steak, salad, and French fries every night."

Though short on space and sometimes overloaded with work, the family was a close-knit one and remains so today.

"When we were kids," Steve remembers, "we had our normal fights like all kids do, even a couple fistfights in our early years in high school. But I can't remember a time after we became adults that anyone in our family ever physically had a fight with another one. We were raised to respect each other and each other's ideas. Even if we disagreed with each other, we still respected the other one's opinion. And we never argued with our mother, no matter what, even to this day."

Dale, too, has plenty of warm childhood memories. But they're colored by a darker kind of introspection. The images and recollections start simply enough before giving way to something less storybook.

"I was given a colt to break when I was about twelve," he says, tracing his memory. "I rode him bareback and very seldom used a saddle. I could race him as fast as he could go with no saddle or blanket. I wore tennis shoes and Levis but no shirt during the summer, and you can't believe how many people stopped me alongside the road to take a picture of me on my horse against the Beartooth Mountains in the background."

He continues, "I guess I had a quite happy childhood, although I never had any privacy during that time because the houses we lived in all had just one big room for all four of us boys. I think, now that I look back, I was probably a pretty moody child and quite contrary. I know I used to argue with my dad a lot, and that would upset my mom. But I did break the way for my younger brothers and sister to do things at an earlier age or do things I wasn't allowed to do."

The responsibility inherent in being the oldest of five often weighed heavily on Dale as he was growing up. He remembers his youth differently than Steve, whose recollections are unclouded and even idyllic.

Not surprisingly, Dale rebelled.

"I used to sneak out of the bunkhouse and walk to town or to my friend's house and push his car away from the house and drive to town to party," he says. "I did a lot of drinking in high school, but never during football season."

Dale, a stocky five-foot-nine, excelled on the gridiron. But he wasn't a stereotypical jock. From junior high on, he always had his nose in a book in order to, in his words, "escape my life." He eventually discovered acting and landed roles in several school plays. He even won a couple of acting awards while in high school. And he could type faster than most people drove the highway to Billings.

"He was always the smart one in the family," Steve says.

Because he wore glasses – a condition no longer considered a liability – Dale was refused admission to the Air Force Academy toward the tail end of his senior year. He drifted the following fall, deflated and aimless. He enrolled at a small junior college in Powell, Wyoming, where his girlfriend and best friend from high school also attended. But he spent more time partying than he did studying.

"I think a lot of that was getting away from all my brothers and sister and being on my own for the first time," he concludes. "I didn't know how to make the right decisions."

His next decision would affect the rest of his life. But like most vets who went to Viet Nam (including his brother), he insists he would do the same in a heartbeat.

#

In March 1968, Steve, a senior in high school, signed up for the Marines. Partly, he admits, he did so because it was better than being drafted. But he had other reasons, as well.

"I feel in some ways the U.S. government was a little arrogant to think they could solve the problems between North and South Viet Nam," he says. "To try to do that cost a lot of people their lives. But I'd do the same thing over again because from the moment the first American died, it was my war, too."

He wouldn't be alone. As soon as he got wind of his younger brother's decision to join the Marines, Dale signed up alongside Steve.

"I think a lot had to do with the fact that I wasn't doing a very good job in college," Dale explains, "and I always thought that I would like to make the military a career. I thought I was tough because no one ever tried to fight me in high school, and they all had a lot of respect for my toughness on the football field. Also, I took to riding broncos and bulls while in college, so I thought I was a pretty mean SOB.

"As far as joining because of Steve, maybe that was part of it. I don't know. I had been in charge of my brothers since we were young, and the habit is hard to break."

In June, the two Webb brothers traveled to boot camp in San Diego as part of an eighty-man, all-Montana platoon. After eight weeks of boot camp, they were separated, with Dale sent to office administrative school and Steve sent to

ITR, or Intensive Training Regiment. Dale wasted little time in earning an E5 sergeant ranking, garnering one meritorious promotion after another. Steve finished ITR and then basic infantry training before going to the staging battalion, where he awaited orders for Viet Nam. After three months of Viet Namese language school, he joined the war on March 6, 1969.

"When I heard that Steve was in Viet Nam and was with Kilo Company, Third Battalion, Ninth Marines, I was scared," says Dale, who would be stationed another year in San Diego. "They were called 'the walking dead.'"

#

"It seemed like we were always on edge," Steve says of combat in Viet Nam. "You spent hours on edge waiting for something to happen. And then most of it, when it did happen, didn't last but a few minutes, and then it was over."

Stationed near the Rock Pile and the DMZ, Steve's unit went on daily patrols, swept for mines, and conducted other infantry-related operations. They found themselves in plenty of firefights, one lasting over five hours, and were pitted against NVA regulars. While in the bush, Steve survived tainted water, rivers full of leaches, a helicopter crash, and one fateful day he was certain would be his last.

"Every morning when we woke up," he remembers, "there was always someone in my platoon who said, 'I know I'm gonna die today.' Well, the day I said that I was walking point, and we came upon a location that was supposed to have been abandoned by a Marine company. But we saw movement there. I almost opened up. And they almost opened up."

The Marine company was still there. Last-minute radio contact saved more than a few lives.

"I realized that I almost talked myself into making a mistake," Steve says. "I never said it again. Little things like that could get you killed."

After six months in Viet Nam, Steve got out. Without a scratch. The Third Battalion, Ninth Marines had been the first marines to arrive in Viet Nam as the war was escalating. Now, as part of an incremental withdrawal, they would be the first to be shipped out.

"The whole unit was being pulled out, and I had had enough operations to my credit that I could go out or stay in Viet Nam," Steve recalls. "My commanding officer approached me and said my brother Dale wanted to go to Viet Nam, but the government had a rule that only one family member could go to Viet Nam at a time."

He had a choice: switch units, or stay with his and go to Okinawa.

"I told my lieutenant, 'I'm ready,'" Steve remembers. "'Get me out of here. I've seen enough of this.'"

#

"The first thing I did in Viet Nam was look at the old timers," Dale says. "I did whatever they did. When in the barracks, I undressed if they did and slept in my clothes if they did. I had read that the worst and best time to die over there was your first thirty days and your last thirty days.

"My first night in Danang was spent in a wooden barracks, and I was on the third floor. Like I said, I watched the old timers. Since they only took off their boots, I did the same. About three o'clock in the morning when we were all asleep, the VC started sending in rockets. My first time, and God, I was scared! But I watched the old timers, and I was one of the first out of the building because I didn't have to get dressed. All I had to do was put my boots on. It was quite an experience, but I can remember it like it was yesterday."

Dale wasn't given long to find his bearings. The next morning he was issued orders to help organize a move to Marble Mountain, where, upon arrival, he was made chief clerk for the general. His primary responsibility: churning out daily reports for each squadron.

"After about two months, I volunteered to be a gunner on a helicopter," he says. "But my general refused to let me go on any missions. Well, what I did was make friends with some pilots. They knew you didn't mess with your office personnel because of records, payroll, and other things that could get fouled up. So any time the general was out of the area, they would let me fly as a machine gunner on a CH-46. But since it was against the general's orders, I couldn't put in for flight pay, wings, or anything else that would show that I flew. I usually went up on medevac runs and worked with the corpsman. I did do some inserts and extracts, too, although I blocked a lot of that out of my mind.

"I can remember one extract where it was such a hot zone that I wasn't supposed to be there. We couldn't land to pick up a recon team, so we sent down a one-hundred-foot ladder. Well, out of seven men, four were wounded, and they came up the ladder first. They were shot in the legs, arms, and one in the side, but they were all mobile. Anyway, they only came up the ladder far enough so that every one of them could get on the ladder. Then I can remember how they started laughing and twirling the ladder so they could fire down at the VC on the ground. My pilot called them crazy sons of bitches who didn't deserve to be brought out, but I always remember them as an example of what I thought the Marine Corps was all about."

Why would someone who had a relatively safe job as a desk jockey volunteer to go into a hot LZ? Why would someone disobey orders just to get a taste of the fighting?

"I had been going with the same girl since we were sophomores in high school," Dale recalls. "We even went to college together until I enlisted in the Marine Corps. She went with my parents to see me off at the airport when we left. On a couple of my leaves while in California, I would go home for fifteen days and visit her. Well, while in Viet Nam, I got a Dear John letter from her. It wasn't quite the best place to get one, and I really wasn't aware of the dangers I put myself through for the next two months. But survival is a matter that tends to bring us back to reality. So I got over it finally."

Despite his furtive helicopter missions, Dale remained in the general's good graces, earning frequent three-day passes to exotic cities like Bangkok, Hong Kong, Singapore, and Tokyo. In Viet Nam, he regularly frequented a nightclub where he paid the waitress one dollar a month to reserve him a table in front of the stage. After a year's tour, he packed his things for home.

"My base at Marble Mountain was being turned over to the Army because all marines were supposed to be leaving Viet Nam," he explains. "My general made sure I was one of the last marines on the mountain. Then he put me on a champagne flight to Okinawa. There were photographers and news people aboard, but I can't remember what I said to them because I was too busy drinking champagne.

"We landed in Okinawa, and I spent three days there before flying into LA International and then hopping a plane right on to Montana."

Dale would log another year in the Marines, during which time he was stationed in Washington, D.C. before obtaining an early release in March 1972 to attend college. Steve, meanwhile, remained in the Marines long enough to re-enlist, performing his duties stateside from 1970-1972 and then serving in Okinawa and off the coast of Viet Nam for another year.

Their paths, though, continued to diverge after the war, with Steve shaking the nightmare loose and Dale sinking into its lingering aftermath.

#

"My uncle had a bar-type counter between his kitchen and dining room," Dale says, recalling the day he came home on leave after returning from Viet Nam. "I was sitting at the counter. I had an arm around my mom on one side and my uncle on the other. My aunt, who was real short and could just barely see over the counter, was making us some iced tea. A sonic boom went off, and before my mom or my uncle knew what happened, I had them both on the floor under the table. I realized as soon as I hit the floor what had happened – that the sonic boom sounded just like rockets in Viet Nam. I got up laughing, but my mom and my uncle weren't laughing very hard. My aunt was scared because one second we were at the counter, and the next we were gone."

He adds, "One thing my family found out in a hurry after I came back from Viet Nam was that if I fell asleep on the couch, it was best to holler to wake me up and not touch me. My four-year-old nephew didn't know any better and came in and saw me asleep on the couch and ran to give me a big hug. I was asleep, and as soon as he touched me, I swung my fist and hit him. Luckily, I didn't hurt him. But he wouldn't have much to do with me for several days after that."

Dale finished his stateside tour early in order to return to college. But his second stint, this one at Mesa College in Grand Junction, Colorado, didn't last much longer than his first stab at higher education. He partied a lot. Played a little football. Joined a rodeo that spring. After that, he tried his hand at a few odd jobs, acting as a cowboy and ranch hand. But nothing stuck.

He also got to know his grandfather, William B. Webb, a fierce patriot and charter member of the local American Legion, who seemed to have a newfound respect for his grandson.

"When he died in January of 1973," Dale says, "I don't think that had anything to do with me moving on, but I couldn't be satisfied anywhere I went. I went to Seattle and worked for Boeing, then off to California and tried to break into stunts. Then I went back to Oregon, and finally I ended up back in Washington, D.C. From there for the next three years I traveled all over the United States. I don't think there is a state that I haven't been in or worked in. I was pretty lax in keeping in contact with my family. There were times that nobody knew where I was for a year or so, then I would tell someone and get back in contact with my family. It's hard to remember exactly what I did or who I knew during this time period. I can remember all of the places I worked, but very few names and no one who I kept in contact with."

One of the hallmarks of PTSD is an inability to remember names, faces, dates – even important events. Trauma acts like a mudslide, burying the past and reducing history to a disjointed tangle of hazy recollections and confusing emotions. Often, a victim of PTSD is more in tune with the distorted offspring of a crucial moment than he is with the actual trigger, now nothing more than a dim recollection.

Instead of seeing an orderly past that reads like a book, Dale struggles to make out his life's progression since joining the Marines in 1968.

"Steve made lots of friends in boot camp, but I can't remember one," he says. "The only ones I remember all died in Viet Nam."

What happened after boot camp? He remembers few names of the men he served with; even the name of his general in Viet Nam escapes him.

"I can remember going on liberty [while still stateside], and it seems that ninety percent of the time I went by myself," he says. "I can't remember anyone else going with me, or at least their names. I went to Las Vegas, Los Angeles, Tijuana, and other places just to get away. I can remember going to towns and watching people. But I can't remember who I was with."

College life?

"I can't even remember my roommate's name," he says, "nor anybody else from there. I can remember the name of the bar we all went to called 'Teddy's Place' that we drank and danced at. Teddy would even lend some of us cowboys money for a rodeo if we needed help paying our entry fees."

Dale didn't abuse drugs, although he would be the first to admit that he drank too much in those days. Mostly, though, he was addicted to change. Like a hummingbird moving from flower to flower, he never stayed anywhere long enough to see his own shadow.

"I remember walking into New York City in 1976," he says, "and I had $2.95 in my pockets. That was at ten o'clock in the morning. By nightfall, I had a job and a place to stay. During this time period, I could usually find a job because all I had to say was that I was a farm boy from Montana and people would hire me because I knew how to work. Also, the Marine Corps had trained me as a personnel clerk, so I could work for Kelly Girls [a temporary work agency]."

In 1978, his father and his brother Ed started their own oilfield maintenance company back in Montana, and, like the prodigal son, Dale returned to his hometown to live and work. He worked with them until 1990 and continued to work odd jobs in Montana until 2002. That year, a slew of health problems and his struggle with PTSD finally inspired him to travel to the VA Hospital in Breckenridge, Ohio, which specializes in helping PTSD victims find the road to recovery.

"I had open-heart surgery in 2001," he says, "and the doctor laughed and said I had three strikes against me: Viet Nam, Agent Orange, and diabetes."

The latter, incidentally, has been linked to Agent Orange exposure. But Dale has had little luck in wresting disability compensation from the government. After getting treatment in Ohio, he moved to Virginia to live near his brother, John, and to hook up with a highly regarded counseling program at the McGuire VA Clinic in Fredericksburg.

"The counseling made me worse, and I was getting more depressed," he said. "I haven't drank since 1991 and was wanting to start again while in counseling. I didn't have that feeling when I quit. So I quit and haven't felt like drinking since. I haven't gone back to either counselor."

Adds Dale, "They weren't trying to get me disability. All they did was ask me questions about whether or not I masturbated a lot and why I didn't join a singles group and try to get involved with some women there. That wasn't why I was going to them. I could have done that on my own."

Meanwhile, his health problems multiplied.

"I have discovered that I have an infection in my other foot, and my diabetes is out of control," he says, having already lost a toe on his left foot due to an infection. "So I don't know what to do. I need to try and get on disability, but I don't know how to live while I'm waiting for approval or disapproval. I really think Viet Nam was responsible for my being a non-sociable person and traveling all over the U.S. I know that I couldn't form a lasting relationship with any person after I came back."

Dale maintains that often the look on his face is enough to thwart any would-be friends. In fact, when he recalls his travels, he remembers that he often frequented bars and taverns in countless seedy neighborhoods from San Francisco to New York. Everybody – barflies, hustlers, drug dealers, and bikers – gave him a wide berth.

"I was never afraid to go anyplace after Viet Nam," he says.

Anyplace, it seems, save perhaps the source of what haunts him.

He was old enough to fight – and die – for his country halfway across the world. But he wasn't old enough to drink a beer when he got home. The incident still sticks in Steve's craw, although he can laugh about it now.

"My parents met me at the airport in Billings," he recalls of his return home after the war. "I was only twenty years old. We stopped at a local bar. Nobody was in the bar except me and my dad and mom. My dad wanted to buy me a drink. The barmaid refused to serve me a drink, even though I was in uniform. My dad even asked her, 'Why don't you give him a glass of Coke and put a shot of whiskey in it?' She refused to do even that. That's something I'll never forget."

A minor incident, but one that came on the heels of being called a baby killer only a few days before back in California.

"I think those things are bitter memories because to me that's a form of disrespect," he says. "Even though maybe I hadn't earned respect in their eyes, they still should have respected where I had been and what I had done. Maybe that's part of the problem with all Viet Nam vets: we don't feel we were ever given the respect we should've been given for what we did.

"Everybody likes to be recognized – I don't care who you are, whether you're a kid or an adult. It's something you need. Even in the job I have today, I've gotten three letters of commendation, and that still makes you feel good, even at the age of fifty-two."

Though by no means tragedy-free, Steve's road out of Viet Nam has been smoother than his older brother's. He has had his share of problems since the shooting stopped: two divorces, another wife lost to cancer, and his eldest daughter lost to a heart problem complicated by heroin addiction. He has nightmares about the war on occasion. And he can't watch violent movies, especially ones about war, without getting the shakes. But he has carved out a life largely free of Viet Nam and its legacy.

"I've been lucky," he says. "I've been lucky enough to love four women in my life [including his current girlfriend]. I've had five of my own kids, plus step kids. If you want to count things, you count them all as blessings, not bad things that have happened to you."

A detention officer at the county jail in Yellowstone County since 1990, he lives in Billings and hopes to someday buy a little land out of town. In his spare time, he sings and plays guitar. With his father on fiddle and his youngest brother Ed on electric bass, he heads up a country western band called Five-Star Country. And he's the president of the Montana State District 4 Fiddlers Association, which hosts a big jam every other Sunday at the local tavern.

His biggest fan is his stepdaughter, Kris Dance, although it's not his music that has won her admiration. She was almost out of the house by the time he married her mom, and the marriage didn't last. But she considers him her true father.

"My grandfather [Elmer] and my dad are the most honest people I've ever met in my life," says Kris, a college student and secretary at a hospital in Dallas, Texas. "When I had my daughter, my dad was in the delivery room with me. He gave me as much love as he gave his own children and never thought twice about it.

"He gave me respect for myself, my country. He gave me a good work ethic. He taught me how to be proud without being arrogant. Strong. Honest. And forgiving. In a few short years with my dad, I was able to learn every lesson that a child should learn.

"He's my hero."

#

What happened? How did two brothers from rural Montana return from the war with such different outlooks? Why has one managed for the most part to put the war behind him while the other has struggled to escape its grip? Why is there no apparent correlation between what they saw in Viet Nam and how they've gone on since?

The answer, both Dale and Steve insist, is fairly simple. In the end, combat played second fiddle to personality in shaping their experiences in Viet Nam.

God, I am a lonely man, for I am lost and know not where I am, Dale began his first poem while atop Marble Mountain in Viet Nam on June 24, 1970. *My life is like a caravan that travels forever and stops not even for a traffic jam.*

The poem continues:

> *I go from here to there*
>
> *and try to find a quiet place*
>
> *to put down a root.*
>
> *But friends elude me everywhere,*
>
> *and I keep traveling and praying*
>
> *for I am very destitute.*
>
> *But I know you will hear,*
>
> *and then you will come to answer*
>
> *all my prayers.*
>
> *Maybe not this year,*
>
> *but your answer when it comes will be*
>
> *like a burst of light from a flare.*

Though the oldest of five children, though perfectly capable of leading by example, meeting his responsibilities and interacting with the family, Dale is at heart a loner. Shirtless and windblown, his shadow a streaking silhouette against the jagged Beartooth Mountains, he's still breaking in that colt.

"Dale is the type who withdraws into himself a lot," Steve says. "He's very sociable when he's around people. But at the same time, he can be extremely withdrawn and antisocial. It's almost like mood swings. Sometimes when Dale's here, you can sit down and visit with him about anything and everything. The next time you talk to him, he doesn't want to look at anybody. He doesn't want to talk to anybody. He just wants to be left alone."

If Dale naturally gravitates toward playing the part of the loner, Steve is the affable one who likes to chew the fat. He's laid back. He likes a good laugh. Underneath it all is a steely reserve, an almost cocky confidence that can't wait for the next challenge.

"I've always felt I could handle myself in certain situations better than some people," he says. "That may sound a little arrogant, but it's just one of those things I feel inside. Viet Nam had an impact on me, but it didn't change fundamentally who I am. I don't think I'm any different than I was before I went to Viet Nam. My main drive in life is to be the best I can be at something and try to make other people realize that they can rely on me and count on me. That's the way I was when I was growing up on the farm."

Though Dale was at times overwhelmed with the responsibilities inherent in being the oldest brother, Steve openly yearned for them.

"I was more out to please other people and put myself second," he says. "I was more out there to do for other people, because I always felt that was what's necessary in life."

Such a philosophy could backfire if one were hoping for recognition or a reward for good intentions. But Steve's motives, it seems, aren't overly complicated by the ego or its trappings.

How, though, did someone whose aim is to please others pull the trigger? How did someone who was raised to respect the feelings and opinions of others add to a body count without feeling the weight of his own actions? How did he wipe the blood clean?

"I never hated the Viet Namese," he says. "One thing that helped me keep my sanity was that I didn't look at them as human but more as an animal that was trying to kill me. I just did what I had to do. I think everybody justifies what they did in different ways. But that's how I justified it to keep my sanity. Honestly, I believe those who came back and couldn't deal with what happened over there are the ones who couldn't find a justification for what they did."

Nevertheless, it takes a certain amount of resolve to keep a lid on the war and to make sense of the senseless slaughter, even with a mental construct in place.

"Steve's the type to just shut it off," his father says.

His daughter agrees, to an extent. "I think he has it all inside," Kris says. "Some of it is pressed down tightly. Some of it rises to the top every once in a while. But basically he's learned that tolerance is best. He doesn't shoot guns anymore. He always said he shot enough in Viet Nam. He doesn't do much of anything to get a rise out of anybody. He just wants to live his life, find happiness – what we all want."

She adds, "Every single minute of the war is documented in his head. And it hasn't turned him bitter, harsh, or cynical. If anything, it's made him more understanding, stronger, and more tolerant."

If only Dale could find the same sense of catharsis. Instead, he feels trapped in a world of bitterness, unable to let down his guard.

"I still have feelings and lots of empathy for people," he says, "but now I just won't let it show. I can be a very harsh person. Tears don't faze me like they used to. I just don't let my sympathy come out into the open. I mean, I have a hard time giving my mom or sister a hug. My family has always been openly affectionate with each other, but I have a hard time with that sometimes."

#

Dale and Steve don't discuss the war. One would think that two brothers who lived through similar versions of hell would want to trade stories and share each other's heartbreak. Not so, in this case.

"I haven't talked much about Viet Nam," Dale says, "even with other vets. I don't know why that is."

Steve is even more succinct. "We haven't talked about it much," he says.

Neither has the family. Viet Nam has remained an open secret. Not necessarily taboo, but not fodder for daily conversations, either.

That doesn't mean, though, that the family hasn't supported them over the years.

"There was no way we didn't back them," Elmer says of his two sons. "We were proud of them for serving their country, whether it was a lost cause or not."

Their mother and younger sister say the same thing.

"I was very, very proud of them for being there and sticking it out," Marian says.

Adds Elmer, "I'm still proud. Any time it comes up about the service, I say I had two boys in Viet Nam and three who were marines during that era. They did what they thought was right. I'm proud of them. Always have been."

As for the third son who volunteered for the Marines, John served from 1971 to 1974.

"I went into the Marines in May of 1971," he says. "I had gone through boot camp and all that stuff. As I was finishing up my Military Police School, they were withdrawing marines from Viet Nam. Some of the Army guys I graduated with did go to Viet Nam. I always thought I would end up going over. I didn't really feel any regret for not going over, but at the same time I wish I would have had the chance."

A civil servant in Washington, D.C., John lives with his wife and two children in northern Virginia. Until Dale moved out to D.C., he hadn't had much contact with his brothers since the war. But he has an interesting perspective on the war and how it has affected the Webb family.

"Basically, Steve put most of Viet Nam behind him, whereas Dale hasn't," he says. "I really don't know why because I've never sat down with either one of them and talked about what went on while they were over there. Steve hasn't said much at all. Dale spoke a little about his helicopter runs. Dale is quite the loner. He only lives maybe ten miles away from me. We probably talk once every two weeks or so is all, and usually I initiate the call. He is just a loner type person. That's probably why he moves around a lot, too. I know when he was in high school, he hung out with a lot of friends, so he wasn't a loner then. But that doesn't mean he wouldn't have been a loner later on in life after he started working.

"I've never brought the war up around them. I basically felt that if they were going to bring it up, they would talk about it. Some of my curiosity may have been taken out because I was in the military and a lot of people I worked with had been in Viet Nam, and they talked about it a little bit. But even they wouldn't say much. To me, I got the idea from them that, hey, if they wanted to talk about it, they would talk about it."

Adds John, "Probably the biggest effect the war had on our family is the way Dale is now. I think it's affecting my mom for sure, more now than when they first got out. I think it could even be affecting my parents more now than when they were in Viet Nam."

In fact, when the subject comes around to her sons and the war, the concern in Marian's voice is palpable.

"Dale was always so open about the war," she says. "As they got older, it changed. Steve shows his opinions more now, and Dale doesn't."

John, meanwhile, goes on to raise an interesting point. It's difficult to say with utter conviction how or even *if* the war changed his brothers because both Dale and Steve went to Viet Nam while they were maturing. They were still boys, really, as were many of those who served alongside them. Had they gone to Viet Nam later in life after developing careers or starting families of their own, then their personalities would have been much less malleable. Then, perhaps, their family would be able to discern how much Viet Nam had shaped them.

Here the argument comes full circle, however. If the Webb brothers came of age in Viet Nam, then it *must* have shaped them. Because if the war played backdrop to their maturation, if it provided the staging ground for boys on their way to manhood, then it did more than blur the lines between cause and effect. Indeed, it was more than part of the process. It *was* the process. A violent and frightening rite of passage.

#

"I am an artistic type of personality," Dale says. "If you look back through history, you will find that they have always been the ones who couldn't stand reality. This type of personality has a hard enough time in life without having a drastic event take place. I had Viet Nam. And I think that hindered me from becoming something I could have been. My father, my VA doctors, and my VA counselors all get upset with me because I have such a high IQ [144] and I haven't made use of it. Maybe I am just using this personality trait from my astrological sign of Pisces as an excuse for all of my troubles. I don't know."

Steve doesn't buy into Dale's theory, largely because he considers himself an artist of sorts, if only an aspiring songwriter. But such differences of opinion have always coexisted among the Webbs, a patriotic but tolerant family for the last three generations.

Their grandfather fought in World War I. Three of their uncles completed tours, including one in WWII and one in Korea, but their father never served in the military. For their part, Steve and Dale both went to Viet Nam. But John stayed stateside, and Ed followed his own path, sans the military. Though there's a proud sense of military tradition among the Webb men, it has more to do with love of country – and all its voices – than it does love of the armed forces. When Viet Nam went sour, Elmer's primary focus was on his boys' safety.

"My dad was real proud of them going in because he thought any time our country was at war – and Viet Nam was a war – it should have been finished," Elmer recalls. "I could see Viet Nam was a lost cause by '72. Up until about '71, I was kind of gung-ho on it. But I could see the people of the U.S. didn't want to finish it. I was kind of glad to see my boys get out of there by then."

It still hurts to know that someone called his son a baby killer after he dutifully served his country. But Elmer is ready to let bygones be bygones. So are his sons. Their focus is on the future and how, finally, to put Viet Nam to rest. It helps that the country's mood has shifted and that their role in history is no longer reviled.

"I have more people nowadays asking me about Viet Nam and wanting to hear what I have to say than I did probably the first twenty years after I came back," Steve says, adding, "I was raised you never start a fight. But if one comes along, you do what you have to do to win it. Let's choose the battles we fight."

Dale, too, can see a change in how Viet Nam veterans are being treated these days. For his part, he's ready to make one last move before tackling once and for all his health problems, physical and existential.

"I would really like to come back to Montana if I could just get the money to move back and find a job of some sort," he says. "I hate to leave my doctor out here, but I think I can find one in Montana probably as good, or maybe even get back with the VA out there. I really think I would heal better in the mountain air."

#

One thing Steve has never been is a worrier. His job brings him into daily contact with prisoners, some of them harmless, some of them potentially lethal. What if an inmate attacked him with a crudely built knife? The dangers are real. And unpredictable.

"I try very hard not to anticipate what's going to come tomorrow," he says. "If it happens, I'll deal with it. But I'm not going to spend my whole life worrying about what's going to happen tomorrow."

His philosophy extends to his family, although admittedly not very easily.

Sharon, still his baby sister even if she is forty-six years old, is battling ovarian cancer. The cancer has spread to her liver and spleen and doesn't seem to be responding to chemotherapy. She's living day to day, exhausted but hopeful. Her struggle is one shared by everyone in the family.

Steve has just gotten off the phone with his mother, who called with an update. The latest news isn't good. But he refuses to give in to fear. In Viet Nam, he learned how to do more than survive. He somehow learned how to view each moment as a gift.

"You can play the what-if game," he says. "Maybe she ate the wrong food or was exposed to too much secondhand smoke – whatever. If she does pass away, it's gonna tear me up. But you deal with it when it happens. And that's when you rely on your friends and family."

(Postscript: Sharon passed away on March 30, 2003, a month after Steve's last interview. She was survived by her parents, Elmer and Marian; her brothers, Dale, Steve, John, and Ed; and her son, Boyd Joseph. She was forty-six.)

PART II:
HEALTH OF A NATION

When I joined the military in early 1944, the U.S. Army promised me, among other things, lifetime health care. After twenty years of active military service, including stints in Italy, Iceland, and two long tours in West Germany, I would be entitled to this hard-earned safety net. My family of twelve years endured a gypsy's lifestyle as I dragged them to various parts of the world. This health care entitlement would serve as a down payment for our future.

The Army lied. More precisely, they, along with the other branches of the service, under the direction of the original War Department (later designated the Department of Defense), made promises they would not be able to keep except as Congress legislated.

Congress sees fit to change the law by legislation. It is the only authority with the power to insure such promises, and it has done so in a very profound way in the instance of military retirees.

In the mid-1990s, after enduring years of marginal and partial health care, Korean War vets and old-timers from World War II like myself were simply cut off, victims of budget cuts by the same legislators who regularly invoked, and still invoke, the mantra of "support our troops." On attaining age 65 and no longer subject to recall to active duty, we were told to make do with Medicare. Medicare did not even exist when I retired.

Simply put: with the collapse of communism in the former USSR and the resultant Base Realignments and Closures (BRAC) in the late 1980s and early 1990s, hundreds of military posts and bases, along with their associate Military Treatment Facilities (MTF), were closed and put out of business.

Enter retired Colonel George "Bud" Day, a decorated war hero and former prisoner of war in Viet Nam. Bud took the health care fight straight to and through all of the federal courts by galvanizing the media and military retirees who are also veterans from all over the country. He tried to make good on the decades-old claim of plaintiffs Robert L. Reinlie and (the estate of) William O. Schism, two retiree/vets who had fought the system of the late 1950s when the military decided to cap its benefits on retired pay, but more specifically the authorized health care for soldiers who had served twenty years or more.

Bud's bid for restitution of health care for those men – up to fifteen billion dollars' worth representing upwards of 800,000 retirees – made it all the way through the federal courts up to the Supreme Court. At that point, in June 2003, the panel of judges refused to hear the case. At the writing of this book, Day has decided to take his case to Congress in a political move. It's his last hope.

Certainly Day, like the rest of us, expects nothing from the executive branch. From the late Richard Nixon to George W. Bush, presidential hopefuls have been promising to make good on America's debt to its retirees only to balk later, citing, as always, budget constraints. I still have in my possession a letter written in 1970 by Nixon's Secretary of Defense Melvin R. Laird assuring us that " . . . some form of recomputation of retired pay will continue to be a goal of this Administration and this Department."

Well, Mr. Laird, Mr. Nixon, Mr. Bush, et al., we're still waiting. I've paid upwards of $155,000.00 over the years in health insurance and supplements alone. This was my money which my family could have used. This is money I thought I had earned in combat and in peacetime. Medicare Part B (which didn't even exist when I retired), Civilian Health and Medical Program for the Uniformed Services (CHAMPUS), TRICARE – I've outlived enough programs and acronyms to know a lemon when I taste one.

Patriotism, the trump card of the cynical and self-serving or refuge for the scoundrel, is a hollow word to those of us who gave our best only to be forgotten by an ungrateful nation.

The tragicomedy plays out the same with each new generation. A threat is perceived. A call to arms is issued. And mortal sacrifice is demanded from the healthy young, to whom we promise veneration and dignified care in the years to come. When the threat is gone and the healthy young have served their country, we turn to other things. When the young grow old and need a return on their investment more desperately than ever, the same country that gratefully accepted their collective sacrifice denies them.

"Who," the country asks, "are you?"

Chapter 4: Agent Orange
The Twinam Family

Agent Orange.

The mere mention of the phrase, as is so often the case when it comes to the Viet Nam War and its muddled legacy, evokes more than it informs. We see wide swathes of forests reduced to a vast wasteland, a desert in the middle of a teeming jungle. We see American soldiers on the ground enveloped in a chemical sheen but oblivious to the ubiquitous film's potentially lethal effects. We see premature births, spina bifida, cancerous pain – a toxic tether between one generation and the next.

But what do we *know*?

We know that Agent Orange was named after the orange stripe painted on each fifty-five gallon storage drum containing the deadly herbicide. We know that it was a broadleaf defoliant tested in Viet Nam in the early 1960s and used widely in the war until it was discontinued in 1971. We know that more than twenty million gallons of the herbicide rained down on Viet Nam and neighboring Cambodia and Laos during the war.

We know that the carcinogenic mix that makes up Agent Orange contains TCDD, a type of dioxin and a byproduct of production. We know that dioxin kills laboratory animals.

We know that, in the human body, dioxin is stored for years in fatty tissue and the bloodstream, a latent time bomb with little regard for the future. Several American companies, including Dow Chemical, profited from the production of Agent Orange before settling a class-action lawsuit in 1984 for a paltry $180 million, presumably killing any further litigation by American vets and their families even though the fund ran out ten years later.

We know that the Department of Veterans Affairs, despite disagreement within the scientific community and among some in the news media, has recognized a link between Agent Orange exposure and a whole host of diseases. The list is a long one: chloracne, non-Hodgkin's lymphoma, soft tissue sarcoma, Hodgkin's disease, porphyria cutanea tarda (PCT), multiple myeloma, respiratory cancers, prostate cancer, peripheral neuropathy, and Type II diabetes, which was added to the list in 2000. We know that mothers and their unborn children can also be affected; thus, the VA has recognized a link between Agent Orange exposure and spina bifida and other birth defects.

Finally, we know that all of the above barely skims the surface for today's Viet Nam vets with cancer or diabetes who are simply trying to wrest disability compensation from the government or legal restitution from the makers of Agent Orange. Their efforts are often met with barely veiled disinterest or bureaucratic obfuscation. Their primary support invariably comes from their families, not the government who tolerated and condoned the use of this deadly product – the government for whom they were willing to sacrifice everything only three decades ago.

#

Joseph Michael Twinam, who goes by Michael, has noticed a decline in his retention skills lately. Little things – like what he ate for breakfast – occasionally elude him. But his tour in Viet Nam – which he completed more than thirty years ago – might as well have been yesterday. Countless vivid details are still fresh in his mind.

Such a memory has its pluses and minuses. On the one hand, he was able to recount to the VA Medical Center in Albany, New York, precisely when and where he was directly exposed to Agent Orange, thus ensuring for himself full medical treatment and disability compensation. On the other hand, he can't help but shudder every time he recalls the precipitous moment.

"They sprayed [Agent Orange] around the bases to keep the growth down, and we were exposed to it daily," says Michael, who served with the U.S. Army Security Agency and was stationed at Phu Bai. "But what I consider my primary exposure occurred when I had to drink from a stream that was coming out of a defoliated area. At the time, we didn't know anything about Agent Orange. The Army issued us purification tablets to kill the bacteria to make it safe to drink. But no one said anything about dioxin in the water. Even though it has a twenty-year latent period, it still gets you."

Michael, a 55-year-old architect who lives with his wife Pat in Clifton Park, New York, knows firsthand the malignant echo of Agent Orange. He can feel it in his bones. In 1996, after going in for a routine physical, he was diagnosed with multiple myeloma, or bone marrow cancer.

"The doctor kept asking me to come back for more blood work," he recalls. "I went back four or five times. I thought it was kind of funny at the time. Finally he called me at work and told me I had multiple myeloma. I didn't even know what it was. I was kind of shocked. I went home and went online and did some research. Basically, it says you've got three years to live."

That was seven years ago. Michael has gone back every three months since then to check the disease's progress. Early on, he decided to opt out of a bone marrow transplant, a cure that is often more painful – and deadly – than the disease it's designed to fight. Instead, he tried to learn as much as he could about multiple myeloma while monitoring the cancer's steady advance. A Caucasian and only forty-seven at the time he was diagnosed, he was surprised to learn that the disease usually attacks older African-American males.

But that was only the beginning. In June 2000, Michael noticed a lump in his chest.

"It was basically behind my right nipple," he explains. "I have pretty good pecs. But I had this marble under my chest. I told the doctor, 'This is hurting.' He felt it and thought it must be just a cyst. He told me, 'Don't worry about it.'

"A couple months later, I was back again. This time I saw a surgeon, who wanted to lance what she thought was a cyst. She used a huge needle, and it hurt. She was expecting all this fluid to drain out. Nothing came out. At that point, the doctor said, 'Go get a mammogram.' Believe me, if your wife ever tells you these things hurt, she's not exaggerating. They squash your breast like a cracker. It hurt like hell."

The technician found a mass in his breast, and the doctor ordered surgery to have it taken out. As it turned out, the mass was an infiltrating ductal carcinoma – a very rare cancer for men. And the cancer had spread.

"It was in my blood system," Michael says. "They removed twelve out of seventeen lymph nodes from my armpit. The procedure used to remove my breast was a modified radical mastectomy. I also had six cycles or six months of chemotherapy after the surgery. Now I take Tamoxifen, a drug for breast cancer patients. I have to take that for five years."

Two different forms of cancer. Both rare for a white male in his age bracket. Michael had become the poster child for Agent Orange exposure. Less than two years later he added Type II diabetes, osteoporosis (a byproduct of chemotherapy), and cataracts (another byproduct, this time of steroid treatment) to his file.

"I go to the VA for infusions to strengthen and protect my bones every four weeks, and will do so for the rest of my life," Michael says. "The government has approved ten diseases that are attributed to Agent Orange. Breast cancer is not one of them. But I proved to them through research and medical documentation that it was related to dioxin exposure. I now have a one hundred percent VA disability rating from my cancers."

#

Five days a week Pat Twinam delivers U.S. mail in rural Saratoga County. She likes the job. Likes the fresh air. Driving a mail truck offers her peace of mind – something sorely lacking in her previous work when she was an assistant director of operations for a non-profit organization.

As the country roads in Upstate New York unfold in front of her, she soaks in the bucolic scenery while pondering how Agent Orange has affected her own life. Instead of reaping the harvest of a thirty-three-year marriage, instead of dreaming about retirement and vacations and home remodeling projects, she worries about the future. How long will it include her husband? How will she face the future should his health take a drastic turn for the worse?

"With an uncertain future looming in front of us," she says, "it's interesting how we're both reacting. Mike wants to do things now – because he doesn't know how long he'll be able to. I, on the other hand, want to get things in order; pay off all of our debts, including the house; and postpone projects and vacations to be in a good position should something happen to Mike. It's a constant struggle between us.

"I don't know how long I'll have Mike with me. I'm thankful that his illness appears to be smoldering at the moment, but I know that at any time, he could get much worse. While I always have hope that he will be cured, I know that the illnesses he has are not easy to treat and there is no cure at this time. A bone marrow transplant, a last resort, would be a nightmare to go through physically and has a high mortality rate. Those who undergo bone marrow transplants are very susceptible to infections [and often reject the transplanted marrow]. It will be very hard on all of us if and when that time comes. I worry about how I will be able to handle everything with my job and other responsibilities. Where would treatment take place – here or in another city like Boston? Will I be strong enough to help Mike through all of this?"

Born Patricia Elaine Wurth in Johnson City, New York, on July 15, 1948, Pat grew up just a few miles to the southwest in the small town of Vestal. After high school, she attended nearby Keuka College, a women's college at the time, where she studied nursing before changing majors to psychology.

She met Michael in the summer of 1969 when the two were working at IBM in Endicott. He was working the graveyard shift. She was working the day shift. Their paths crossed each morning at the punch clock.

"I was flirting with three nice-looking guys there," she recalls. "One night I received a call from one of them asking me out on a date. I accepted, not knowing which of the three I had made a date with. The next morning I met Mike, and we went out to the movies and had a great time. I was attracted to his laugh, which was deep and hearty. After our date, he sent me roses, which went right to my heart. Two weeks after we met, we were out on a lake in a rowboat and he proposed to me, jokingly, with a Crackerjack box ring. One week later he proposed to me seriously, and I accepted.

"Mike was a romantic. He would leave romantic cards in my locker at work and would send me flowers. He would come over in the wee hours of the morning on his lunch break, and I would try to make him something to eat. I was noted for burning the grilled cheese sandwiches, among other things."

In the fall, Pat went back to school for her senior year, with Michael visiting her on the weekends. On one such occasion, he brought her a diamond ring to formalize their engagement, and a May wedding date was set.

Their budding romance, though, would have to wait. The Viet Nam War, as it would again later on in their marriage, had come between the two, staking a claim on Michael and postponing their honeymoon in the process.

#

Born in Louisville, Kentucky, on June 25, 1948, Michael moved with his family to New Jersey and then Tucson, Arizona, before settling in California. After graduating from high school, he made his way to New York and found a job at IBM, eventually meeting Pat.

"She looked very much like Ali McGraw," Michael reminisces, comparing his then fiancée to the striking, brown-eyed brunette who starred in the movie *Love Story*. "I was very innocent. I just fell head over heels."

Adds Michael, "When you're that age, you're not thinking too much about the future. It was the sixties. We were like most kids. We weren't really hippies, but we were part of the movement. I went to Woodstock before I met Pat. I was a typical kid at that age."

Wide-eyed and optimistic, he would taste reality soon enough. After being drafted by his local draft board (the dreaded lottery had yet to be born), the color-blind and flat-footed kid from Kentucky failed his first physical. The Army, though, invited him back for another stab. He failed again, but they took him anyway. He was ordered to report for induction in December.

He completed his basic training at Fort Dix, where he showed an aptitude for communications and was enrolled in radio school. In May, he flew back to New York for his wedding and a one-night honeymoon at a nearby hotel. Then it was off to Fort Gordon, Georgia, for special training. Pat, meanwhile, completed her final exams and then loaded her car with everything she owned, Georgia-bound.

"She joined me there for a few weeks," Michael says. "I finished my advanced training in radio and teletype school. I picked up a couple other specialties, too. When you go into the service, they give you a battery of tests to determine your aptitude. Most guys just blew it off. Those were the guys who ended up in the infantry or being a cook or something. But I tried real hard. So it behooves you to always try your best."

Says Pat, "We lived in an old mobile home outside the base, and I remember waking up in the wee hours of the morning to make Mike breakfast before he went to the base. He left for Viet Nam at the end of the summer, and I went back home to look for a job. I ended up teaching special education to first graders for the year he was away."

Her husband, meanwhile, landed in Saigon on August 18, 1970. The atmosphere in the South Viet Namese capital was, to say the least, anti-climatic. The headquarters, the trailers, the barracks – everything was air-conditioned. Office clerks busily shuffled reports and crunched numbers. And the bureaucratic juggernaut of the U.S. Army rolled on: impervious, oblivious, and hermetically sealed off from the grim fighting just a short plane ride away.

"In Saigon, you would have never known there was a war going on," Michael says.

After a brief wait, he got his uniform and his orders and was flown into Phu Bai, near the DMZ. For him, at least, the war, gritty and unapologetic, would soon transcend military hierarchy and red tape.

"I flew in wearing short sleeves," he says. "I was just in my khakis. I came in late, in the evening. While we're disembarking, rockets start landing all around us. Everybody has to go to the perimeter. So here I am in a ditch with water up to my waist, no weapon, being eaten by bugs, with rockets and mortars landing around us. It was a rude awakening to Viet Nam. We ended up staying there until morning."

#

Another scene, three months later, stands out vividly in Michael's mind. Exhausted and filthy, he stared in disbelief as a helicopter, loaded down with frozen cargo, landed in the middle of a remote firebase. He had been carrying a radio in the jungle for three months. Today, the Americans were being rewarded for their part in the war – with steak and ice cream. An incongruous scene and fodder for the likes of *Apocalypse Now*, it was the sort of surreal moment Michael had come to expect while hopping from one firebase to the next.

"It was just crazy," he says of his three-month stint in the bush. "It was the unpredictability of war. Things were fluid and changing all the time."

During one sojourn into the jungle, Michael drank from a stream that wound its way out of a defoliated wasteland. At the time, he didn't think twice about the tainted water. He had more immediate concerns. With a radio on his back, he made for an inviting target for NVA snipers. He was a tall one, too, considering he stood at six feet, two inches. Somehow, though, he escaped every engagement without a scratch. Not so for many of his fellow soldiers, American and enemy, who went home in body bags or were left on the battlefield.

After returning from one mission, he was awarded a Bronze Star, a combat medal judiciously handed out for uncommon acts of heroism. But how he earned it will have to wait for another book.

"It's not important," he says, circumspect. "It has nothing to do with Agent Orange."

Neither, fortunately, did the remainder of his tour. After three months, he was plucked from the bush and returned to Phu Bai, where he was handed a ham radio while he waited for the U.S. Army to get him a top-secret security clearance: a $50,000 investment involving, among other things, extensive background checks. Another three months went by in the interim, and Michael passed the time as a MARS (Military Affiliate Radio System) station operator.

"Because it was a ham radio," he remembers, "it was one-way communication, where you give me the number and I would find another ham operator in the U.S. and connect with them. That way, callers were only charged stateside rates. If I got the Pentagon, it was free. Because they were one-way conversations, I had to listen to all the conversations in order to switch from transmitting to receiving. Some were great. Some were terrible. A lot of Dear Johns. One guy hadn't gotten any mail from his wife for quite a while, so he called home. She says, 'I'm leaving you.' He says, 'What about the baby?' She says, 'The baby's not yours.' Normally you only allow soldiers to talk about five minutes. I let this guy talk an hour."

After he got his security clearance, Michael's job changed radically.

"I was in a secret unit that really did not exist," he explains. "We were attached to other units for radio communication interdiction. Our unit was called the 8th Radio Research Group. We were a field unit of the ASA [Army Security Agency]. We gathered info about the VC, most of it being radio communication intercept, although there were branches that did prisoner interrogation. Where we were stationed was kind of a joke. Everybody outside wanted to know what we did, and we couldn't tell 'em. We were in a compound that had six twelve-foot rows of barbed wire around it and about a hundred thousand landmines around us because we couldn't afford to let the enemy get hold of our communications equipment. Rumor was we would be targeted by our own B-52's if we were overrun. We knew if anything happened, we didn't have to worry about the VC getting us. Our own B-52's would take us out. It came close at one point."

\#

While Michael was playing spook in Viet Nam, Pat was busy working stateside. She wrote her new husband daily, with the letters often arriving in Viet Nam in bunches. Michael returned the favor, occasionally sending tapes, which Pat still has to this day. Once a week, they spoke on the telephone via a ham radio operator, their not-so-private conversations punctuated by the requisite "over."

"I remember one time purposely saying something racy to Mike and hearing chuckles down the line," Pat says. "I was thankful for those weekly calls."

When Michael finally earned a week's worth of R&R in March, he traveled to Hawaii, where he met Pat for a delayed honeymoon. He almost had to cancel due to a flurry of top-secret message trading leading up to his departure date, but Pat wouldn't find out until years later.

"A bunch of us wives, girlfriends, etc. were waiting in a building for the men to get there," says Pat. "I was toward the front and literally jumped at Mike when I saw him. I think I scared him. We had a wonderful week, toured the island, went swimming on the beaches, went to a luau, and of course did all of the things newlyweds do. It was hard to go back to the real world again after that."

Back in Viet Nam, Michael went through the motions, waiting, like everyone else, for the "freedom bird" to take him home. Most GI's kept a "Charlie calendar," a hand-drawn calendar divided into 365 days, with the days gone by blacked out. Michael was no different. As his departure day approached, he gradually started to hand over responsibilities to others around him.

The Army, meanwhile, having invested so much in his training and top-secret clearance, tried to convince him to stay, offering him a rank increase (he was a sergeant) and a $10,000 bonus. He refused. He just wanted to go home and be with his new wife. He was anxious to get on with his future, as well – a future that included college.

Before he left, a planeload of American GI's headed for home was downed by enemy rockets, everyone on board killed. The tragedy added fuel to Michael's anxiety. But his own trip home was uneventful. He left Viet Nam on August 18, 1971, aboard an Air America plane and arrived safe and sound at Travis Air Base in California twenty-six hours later. After waiting around five days to get his orders cut, he was released from service and flew home to New York. From there, he caught a bus to the Catskills, where Pat had found a summer job at a tourist resort.

"I surprised her," he recalls. "I came in the middle of the night, sneaked into her room, and scared the begeezes out of her. She was supposed to work a few more days there, but I went down the next day and told her boss she was quitting. I was in my uniform and said, 'We're leaving.' At that point in time, I needed to be with somebody."

Adds Michael, "I got a welcome from my family only. All my exposure to the general public was generally what you've heard: scorn. I was never spat upon, but I did have some names called at me. I had a guy try to pick a fight with me in a bar. I was in a uniform, so I was an easy target. Overall, we got no encouragement, no thank you's. We were just glad to be home. You go back to your family and try to forget it, if you can. You did your duty. But your country was almost embarrassed by having you there. It was a political war. It wasn't a military war. That's what really burns the veterans today. We went there with good intentions of being loyal Americans and doing what our country asked, and we ended up being the scapegoats. Everything we did just got washed away. Right now, it's history. The only people that are connected are the veterans and their families. There's no real understanding of what went on there, why we were there. Even my own kids – they don't know. It's just something they read in textbooks. They see my medals, but they don't understand."

Once stateside again, he tried to make the transition to civilian life as quickly as possible. But it wasn't easy. A year's worth of combat in the field and incoming artillery back at the base had taken a residual toll. He tried to bury the tension. But, like a spring bulb pushing up snow, it found its way to the surface.

"I had been back maybe three or four months," he recalls, "and my wife and I were asleep. For some reason or another, there was a loud noise outside – a pickup truck backfiring or something. Just reflexes caused me to reach over my wife, grab the edge of the mattress, and pull it and us over to the floor with the mattress over us. Afterwards, I was embarrassed. My wife was screaming, not knowing what was going on. That was my letdown from Viet Nam, my residual that worked its way out.

"You look at most vets and they act a certain way. I always have my back against the wall at a restaurant. Most vets are the same way. They don't like to be exposed. They look for all the options and the things you need to be aware of. They train themselves over there to look for all the little things. It carries through even in the States when you're back home. Your senses are skewed, tuned to see the unexpected. It's just a byproduct of Viet Nam.

"As soon as I could, I tried to get back into the mainstream. A lot of guys came back messed up, and some are still messed up. Most of those were the ones that were so close to the immensity and the tragedy of war. I tried to get back in as fast as I could to the mainstream. I got back on August 18 and started college September 3. I ended up working full-time and going to school full-time. Then I had my first son.

"I never did a lot of the normal fun things that many people do when they're in college. One of the reasons Pat and I are still together is because of the hard times we went through. A lot of people today just give up when things get tough. But when you stick it out, there's that bond that you've created. You've invested a lot, and you just don't throw that away. Viet Nam made me grow up early – and quickly."

Michael earned a bachelor's degree in architecture at State University of New York in Buffalo. He followed that up with a master's degree at the University of Miami in Ohio. He found a job shortly thereafter in Carlsbad, New Mexico, moving Pat and their first son, Matt, there. The Twinams lived in Carlsbad for three and a half years, long enough to have their second son, Ken, before moving on to Dallas, then Indiana, and finally back home to New York.

"We loved being parents, but your life definitely changes after that," Pat says. "We could no longer do all the things we used to and, of course, finances were always a struggle, as they are with most young couples just starting out. It was difficult with Mike going to school, working, and a new baby in the picture, but somehow we managed."

Michael and Pat continued to pursue their careers, he a school architect and she a payroll supervisor. As the years passed, Viet Nam continued to shrink from view, a slowly receding blip on the radar screen. The war was history. Or so they thought.

#

"I found out about the multiple myeloma on Valentine's Day," Pat says. "Mike didn't want to tell me and ruin Valentine's Day, but I knew something was on his mind and I made him tell me. Being the calm person that I am, I didn't fall apart when I got the news. I do remember reading about the disease and crying because it sounded so dreadful and painful and there was no cure. What I read made it sound like he wouldn't have long to live – a three-year life expectancy from the time it was diagnosed.

"I also remember the night we told our children. We had told them that we wanted them to be at home on a certain evening but didn't tell them why. Even though we have a happy marriage, they were almost sure that we were going to tell them we were getting a divorce or something. That was the only serious thing they could think of. Mike told them about the disease and that there was no cure. They were both stunned but reacted in different ways. Matt openly cried, but Ken was very quiet. We all hugged. It was a very emotional evening, and who knows how it affected the children."

#

Though it seems unlikely on the surface, the ultimate casualty of the Viet Nam War may have been the very government that perpetuated the conflict. Doubtful? Just listen to Matt Twinam talk about the institution that put his father and hundreds of thousands of others like him in harm's way.

"I'm proud to be an American, and I love the country we live in," he says. "I also know that the business of government is a complicated one and there are certain things they do that must be kept secret. However, I'm also very skeptical and untrusting of the government. I'm beginning to see the government as an imperialistic might that is overstepping its bounds more often than I'm comfortable with. I feel that if we weren't so involved in the world's affairs, maybe we wouldn't have to go to war as often and tragedies such as the Agent Orange spraying would not be necessary. In the future, before the government and chemical companies use a product like Agent Orange, they need to test its use and know the long-term effects."

Adds Matt, "I think the future is uncertain. I wonder if the diseases my father has can be transmitted to me and my brother through heredity. Are my children going to have problems?"

For Matt, a 28-year-old special education teacher who lives and works in Latham, just ten miles away from his parents, Viet Nam would likely have remained a largely enigmatic subject, had his father never become ill. But Michael's fight with bone and breast cancer has brought the war's tangled history simmering to the surface, despite his own reluctance to discuss it.

"For years my father never spoke of the war," Matt explains. "He said that many of his experiences were confidential, so he couldn't tell us. I do remember picking his brain about the war, and after several questions I asked the question I was most curious about: 'Did you ever kill anyone?' For some reason, he broke down and cried. I still don't know the answer to the question.

"My father hasn't spoken much about the health issues related to Agent Orange. He has gone through the treatments without complaint. He answers any questions about his condition but doesn't offer information voluntarily. I don't know if he's protecting the government from ill thoughts from his family. The only negative comment he has made about his chemotherapy was that he would occasionally have explosive vomiting that would come out of nowhere. He has been very strong through the whole experience. He always lightens the mood about his illness by joking."

Indeed, Michael's typical reaction to questions about the war or his health varies between tight-lipped stoicism and humorous sidestepping. This has frustrated no one more than Ken, a 23-year-old college student (at State University of

Willard D. Gray

New York Institute of Technology at Utica-Rome) who often feels left out of the loop.

"My brother is six years younger than me, and I don't think he's ever known what's going on," Matt says. "I don't know that my parents have had conversations with him about my father's illnesses. He knows a lot from what I tell him. But we've actually had problems where we'll find out my father's condition has worsened or something has happened well after the fact. They seem to want to wait for the right time. But I don't always agree about when the right time is. I think they don't want to worry us. Usually when I tell Ken about something, he gets really upset that he's the last to know and that he hasn't found out from them personally. I'm the same way. My mother is loyal to my father, and usually my father is the one who wants to hold off. She won't say anything until he gives her the okay."

Adds Matt, "Our initial response was that, well, they had only given him a few years to live. This was right when I was in college. He was supposed to pass away when I was doing my student teaching. We're eight years out now, and he's still working and doing okay. They feel like bonus years."

It was while Matt was student teaching in Buffalo, in fact, that he began to realize his father's illness, though grave, might not play out as quickly or tragically as predicted. At the elementary school he met another teacher whose own family shared, as it turned out, an uncanny bond with the Twinams.

"We were sitting in the classroom after school chatting one day," Matt recalls, "and for some reason we were talking about her father. She said her father had passed away. I asked her, 'What did he die from?' She said he died from multiple myeloma. It was almost surreal. It was like her lips slowed down, and I just thought, 'Wow.' I barely even knew her! It turns out her father had found out very late in the disease, almost when his bones were deteriorating, and he wasn't very mobile. What I knew was that my father had caught it at the beginning of the disease. Her father still lived seven or eight years after he found out so late, which gave me hope. I thought, 'Well, my father's still walking around and working and he hasn't even reached that stage yet.'"

#

Despite combating a slew of illnesses and despite receiving essentially a terminal sentence from his doctors, Michael has managed to continue working, playing, and moving on with his life. His fortitude while dealing with surgery and chemotherapy and the various other treatments has inspired his wife and sons, all of whom admire his courage and tenacity. He's asked very little in terms of support. So far, at least, he's been able to take charge of his own treatment and recovery.

In fact, he's still just as obstinate and as opinionated as ever – two qualities that often rub Matt the wrong way.

"I know that my relationship with my father is probably very ordinary," says Matt, who married Amanda, a law student, two years ago. "We have opposing viewpoints on most topics. Our communication with each other could have been better while I was growing up. It's better now. But we don't speak as often or as openly as we should."

His father's health problems might have mitigated some of that up front. But the longer Michael defies the odds and the dire predictions of his doctors, the easier it is to get used to life simply staying the same. Old habits die hard. And mortality looms less glaringly.

Even Pat finds herself growing used to the fear.

"At first I was sure we wouldn't have much time together, so I tried to do as much as I could while he was still fairly healthy," she says. "We took a vacation that we might not have taken. I gave him a present on the twenty-fifth of each month, the date of his birthday, for one whole year. I remember crying by myself at work every once in a while when I would hear a certain song or think about what might happen. I was going to start a diary of everything as it happened. I started it but haven't written anything in quite a while.

"Fortunately, both Mike and I are calm people who aren't going to fall apart at the thought of what might happen. We live every day as normal as possible and deal with whatever life brings our way. Mike continues to work as he can, although he'd rather not. He fatigues easily and must get a good night's sleep in order to get through his workday.

"Every day I see more and more things going wrong with his health. He was diagnosed with diabetes and glaucoma and has had occasional pains going from his chest down his arm, which could be heart problems. Again, he has put off seeing a doctor about these concerns, even though I remind him to make an appointment. But I'm very proud of Mike. He has such a good attitude about his illnesses. We both take one day at a time and try not to dwell on his health, although it's always on the back of our minds. He has told me that the only thing he's afraid of is the pain."

#

Who is culpable? The government? The chemical companies? Both? The question matters a great deal to Michael, who is pursuing legal action against the makers of Agent Orange, aiming his indignation at the companies that buttressed their already bulging bank accounts at the expense of his own health.

"I don't hold the government responsible," he says of his exposure to Agent Orange. "I think the government has been very callous and very negligent in the way they've handled the problem. But I don't think they're guilty. They didn't know. What they knew was what the manufacturers told them. They were using a weapon of war. And that's part of war. But the manufacturers didn't tell them what was in the product, and that's the problem. That's why I'm going after the manufacturers. They were very criminal in their actions. It is similar to the tobacco industry, where they knew [cigarette smoke] wasn't good, but they kept it secret."

Though Dow Chemical, Monsanto, and others received a favorable settlement in 1984, Michael is closely following the suit of two other Viet Nam vets who, should they prevail, could pave the way for redressing the rights of those who were left out of the first settlement. Anyone suffering from an Agent Orange-related illness after 1995 and not included in the first class-action settlement can join the fight, which is being headed up by Gerson Smoger, a Dallas attorney with plenty of moxie – and the experience to back it up. He's been advocating for Agent Orange victims for nearly a decade.

Smoger's chief argument rests on the fact that the original settlement didn't speak to any of the countless victims of Agent Orange who had yet to start showing symptoms. The effects of Agent Orange exposure are difficult to track precisely because of dioxin's pattern of lying dormant for decades. To bar those who fell victim to its latent toxicity after the settlement from seeking restitution constitutes the ultimate injustice.

Michael, meanwhile, is working alone with his own attorney for the moment. He's hoping for a favorable Supreme Court decision, thus paving the way for his own lawsuit. If the U.S. Supreme Court upholds the decision of the Second Circuit Court of Appeals, the suit will be presided over by Judge Jack B. Weinstein, the same judge who oversaw the first settlement, and the same judge who has thrown out every Agent Orange case brought to him since.

Regardless of the outcome in the courts, veterans who were exposed to Agent Orange can turn to the Veteran's Administration for help, just as they would for any war-related injury or disease. Of course, there's a catch.

"If you have any disabilities related to Agent Orange and you're a veteran," Michael says, "you're going to have to fight the government for what's due you. They basically turn down probably nine out of ten applications. Their definition of proof is absolute. If it's fifty-fifty, they're not going to give it to you. You have to fight. You have to prove it. It's set up that way. And most veterans don't get it. I'd say only ten to twenty percent of veterans actually get anything from the VA."

The statistics from the nation's capital are actually far starker than Michael's estimates. As of March 2000, according to numbers released by the Department of Veterans Affairs, 297,194 Viet Nam vets had taken part in the Agent Orange registry, an ongoing federal program that was created twenty-five years ago in an attempt to help vets determine if they had any Agent Orange-related diseases. Of those who registered, 99,226 filed claims alleging Agent Orange affected their health. Of those, only 7,520, or seven and a half percent, received disability compensation from the VA.

Jim Benson, a spokesperson for the Department of Veterans Affairs in Washington, D.C., is quick to point out how generous the VA is with American vets compared to institutions from other countries that can't afford to take care of their aging soldiers. He also cites the total number of Viet Nam vets who, as of the beginning of fiscal year 2002, had received some level of disability compensation from the VA: 749,554.

But that number simply shows how truly hard it is for victims of Agent Orange to receive disability compensation from the government they served. Again, only 7,520 veterans, or seven and a half percent of those seeking aid, have received compensation for exposure to Agent Orange since the war ended.

"We presume anybody that was in Viet Nam was exposed to some level of Agent Orange," Benson says. "If you present with any of the diseases on the list, then it is presumed that that disease is linked to your service in Viet Nam. This includes those stateside or elsewhere who were involved in production, storage, handling, or shipping of Agent Orange."

Sounds fair. But the numbers prove otherwise.

The battle for disability compensation, like the battle for legal restitution, is an uphill one. Press on or give up? For vets like Michael, it's a matter of life or death.

#

"It is only by going down into the abyss," the eminent mythologist Joseph Campbell once wrote, "that we recover the treasures of life. When you stumble, there lies your treasure. The very cave you are afraid to enter turns out to be the very source of what you were looking for."

Every month Michael drives to the VA Medical Center in Albany for a bone infusion. He sits in a chair for five hours while a machine pumps medicine into him to resurrect his bones. He's more susceptible to colds these days. And his platelets, like his red and white blood cells, are low. So too is his hemoglobin. He bruises easily. Fatigues easily. His bones, despite the monthly infusions, are slowly dissolving.

For a while, he experimented with soybean extract, wheat germ, and other homeopathic remedies. The regimen improved his immunity. It also sped the advance of the multiple myeloma. He was tempted to go back to drinking Coke and eating junk food. But he found middle ground. Likewise, the former workaholic eased up on his job. Slowed down. Took a deep breath. And started eating his dessert first.

One day a week, he and Pat try to make time for a date. Sometimes that means going into Albany to enjoy a play at the Repertory Theater, where they have season tickets. Sometimes it means working in the garden, taking a dip in their swimming pool, or visiting with their grown-up kids. Sometimes it means renting a video and spending a quiet night at home together curled up on the couch.

Joseph Michael Twinam, despite living his life in the hovering shadow of his own mortality, has faith in the future.

A combination of military training and religious conviction, the latter found after being born again in arid New Mexico, has given him the strength to push on.

"There have been times when I've been down physically," he says, "where I could have basically stayed down and not gone back to work and just resigned or retired. But I can't do it. I have to keep busy. I have to keep moving. I have to keep objectives in my life because, if you stop, you might as well roll over. You've got to keep fighting. So that's what I'm doing. I'm not going to give up."

Chapter 5: PTSD
The Ken Hayes Family

As the 1980s came to a close, the Veterans Administration went public with a study that had far-reaching, if bleak, implications. Three million men and women had served in Viet Nam, the survey noted, and an estimated 500,000 had come home with Post-Traumatic Stress Disorder. It had been fifteen years since the end of the war, but PTSD, an evocative yet dimly understood acronym, was just rising to the surface of the American psyche. Suddenly, it could be found lurking beneath alcoholism, domestic violence, chronic unemployment, homelessness, suicide, and numerous other social ills.

In the American heartland, meanwhile, life went on as it had before the war. Fields needed to be plowed. Machinery needed to be repaired. Shelves needed to be stocked. Bills needed to be paid. If PTSD had penetrated the Midwest vernacular, no one was talking.

#

When Penny Hayes looks back at her marriage of seventeen years, she doesn't know where to start.

She holds onto the good memories – playing cards with friends, taking the kids fishing, watching her husband lose a game of tick-tack-toe to a chicken. And she remembers the quirks – how Kenny was always cold, how he wore long underwear nearly year round, taking a sabbatical from his longjohns in summer only.

She remembers how he hated snakes. And rice. How, when she brought a box of rice home to feed their six-month-old daughter, he made her throw it out. It reminded him of Viet Nam, he said. He'd had his fill in the bush, where maggots masqueraded as white rice.

She remembers, too, how he hated water, even if dropping a hook in Olney Lake, his favorite fishing hole, was the only way he could wind down.

"Looking out over the lake," she says, "I can see why it's beautiful. It's peaceful. It's quiet. It was the one peaceful place he could go. I guess I have tried to forget the bad past. I've tried to forget what it was like to wake up with a gun pointed at me. I've tried to forget what it was like to be put into a neck hold, with him threatening to kill me. I've tried to forget the swollen face, black and blue bruises. I've tried to forget what it was like to have someone beside you thinking you were the enemy."

Experience. Relive. Avoid. Erupt. Implode.

Penny Hayes rode the waves of her husband's anxiety disorder for the better part of two decades, surviving one stage after another. It was the only life she knew until September 17, 1991, when Kenny disappeared for seventy-four hours beneath the tranquil surface of Olney Lake.

\#

Penny Jean Hayes, then Barcroft, spent most of her youth on the move, calling several towns in the Midwest home. Her parents got a divorce when she was a freshman in high school, and she and her two younger sisters moved in with their mother in Sumner, Illinois.

She met Kenneth David Hayes, an affable local boy who had recently returned home from a tour in Viet Nam, in the summer of 1972, just before her junior year in high school. Kenny, who was eight years her senior, came from a big family. He and his nine brothers and sisters were a close-knit bunch. Their mother had passed away when the kids were young, and their father, because he had to provide for ten children, wasn't around much. As a result, the children formed a tight bond that would flourish well into their adult years.

At the time, one of Kenny's brothers was dating Penny's best friend. Running with the same crowd and sharing the same friends, Kenny and Penny seemed a natural fit. They got married a little more than a year later in August 1973. Penny was only seventeen.

"After we got married," Penny recalls, "Kenny's family told me that if he ever got pneumonia, I would have to tie him down or something. He had gotten really sick right after he came home from Viet Nam and had come downstairs with a gun aimed at his family."

The family had survived the incident, wrestling the gun away from Kenny. But it proved an ominous portent of things to come.

#

Details of Kenny's service in Viet Nam are sketchy at best. His two-year tour was over before he met Penny. A fire at his family's home destroyed most of his records and, though the U.S. Army reissued his medals and citations ten years into his marriage, Penny has since misplaced them. Like her late husband, she would rather forget.

Kenny was stationed in Danang and served his tour as a heavy equipment operator with the Army engineers in 1969. His experiences in the bush left a bad taste in his mouth.

"He wouldn't talk much about the service," Penny says. "He just said, 'Our son won't go; I'll go back first. I won't put him through that.' I told him I didn't think it worked that way. It turns out our son had knee problems, and the Air Force turned him down. Anyway, once in a while, Kenny said something about them being called baby killers when they arrived back in the States. He didn't like that he had to shoot kids, even though he was only about eighteen at the time. But they were about fifteen.

"He talked about how they were just kids and how they had been taught to kill or be killed, that most often the Vietcong were booby-trapped and that they would shoot first. Kill or be killed. He did make me promise that if he died first, he didn't want Taps played at the funeral. He didn't like anything connected to the service after Viet Nam."

Adds Penny, "He often commented on Agent Orange and how he knew what it did to things over there. 'How could it not affect us?' he said. 'We were in the middle of it!' After all, it killed the animals, vegetation, trees, etc. He often wondered if it would affect our two kids somewhere down the line, or if it affected him."

He was less inclined to worry about the psychological effects of fighting a war with no front, often no discernible enemy, and waning public support back home.

\#

PTSD, according to The Post-Traumatic Stress Disorder Sourcebook by Glenn R. Schiraldi, Ph.D., can be broken down into five somewhat predictable stages. First, the victim experiences a traumatic event or series of events. Second, the victim then relives the event or events repeatedly, either through nightmares, flashbacks, or unbidden memories. Third, the victim starts to avoid people, places, and thoughts that trigger the memory, thus retreating into a shell that excludes joy in life's simple pleasures, attachment to and intimacy with loved ones, and faith in the future. Fourth, the victim begins to maintain a constant state of arousal, as hyper-vigilance and irritability replace sound sleep and the ability to concentrate. Finally, the draining effects of the disorder begin to take a toll on the victim's personal and professional life; relationships suffer, and jobs are lost.

Not necessarily spelled out, but no doubt implied in the above explanation, is one minor detail: victims of PTSD claim their own victims, as well.

"He beat me every night for about ten years," Penny says, recalling the underside of her marriage. "I really thought I deserved it. I was young. I didn't know any better."

The same could be said for Kenny, who had yet to decompress from Viet Nam. His marriage became the war's only outlet, a funnel through which he poured his darkest moments. Alcohol, as is so often the case, played a defining role.

"I can't say that drinking of alcohol became worse after he came home from the service," Penny explains, "but it seemed to play a big part in our marriage. He could go from Dr. Jekyll to Mr. Hyde at any time. I was always in the wrong place if supper wasn't fixed right. It went on the floor, along with me."

Those close to Kenny insist he wasn't a full-fledged alcoholic, even if he abused the stuff on a regular basis. He was, however, a workaholic. He worked the oil fields by day and ran his own drywall company at night. He was always on the go, always working, and rarely took time to relax. Somehow, he always showed up for work bright and early each morning, regardless of how much he had drunk or how late he had stayed up the night before.

He worked to stave off the ghosts of Viet Nam. But at night, when he collapsed in bed after a fourteen-hour workday, the memories returned.

His daughter Tracy, now twenty-nine, listened intently at night as her father fought the Viet Nam War all over again in the next room.

"It didn't sound all that great," she remembers. "You could almost get a picture of what happened from the way he acted. It was scary. You didn't know when he was gonna have a flashback or an episode of any kind. We just went day by day, hoping he wouldn't have one and hoping he wouldn't think back to what happened while he was over there."

Her mother adds, "The nightmares were unreal. He would wake up screaming, shouting, punching at things that weren't there. Sometimes he thought he had a gun in his hand, and he was pretending he was shooting. Sometimes it was a real gun in his hand."

When things got rough, Penny usually turned to her brother-in-law, Mike Hayes, and his wife Sheila for help. Mike had a calming effect on Kenny and could defuse his brother's anger. Sheila, meanwhile, focused on Penny and the kids, often whisking them away in the middle of the night during one of Kenny's episodes.

"Kenny and I had an understanding," Sheila recalls. "I would go get Penny and the kids, and he knew I had to."

Adds Sheila, "He always called me 'Penny's f---ing bodyguard.'"

During one episode, Sheila returned with Penny and the kids only to find that Kenny had boarded up the house and was holed up inside with a gun. Other moments were tinged with black comedy.

"The neighbor lady would come out on her porch because Kenny would be screaming at Penny," Sheila recounts. "And the kids would be coming out with their pillows. Kenny would be out on the porch in his underwear, screaming at me as I went in to get Penny."

To this day, Jeremy, who was a wee little one during most of the turmoil, doesn't remember such incidents. In general, he and his sister were spared their father's struggle. As adults today, they hold onto the good times, not the bad.

"I just remember how much he enjoyed life," Jeremy says. "We spent a lot of time on the lake fishing and hunting out in the woods. Usually rabbits. Sometimes squirrels and doves."

Says Tracy, "I used to go to work with him on Sundays. We'd go on his routes in the oil field. We played basketball and games together. Just being with him when he wasn't drinking had a lot to do with it . . . because Dad and I were really close."

Even Penny's bodyguard remembers Kenny fondly.

"He was a hard worker, a truly loyal friend," Sheila insists. "He would help you out any way he could. But he was a bad husband when he drank. He was not good to Penny. He would become very enraged and start knocking the crap out of her. But you should have seen his funeral. It was one of the largest funerals I've ever seen because he had so many friends. He was a very, very highly thought of person. Nobody saw his dark side . . . or at least nobody talked about it."

#

Kenny Hayes, larger than life in person, only weighed in at about 150 pounds.

"Soaking wet," Penny adds with a laugh.

At five feet seven inches tall, he was wiry – but strong.

"He had a lot of freaky things happen," Penny remembers. "He had nine lives. He was so little, he never got hurt."

In fact, he was involved in several car accidents and somehow managed to walk away every time. In one accident, he broadsided a small herd of cows. With his truck in the ditch and his air compressor in the middle of the highway, he stood by the side of the road, ranting and raving in an alcohol-induced rage. His knee had been torn up, but he refused to go to the hospital. Finally, Mike, as usual, came to the rescue and convinced his older brother to seek medical help.

In another accident, he collided head-on with a teenager, who was killed. Both were cited as partially at fault – Kenny for driving drunk, the teenager for pulling out onto the highway on a blind curve, his engine stalling at just the wrong time.

Kenny's luck ran out on a chilly day in September 1991. He had just worked three straight weeks and was finally going to enjoy some down time. He had made plans to go fishing with his son and his friend, Mike Weiss. But for some reason, he decided not to wait for either and went to Olney Lake alone.

"That's a day that kind of sticks and won't go away," Jeremy says. "I remember sitting there on the side of the lake while the search boats were out there looking, and the TV cameras and everybody were all around. It was just total shock, especially the way it happened – a total accident and everything. It was unbelievable. No matter how long we sat there, we kept thinking he would come home. We just couldn't believe it."

Somehow, Kenny had gone overboard and gotten tangled up with the propeller, which had then caught him in the face. He had just bought the engine used, and investigators afterward determined it had a defective safety.

When Mike Weiss went out to check on Kenny, he found his boat spinning circles in the middle of the lake. Later, the family would find out that a young woman driving by the lake had seen Kenny go down. She stopped and ran to the lake, but he disappeared before she could get to him.

Mike, meanwhile, went straight to Penny's and told her she needed to get out there. Something was wrong. About that time, the police arrived and requested that she accompany them to the lake.

At the lake, the police asked Penny if there was anything they could do. She numbly asked for her brother-in-law, Mike Hayes, who, until then, had always been able to run damage control where his older brother was concerned. When he heard the news, Mike, who was umpiring a baseball game, dropped everything and hurried to the lake.

Meanwhile, Sheila broke the news to the kids. Jeremy leaned over and cried. Tracy sat in stunned silence, unable to look up from her homework. Sheila then took the kids to their Aunt Cathy's house before meeting Penny at the lake.

"Penny was just marching back and forth, pacing," Sheila recalls. "It was awful. His friends were there, and his family was there, and everybody was looking for him, and he was under the water."

A team of divers and a television crew added to the surreal drama.

Adds Sheila, "A lot of times she was angry with him, but she didn't want anything like this to happen to him. I had mentioned a few times it would be nice if he dropped off the face of the earth so he wouldn't hurt her anymore. I think she felt some guilt for that, even though I was the one who said it. The kids were pretty devastated. I'll never forget that day. I think for a long time Penny just expected Kenny to show up because, despite all the accidents he'd had, he always came out of it banged up but okay. It's Kenny. He's not gonna get hurt. He never gets hurt. Seventy-four hours after his body went down, it surfaced."

"What do you do?" Penny would ask years later. "Do you laugh or cry? Or do you just sit down and forget?"

#

Two distinct moments. Years apart. They're held together by irony and a bittersweet sense of déjà vu.

"One day we went fishing over at Olney Lake," Jeremy explains, his steady voice masking the pain. "We got done for the day, and we were about to head home. We parked the boat at the dock, and he went to get the truck and told me to hold the boat there at the dock. At the time, I was about seven or eight. The boat started to slip away. When I reached out for it, I fell in. I had no idea how to swim, and I was just struggling. I could feel myself sinking, and I remember seeing his arm coming toward me as he reached in and pulled me out of the water."

Jeremy still wishes he could have returned the favor years later at the same lake. He wonders why his father couldn't wait for him to get home from school.

"I always thought that if he had waited," he says, "I could have helped him. But if he thought it was gonna rain or something, he didn't wait around."

After his father's death, Jeremy and his family were left to pick up the pieces. It wasn't easy.

"I had a lot of good friends and relatives that helped me through most of it," says Tracy, who still can't talk about the day she lost her father. "I think I felt more sorry for myself than I should have. I could have handled the situation afterwards, especially after I got out of school, a little better. I could have stayed home with mom. Instead, after I was of age, I was out and about and didn't want to think about what happened."

These days, Tracy says, she looks at things differently. She thinks things through. After all, she had to grow up quicker than most of her friends.

Says Jeremy, "I guess I discovered how to do a lot of things more on my own and teach myself a lot about life that I would have normally asked him about."

For Penny, the next decade would be a painful one as she mourned the loss of her husband. Despite his battle with PTSD, Kenny was a loveable guy. And, as those who were in his inner circle attest, he had been learning a different way to live before his life was cut short.

"He was starting to get it together toward the end," Sheila says. "Slowly. Mike found out about the way he was hurting Penny. There was a time when we had a talk with him. He stopped hitting Penny. He would do other things, but he stopped hitting her. He started to show more care for her. He was home more."

Says Tracy, "It seemed like when he got older, he thought about [the war] less. And he didn't cause a lot of fights. He was caring. Of course, he towed you to the point. He didn't beat around the bush or say something he didn't mean. He always said what he meant. But he had a lot of friends and didn't have hardly any enemies. People just got along with him."

Much of Penny's healing process, though, boiled down to the abuse. Why did she put up with it for so long? Why did the community turn a blind eye toward her family's struggle? Why, for that matter, had her husband, who had served his country faithfully, essentially been left to his own devices after the war? Where was the support?

In his last years, he got involved with the local Eagles lodge, as well as the local chapter of the American Legion. But for the first ten years of his marriage, Kenny fought the demons alone, his wife bearing the physical evidence of his inner turmoil.

"She would have no real obvious injuries," Sheila recalls. "Sometimes there was a bruise on her cheek or scratches on her arm where her shirt could cover it. Penny would always come to me because we were good friends. I would say, 'You need to get it on record that he did this.' And it was always, 'No, they won't do anything.' She was very loyal about protecting his dark side."

Adds Sheila, "In all fairness, the community didn't know anything about Kenny, other than he was a joker and a hard worker and a nice guy. He didn't show anything like that in the public or at family get-togethers."

His family, as it always had, remained tight and supportive of Kenny, even after his death. But Mike, while standing strong for his siblings, stood up for Penny, too.

"After Kenny died, he took Penny to the funeral home to see the body," Sheila remembers. "He helped make funeral arrangements. She stayed at our house. We sat down, her and I, and worked out what to say at the funeral. Mike was very, very strong for Penny because he knew that's what Kenny would want.

"He doesn't talk about it now. He and the rest of the family always talk about Kenny as far as playing cards, what he would say, and how he'd act. But they never talk about his death or anything, except that it's been ten years."

While he was alive, Kenny scoffed at the idea of getting help.

"He thought that was stupid," Penny says. "He thought he didn't have any problems. He wouldn't talk about the service much. I think we watched *Good Morning, Viet Nam*, and he said the scenery was pretty accurate. But he just didn't make too many remarks. He hated it and didn't want anything to do with it."

What of the government? It trained men how to wage war but not how to cope with the fruit of their actions.

"How many lost their lives over there?" Penny asks. "How many more will die here? How many other families will have to pay the price? I can forget the bruises, but I'll never forget the hate in him that had nowhere to go . . . I hung in there because I loved Ken and our two children and thought it would someday go away. This isn't the way I wanted it to end."

Chapter 6: Home Life
The Frank Hayes Family

"You see, I had been riding with the storm clouds, and had come to earth as rain, and it was drought that I had killed with the power that the Six Grandfathers gave me."

– Black Elk, from *Black Elk Speaks*

War, like a slash-and-burn fire, never dies. It simply hops from one field to the next, burning everything in its wake. When the Americans slung their rifles and went home, they took the Viet Nam War with them. And the war, ostensibly over, went into a slow burn, smoldering beneath the public radar, but burning just the same. Agent Orange. Suicide. PTSD. The casualty list continues to pile up even today. It stretches beyond the vets who fought in Viet Nam.

But don't count Weatalo Francesca Hayes among the victims of the war. As far as she is concerned, Viet Nam ended with her father.

"Instead of repeating our parents' mistakes," she says, "we've made a very conscious effort to learn from them."

A 23-year-old English major at the University of Maine, Weatalo, like her two brothers, has never been to Viet Nam.

She never fired a shot in the war that still consumes her father, Frank Hayes. Never wandered the mountainous jungles of the Central Highlands in search of a body count. Never watched her hand shake as she set fire to some villager's hut.

She was born in 1980, seven years after the last American troops left Viet Nam. And her father has shared little about his war in Viet Nam. But since an early age she has watched him wage his own battles on a psychological landscape that doles out its own kind of carnage.

"We've all realized that a lot of Dad's anger is because of Viet Nam, and it's not because of us," she says. "That was a really big realization with us. Viet Nam was so hard on my dad. I went through it, but I didn't understand it because he never talked about it. There was a lot of fear, especially in the early days."

Startling noises made her father recoil in fear. To a lesser extent, so did crowded places. And unbidden memories. The horror of Viet Nam had found its way into his fast-twitch muscles, unspeakable atrocity turned into jerking reflex.

"One time we were at his friend's house on a mountain," his daughter recalls. "I was five at the most. A helicopter went over really low, and they both dove to the floor. That was really scary. I didn't understand. They didn't try to protect me. It was like they were eighteen again and in Viet Nam. Other times, he'd be out drinking on a snowy night, and we'd be worried about him. He'd be mad when he came home because we were up waiting for him."

What actually buzzed the mountain that day was a low-flying jet, the sound of which the two vets instinctively associated with falling ordinance. But such details sometimes escaped – and still escape – those like Weatalo who lived the war secondhand. She had other concerns.

"Waking him up at night was very dangerous," Weatalo continues, "and should never be done. He was ready to fight for his life. The look in his eyes was, 'I need to be awake.' And it was panic."

If her father could only shoot at what haunts him now.

"In Viet Nam," Weatalo says, "he had to defile what he believed in."

#

An eight-year-old kid watches from outside the hash marks as bodies hurtle toward each other. Like a herd of wild buffalo tumbling over a cliff, older boys in pads and helmets thunder down the sidelines, shaking the earth as they rumble by. They collide with a reverberating thud, and cleats that were chewing up muddy sod a split second before go airborne, still churning, still cranking. Whistles blow as bodies continue to crack against each other, and the bloodied and bruised teenagers gasp for air.

The eight-year-old kid's eyes widen.

"I found out in Viet Nam that bullets crush and rip and destroy," the eight-year-old kid would say decades later. "Blood is warm. And a skull will break like a coconut."

Frank Irving Hayes grew up a stone's throw from the Eliot High School football field in Eliot, Maine. He walked the quiet woods every afternoon to the football field, where blood sport and male adolescence fused in a warlike rite of passage.

With a population hovering near three thousand in the 1950s and '60s, Eliot served as a bedroom community for a naval shipyard nearby and its airbase counterpart in New Hampshire. Everybody knew everybody. And the rural, sleepy town evoked an atmosphere that would, years later, utterly drip with nostalgia.

By the time Frank was a student at Eliot High, he, too, donned pads and helmet each day after school, partaking in the ritual with as much passion and lust as he could muster.

"Football was in my blood," he remembers. "It was kind of a prelude, that adrenaline rush. The only thing I found that was similar to that was combat."

After the football season came to an end during his senior year, Frank quit high school, spurned on, as it were, by President Kennedy's mantra of collective self-sacrifice. He joined the Army and tore through boot camp in Fort Dix, New Jersey; infantry training at Fort Gordon, Georgia; and then paratrooper school and special forces training at Fort Benning, also in Georgia.

September 1966 found him a member of the U.S. Army's 101st Airborne Tiger Force at Phan Rang base camp in Viet Nam. He volunteered for a reconnaissance team that had been depleted by casualties. And the war became personal in short order.

"We'd go out into the jungle before everybody else and recon in eight-man teams," he recalls. "We'd check out areas for enemy activity, take prisoners, mostly just look for the enemy and record what they were doing. We weren't supposed to engage them. But sometimes you just run into them face to face. *What do I do? What do I do? Kill! Kill! K-I-L-L!*"

Pulling the trigger unleashed all sorts of demons for Frank, whose first impulse was compassion, not violence.

"The Army training just overrides your spiritual side," he explains. "I lost myself. I lost my country. My mom told me before the war that if I ever got into a situation where I didn't know what to do, I should ask myself what Christ would do. Viet Nam was a constant challenge. You don't hesitate, or you're dead.

"Sometimes we'd form a platoon and attack villages. We'd take the trail to the village. If anyone was there, they were history. We'd kill the livestock. Burn the village sometimes. Sometimes we'd just move right through. It was kind of your choice out there. You could play God. If you found somebody out there, you could kill 'em. Some did. I chose not to. Seemed like everyone we ran into was the Vietcong. If they didn't end up dead, they ended up prisoner. You're way out in the frick'n jungle, and there's eight of you. You're trying to get a body count, but you don't want to be there. I think most people just wanted to be home.

"I realized early on we weren't wearing the white hats. If you're going to go into a village, kill the old people, and poison the rice harvest, you're not going to win the war. It was then that I realized we were evil, that we were the frontrunners of an evil force: the rest of the Army behind us and the corporations behind them. You don't know who the enemy is, but I know a little kid running down the trail is not my enemy. He's *not* my enemy. I'm not gonna kill him. Some guys would. It was open season. But I realized this was morally wrong, politically wrong, philosophically wrong. This was wrong, wrong, wrong."

Nevertheless, peer pressure – and a lack of accountability – at times overwhelmed Frank's instincts in the jungle.

"I'd light my lighter and look at this dry hut," he says. "Something inside me said it was wrong. But you did it anyway. I complained when a sergeant killed an old lady, but I learned not to say anything. Who could you protest to? It was the law of the jungle."

The random brutality of war was often juxtaposed against military absurdity. One day in late November – the same day the sergeant executed the old lady – a helicopter picked up Frank and his unit from a hot landing zone, whisking them away while taking fire. It dropped the eight men on a remote hillside to enjoy a huge Thanksgiving dinner. The Americans gorged on turkey, mashed potatoes, and even ice cream. Victims of the tasteless monotony of C-rations, they savored every bite and then collapsed in a gluttonous stupor. As they lingered afterward, some nearly sick, others simply stuffed to the gills, the helicopter returned. A few minutes later, they were flown to another drop zone, full-bellied and on full alert.

#

Frank left Viet Nam a hero. He had sustained injuries, earning a Purple Heart in the process while defending a listening post on a lonely ridge extending like a finger from HQ Company's command post. With two other Americans sleeping next to him in the foxhole, he fought off a grenade attack by an NVA probe, sweeping his M-60 360 degrees and then lobbing grenades near and far. The NVA never fired back.

"I didn't know how good I was doing until the sun came up and there was blood and bandages all over the ridge," he says. "They were dragging 'em down the mountain when the sun came up. When I flew out by medevac chopper, I looked down at the position. There must have been fourteen holes around our foxhole, with some in the sandbags."

Natural athleticism and a childhood spent wandering the woods in Maine had saved his life, as well as the lives of the two Americans with him. But when Frank returned home a few months later, he didn't feel like a hero.

"I remember looking in the mirror one morning after coming back," he says. "I saw General Custer."

It was an image that didn't square with his upbringing nor with the person he aspired to be.

"My mother was very spiritual," Frank recalls. "In summers in junior high, we'd go out and work in the garden. Then she'd hand us Thoreau or James Fenimore Cooper to read for an hour. That's the way she brought us up. She schooled us in a bunch of different religions."

God died in the Central Highlands, replaced by the whim of men with automatic rifles.

"When you go through something like Viet Nam," Frank says, "it makes you feel soiled inside."

It didn't take long for the grief he had internalized to manifest itself in his behavior. Frank still had well over a year and a half left of his three-year stint to finish stateside. He spent the next nine months at Fort Dix, where he served as a drill instructor. As the river of Americans sent home from Viet Nam in body bags continued to rise, he trained the next wave of soldiers, treating the men under him with respect and empathy and earning the nickname Sergeant Pepper.

"I bonded with these kids coming through," he remembers. "I did what I could for them, giving them advice on the jungle and building their self-confidence."

But he was only nineteen years old. And he had lost all faith in the war and its blunt instrument, the U.S. Army. After verbally jousting with a superior, he was reprimanded and handed an Article 15 (a misdemeanor).

"That was the beginning of the end of my Army career," he says. "I had already had a relapse of malaria. I had been back nine months."

Frank was cut orders for Panama to help guard the canal. Before leaving, he extended what was supposed to be a short break by a month, sitting in on philosophy classes with a friend at the University of New Hampshire. He was, in essence, AWOL. When a police officer picked him up on a New York City turnpike for hitchhiking (he was on his way to North Carolina to report for duty), he found himself in the 12th Precinct jail. He was sent back the next day in handcuffs to Fort Dix, where he was court-martialed and busted down to E3.

#

One of the amazing things about the human body is its uncanny ability to adapt to almost any condition, however brutal, however counterintuitive to healthy physiology. In

Viet Nam, Frank learned how to get by without sleeping more than a few minutes at a time. For a year his body remained alert, clenched, ready to react to the slightest provocation.

In Panama, what had been a finely tuned skill was now a debilitating liability: he couldn't sleep. So he started smoking marijuana in the evenings, sneaking off to a ball field on the base where he would sit on the bleachers in the dark and wind down with a joint. One night, a CID agent caught the glowing embers in his night scope. A pair of detectives greeted Frank back at the barracks.

Facing his second court martial, Frank was busted down to E1 and sent to six months of hard labor in the stockade. He lost all his pay, as well.

"I played the game for a while, playing basketball in the courtyard – more degrading bullshit. One day, I was laying in my cell, and this officer comes by and says, 'Attention!' I didn't come to attention. I didn't move. He kept saying, 'Attention!' Finally, I said, 'Fuck you, too!'"

The show of disrespect earned Frank solitary confinement and meals consisting largely of stale bread, Spam, and lukewarm water. He actually tried to escape at one point but collapsed in fatigue during his attempt. After a month and a half in solitary, he was released on the orders of a new battalion commander, who, upon taking over, recognized Frank's flawless combat record.

The irony surrounding his jail time, meanwhile, didn't escape Frank. In the jungles of Viet Nam, where men played God and snuffed out lives as they pleased, he had conducted himself admirably and with restraint, riding the razor-thin edge between military duty and the moral high ground as best he could. Back home, he was sent to jail for smoking an herb.

"In Viet Nam, I was given medals for committing genocide," he grouses, adding, "I had a sleep disorder. I told the doctor early on that I was having a hard time sleeping. But they didn't do anything."

After the new battalion commander released him, he was reassigned to the west coast of Panama. But he still resented the Army and chafed under its command.

"I had an attitude," he says. "I wanted out."

Frank played cat and mouse with the base MP's, sneaking into town, cutting out of work, and flouting authority at every turn. Before they could catch him red-handed, he bottomed out and committed himself to a mental institute.

"I really had to get out," he says. "I couldn't sleep at night. I was having all these problems. They weren't gonna help me. I checked into this international mental hospital. I had two bottles of speed with me and committed myself. I didn't care what kind of discharge they gave me. I just wanted out. I did start talking to a psychiatrist about Viet Nam. But basically I was on this ward with coke addicts and schizos, guys from all over the world. One day I got bored and started passing out these Bennies to the guys. So I got the whole ward going, rushing around, fighting. I'm just sitting back, laughing. I incited a riot. They had a lockdown and found the Bennies. They wrestled me down. One of the attendees ended up with stitches. They wanted me out of there! Can you imagine that? They wanted to kick me out of a mental institution!

"So I got out. They took me right back to my unit. And I got saved. I had three months left, and they were having softball tryouts for the battalion team. I was one of the best players. Suddenly, I went from screw-up to hero. I was golden. I'd go to the beach all day and practice in the evenings. I loved it. Nobody was bugging me. We were playing under the lights. I was in left field. One night I lit a joint before the game started. I knew they didn't have a sense of humor, but I was trying to piss them off. I asked the center fielder if he wanted a hit. He was trying to get away from me. Nobody ever said a word about it. We won all our games. We won the league."

Frank survived his final month, instigating a few more minor "incidents" along the way, and earned an honorable discharge. He burned his uniform, burned his papers, and started growing his hair long the moment he left the base. He was finally free.

#

Consider this. Perhaps Viet Nam, in the end, was nothing more than a stone the size of a fist. Someone in heaven or, more likely, the underworld took that stone and lobbed it toward a tranquil lake that had been undisturbed for the better part of a generation: serene, picturesque, a plate-glass reflection of a world without ugliness.

The stone changed everything. Along with piercing the calm, it shattered the lives of anyone and everyone caught searching for their own reflection. It sent out a series of ripples that are widening still.

"Post-Traumatic Stress Disorder in a way is transferable," says Dr. Bruce Letsch, a clinical psychiatrist at Togus VA Hospital just outside of Augusta, Maine. "You can call it 'secondary PTSD' or 'PTSD by adaptation.' Some of it is a learned or modeled response. It's a contagion, in a sense."

For almost twenty years, Jeanne Peacock fought the illness. And then she walked away. Frank still remembers his ex-wife's gritty farewell.

"You can't get away from Viet Nam," she told her husband, "but I can."

The two met in the summer of 1972 in York on the coast of Maine, where her parents were vacationing and Jeanne was working a summer job. Five years his junior, she found herself instantly attracted to Frank, a Viet Nam vet turned hippie war protestor.

"He is a charmer," she says. "He knows how to play the charming card very well to get what he wants. At that time my mom had a Mercedes Benz. The first time I showed up in it, I think he said, 'That's the one for me.'"

Frank remembers it differently. "Jeanne came from a wealthy family," he says. "She had never been anywhere. She used to pick me up in her Mercedes. I was kind of her way out. I could get her out of that upper middle class rut she had been in and expose her to the world."

The oldest of four in a close family, Jeanne had just turned twenty. Rebellious and plenty naïve, she ignored her parents' objections and, two months after meeting Frank, followed him on a backpacking trip to Panama. They were married on the island of Bocas Del Toro (Mouth of the Bull) soon after.

"She was pretty tough," Frank says. "Tougher than I thought. She saw a lot of starvation and poverty she had never seen before. It was good for her. She saw what the rest of the world lived like."

The wedding ceremony was small and simple.

"The vows were in Spanish," Jeanne recalls. "They said something to the effect that, if he couldn't find a good way to go in life as the leader, then I should be the leader. But they were just words. That part never worked out."

The young couple returned from Panama and took a train across Canada, from Montreal to Vancouver. From there, they traveled south to Seattle and then rented a car to head east over the Cascade Mountains. They ended up at the Colville Indian Reservation, a 1.3-million-acre reservation just north of Grand Coulee Dam. Sparsely populated, the reservation offered a kind of desolate beauty – just the place for Frank to forget the savagery of Viet Nam.

"It was mostly wildlife there," he remembers. "Beautiful place. Beautiful people. We fell in love with them. We lived on top of a mountain at a fire lookout. That was our job. I'd work five days a week. Jeanne would work the weekends. A helicopter brought our supplies in. It was a three-month stint. Then we came down. Jeanne got a job with the tribal daycare.

I got a job as an assistant at the school, where I tutored kids, worked in the gym, coached athletics. Then we had our first child, Joe. We were there for three years.

"After that, we drove down to New Mexico and spent a few months with my brother. Then we came back east to the Moosehead Lakes Region in central Maine, and we lived with our backs to the mountains again. There was a pattern here. I was trying to live my life like a recluse. We lived in teepees on the reservation, lived in log cabins, lived in one place with a dirt floor, always living in remote areas. We eventually moved to Shirley, Maine, and got our own little farm with chickens, turkeys, a goat. We had a pony for the kids to ride on, had a garden, and raised our kids on Native American cradle boards until they were two."

Though Jeanne has equally fond memories of the early years, she also has bitter ones, especially of Colville. Frank drank too much too often. Even when sober, he was angry much of the time.

"I remember a lot of heavy drinking," she says, "and I wasn't the one doing the drinking. Pretty much I had no support system, so I wanted to come back to the East Coast to be near my family. A lot of the spirituality of the Native Americans is long gone. They were pretty much into heavy drinking. The town was dominated by the War Bonnet Tavern. It was the only business in town, other than the variety store, and a lot of people got involved in that. They were big, heavy drinkers, and they didn't take good care of their kids. A lot of time I ended up taking care of their kids. At one point, I was taking care of a ten-month-old baby.

"One time we were going with some relatives to see an Indian celebration. We went to a rodeo that had a suicide race, where horses are stampeded down this steep hill. That was the first time I could profoundly think about hell – that's what it made me think of. I said, 'There's no way I'm gonna be a part of this.' So I sat in the car for the rest of the evening.

But I have a sense that that's what it's like when there are atrocities. It gave me a tiny glimpse of what it must have been like in Viet Nam. But you couldn't just get in a car and go home if you were in Viet Nam – seeing people dying around you, and wondering if you'll even get out alive."

Her empathy, though, was tempered by Frank's day-to-day excesses.

"Anger and alcohol were the two biggest factors," she explains, "and they often blurred together."

#

Which came first: the war or the anger? The anger or the alcohol? For those on the receiving end, did it matter?

Samuel John "Running Bear" Hayes, the youngest of Frank and Jeanne's three children, was born on August 31, 1982 in Dover-FoxCroft, Maine. He spent most of his early childhood on the family farm in Shirley.

"I think it was even before the war," the young carpenter says of his father's battle with anger and alcohol. "I know alcoholism runs in my dad's family."

Frank's father Charles was a decorated World War II veteran. He said goodbye to a professional baseball career with the Boston Braves when he was injured by shrapnel in the Philippines and earned a Purple Heart. He had nightmares long after the war, abused alcohol, and had a quick temper.

His bitterness, no doubt, could be attributed at least partially to his lost opportunity on the baseball diamond. He was a left-handed pitcher with plenty of promise when, just after being called up to the major leagues, he answered the call to war. The Braves organization, incidentally, nearly suffered a similar fate as attendance slipped mightily after the war. Five years after winning the World Series in 1948, the Braves, on the brink of extinction, pulled up stakes from Boston and moved to Milwaukee before finally settling in Atlanta.

By then, baseball, like the war, was a painful memory for Frank's father.

"I feel like I'm really the only one in the family who understood him because I went to war and know what he was going through," Frank says. "But he could be explosive. He had a temper sometimes. As a kid, I probably bore the brunt of it more than the other kids. But that was the way it was back then. Everybody got the hand from their father or a kick in the ass. That was normal back then. But I've talked to a lot of my friends, and that stopped with our generation. We never abused our children."

"Frank's father was a situational alcoholic," Jeanne explains. "He was a loud, mean drunk who was very tough on his wife. He got his act together somewhat later on and treated his family better. But he was a male chauvinist. His wife supported his chauvinist behavior, even to the point of saying to Sam that I had deserted my husband and children, that no matter how bad it was, at least she stayed."

Frank insists it was never that bad. Although his father lost his temper on occasion, he took the kids fishing, taught them how to play sports, and for the most part raised them well. Regardless, whether it was Viet Nam, his upbringing, or a combination of both, Frank, like his father, struggled with his temper. Drinking didn't help.

"There were some rough moments," Jeanne says. "But I don't want to get into that."

Sam and Weatalo remember a simmering rage that often boiled over.

"We saw him explode into anger almost nightly," Weatalo says. "He frequently yelled and used threatening gestures, toward my mother especially."

"It's weird," Sam says. "Just little things, like he'll drop a fork on the floor and go, 'Fuck!' really loud. He'll get really worked up over stuff and just really get down and mope about it and swear and pace around. He takes more stress out of things than is needed."

Dr. Letsch calls it "the old kick-the-dog syndrome."

"It's very unfortunate but true that many vets take it out inadvertently on their families," he explains. "The problem comes from two things: anger and a fear of intimacy.

"The anger really isn't directed at the family, but they're close at hand. Regardless, the ability to control it is not there. The military trained people to use their anger. The most useful emotion you could have in Viet Nam was anger, and that conditioning was still there when these guys came home. If you don't do things right, you or someone else in your unit might not make it home alive. That's why seemingly trivial things have to be done right.

"The other difficulty is in closeness and intimacy. The softer emotions – love, caring, affection – that ability was really covered over in their training and experiences. It atrophied. It makes it hard to be close to someone who won't be close to you. Also, many guys lost close friends in Viet Nam, so getting close became risky. That gets generalized and comes back here to civilian life. It's a self-protective mechanism."

Frank's experiences, in fact, were true to the stereotype.

"I was told when I reported for my recon platoon, 'Don't make friends,'" he recalls. "I did see a lot of people die and lost a lot of people around me. You have to harden yourself to death. You have to be able to look away from it. In that sense, I never made any friends in Viet Nam.

"With Jeanne, I couldn't pull her close and let her get inside of me, which you have to do in a long-term relationship. I couldn't look her in the eyes and make that commitment. I could with my kids, but not with Jeanne. I was having problems with dreams. I drank a six-pack a day. I worked hard during the day and then had a six-pack in the evening. Then I could sleep. But you're doing damage to your relationship when you're self-medicating. You're either ignoring someone's needs or abusing them. I couldn't be what she wanted me to be. I would have had a much better relationship had I not gone. But I never wanted to open up to her."

In the end, it cost him his marriage.

"I found him to be a very angry person," Jeanne says. "He has been obsessed with Viet Nam since I've known him. Because I was the person in front of his face, I absorbed a lot of that anger. It just reached the point where I said, 'Enough already. I'm out of here.'"

#

It wouldn't be Frank's first divorce. While stationed in Panama, he met a young woman of Peruvian descent named Marina. She was, as Frank calls her, a "beautiful lost child of the planet." She was also pregnant by another American soldier. Frank, who managed to live off base for part of his tour in Panama, married Marina, hoping to undo a host of wrongs.

"I got her and her daughter, Jana, to the U.S.," he recalls. "We stayed together for a year. We had a child together. Her name is Jessica. She was born in the States. I felt so bad. It was a guilt thing. I thought that if I could help other people, I might be able to undo the bad karma and energy I had. So I tried to fix things where I saw America had screwed up. I thought, 'I can't leave her.' I'm sure I felt something for her, but it was just to get some good karma going. But I was sacrificing my own future.

"Now Marina's in California. She's a nurse. Jana's in her thirties now. She went into the military. She's a nurse now, too. She eventually found her father right before he died of Agent Orange exposure. Jessica had a child. She's almost thirty. She runs a daycare."

After his discharge in 1969, Frank brought Marina and Jana to York, not far from Portsmouth, where Jessica was delivered. But they were divorced a year later.

"I tried, and she tried," he says. "But I wasn't ready for it. I was medicating myself with just about anything that came along at that point: pot, acid."

Despite the divorce, Frank managed to maintain a relationship with his birth daughter, Jessica, who lived with Frank and Jeanne off and on over the years.

His divorce from Jeanne, meanwhile, coming as it did years after the couple had children, had a more dramatic impact on the family, especially Sam.

"It was a really hard time for me," Sam says of the divorce, which became official in 1992. "That really stands out from my childhood. I was in the fourth grade. My brother and sister were older and busy. I didn't have anyone to talk to about what I was going through.

"I had a really tough relationship with my mom afterward because I lived with my dad, and she moved farther away. So she wasn't really a mother figure for me. I tried moving down there [Lewiston] because I got in trouble in school, but I ended up in jail."

Sam was in the eighth grade and was on probation for breaking a window. When he skipped school after moving in with his mother and her new husband, Jeanne notified the authorities.

"She called the cops on me," Sam remembers. "You can imagine I was not very happy for a few years. My dad had to come down and bail me out of jail. That's why I went back up to live with him. She wasn't really there like a mother was supposed to be, and that was because I was with my dad. He was a more relaxed guy and easier to get along with. He was like a father *and* a mother to me."

Weatalo, too, tried to move in with her mother. But the arrangement didn't work for similar reasons.

"I thought the kids would naturally come with me after the divorce," Jeanne says. "But because Frank hadn't worked much, I was not home. I was at work. And the kids were supervised by Frank. So when I left and brought the kids with me, pretty much what happened was that I was still at work and they were unsupervised. They felt more comfortable with their father. And I didn't realize it until then. I had moved out, gotten my own place. Especially Sam was back and forth a lot. The older kids were there most of the time. A year and a half afterward, when I met my husband [John Peacock], Weatalo was fourteen. John is not a drinker. He's kind – a very nice person. But he believes in firmness and fairness with accountability. The kids never gave it a chance. Weatalo lasted one day. They spent most of the rest of their childhood with Frank. That was a shock to me, very difficult."

#

Before Frank ever met Jeanne, he checked himself into the VA hospital in Tongus. The year: 1970. No one knew what PTSD was. The VA's answer for sleeplessness, startle reaction, and interminable nightmares was medication.

"My mother saw it," Frank says of the conditions. "So she had me commit myself. They gave me Thorazine and put me back out on the streets. Yeah, you can sleep, but you can't do anything else. The longer you took it, the more debilitated you became. I stopped after three times and never went back."

Never, that is, until Jeanne, desperately searching for that magic bullet to save their crumbling marriage, begged and pleaded with Frank to go to the VA two decades later.

"We were living in Moosehead," Frank recalls. "I was working at a sawmill at the time. There was an AmVet Outreach bus coming to Greenville, and Jeanne pointed it out in the paper to me. She said, 'For my sake and the kids, I want you to go.' I agreed and went in and talked with 'em.

That's when I got ten percent disability, then thirty percent, then one hundred percent. I would never have gone there or had anything to do with the VA or the government, but I did it because of Jeanne and for the children."

#

Chaos.

When Hopi Joseph Hayes talks about his childhood, he talks about a father who wasn't ready to be one and a mother who desperately sought stability from her oldest son. He talks about alcohol and rage, abuse and defiance. He talks about growing up with no ground beneath him. About spiritual free-fall. He talks about chaos.

"I think in a lot of ways I grew up quickly," says Joe, a teacher-to-be who, like his sister, is studying English at the University of Maine.

Born on the Colville Indian Reservation on April 3, 1976, and named after Chief Joseph, Joe lived his first year on the reservation before the family moved back to the East Coast. As the oldest child, he learned early on that he bore a special burden. Along with sometimes playing the role of father to his younger siblings, he developed a close relationship with his mother, who appreciated his maturity and dedication to the family. And he developed a combative relationship with his father, who, in Joe's estimation, finally learned to respect him after the two came to blows while Joe was a sophomore in high school.

"He used to threaten us, saying he could freak out and have a blackout or whatever," Joe recalls. "As an adult now, I'm really glad I was able to stand up to him amidst all the chaos and say, 'What you're doing is wrong, and I don't care how big you are.'"

At five-feet-seven and 150 pounds, Joe didn't exactly intimidate his father, who was three inches taller and eighty pounds heavier. But he stood his ground. He did his best to put an end to his father's emotional abuse. Viet Nam, alcoholism, and anger would stop with his father.

"I'm glad it made him feel better," Frank says of the confrontation, "because it made me sick. What I actually used to say was that I don't like to fight anyone because I might black out and be back in Viet Nam. But that taught me a lesson: I should have just let Joe hit me. I cried after that. It hurt me more than it hurt him."

Joe, meanwhile, can trace his maturation to another pivotal moment, as well.

"When I was in the seventh grade, my mom sent me in to see a psychiatrist once a week," he remembers. "I gained so much from that as a person. To see alcoholism and how it affects the family, to see the war, and to see how very closely related these symptoms are – I learned our family wasn't crazy all by themselves. This was happening all the time all over the place."

Still, knowing what was happening and finding a way to rise above it were two different things. For Joe, that meant carving out his own life and holding steadfast to his own opinions.

One thing Frank tried to emphasize with his children, especially his two boys, was the importance of sports in helping to shape one's life and in building character and discipline. He taught his children several sports, even coaching their teams on occasion. Sam took his father's advice to heart, eventually earning a spot on the state's all-star football team while a senior at Belfast High. But Joe rejected it outright. As he did alcohol.

"I hate alcohol," he says. "I don't drink, period. Alcoholism and the effects of Viet Nam stopped with my generation. That happened with my dad and his dad."

One thing that Frank *has* passed on to his children is his own spiritual quest, which started with traditional Christianity before moving on to Native American religion and paganism.

"That allowed me to have an open mind," Joe says, "because I wasn't immersed in any organized religion growing up."

Says Weatalo, "In class discussions, a lot of people pick up on our values being different from the norm, especially pertaining to government and religion. We're critical of the government and open on a religious level."

"Since we were kids," Sam adds, "he's brought us out in the woods, brought us hunting, up to the pretty spots, watching sunsets. He's really a spiritual person. He thinks Mother Nature is his church. And I love him for that. That's the same track I'm on."

#

While the divorce was difficult for Sam, it came as no surprise to anyone. Joe, for one, was actually relieved.

"I was so close to my mom at the time and we had such a direct relationship that, when she told me they were getting a divorce, I said, 'Thank God,'" Joe remembers. "They were just not getting along whatsoever."

Jeanne's decision to leave, though it hurt up front, ultimately paid off. Like an austerity program administered to a bloated, corrupt bureaucracy, her departure forced everyone, including herself, to grow.

"Jeanne had her own problems, too," Frank asserts, "but seventy-five percent of our problems related back to me and Viet Nam. I think she's just finding herself now. She left the kids at a very critical time in their lives, and she left me to play both mom and dad. But she had no choice, I guess."

Jeanne, a registered nurse, works at a nursing home in Lewiston, Maine. She enjoys healthy relationships with all three of her children. And she's happily married.

"I look at the bigger picture in life," she says. "What are we here for? I must have had some very heavy karma to undo. And I went through it and came out on the other side.

"It seems as though I had to go through what I did to get to the place I am now. I have three wonderful kids, and I love them dearly. I used to have guilt about the kids, but no longer. They had a tough childhood, but they can make the second part of their lives good. More importantly, they're not naïve like I was at their stage in life. They are coming into adulthood with their eyes wide open."

As for her former husband, she says, "Unfortunately, when you have tough times, they tend to blur the good times. It doesn't take many of those tough times to lose trust, to be frightened. I felt like I was carrying around so much anger and just living in it. And I felt I had to forgive him. I knew he was doing the best he could with what he had. I had faith in him and humanity that most of us do the best we can with what we have. That was very healing. Emotionally, I'm over this. I don't carry around anger and hate. I just let it go."

Weatalo maintains that, though her relationship with her mother was strained early on, it has recovered. They don't always understand each other, but they communicate well now and interact positively. Things with her father, too, have improved.

"We have a really good relationship now," she says. "We still don't talk about the war. But I read poetry to him, and he's very responsive, more so than some people in my family. It's like therapy."

Joe, meanwhile, still has close ties with his mother. He appreciates to this day what she gave to the family early on.

"She was the leader of the family," he says. "She did *everything*. She was the glue that kept the family together. It's amazing she was able to be so strong for us."

But what of Joe's father? Has he learned anything from Viet Nam? Does the war still resonate as intensely and immediately with Frank as it did the day he came home?

"He's more open and more decent as an individual than he's ever been," Joe says. "I'm sad that he's leaving."

#

It's Frank's last night here, at least for the time being. For the last year or so, he has lived in this two-story cabin in Monson, Maine, on the edge of the One-Hundred-Mile Wilderness, a vast expanse that stretches all the way to Mount Katahdin, the state's largest peak at 5,268 feet. He has spent most of his days reading, wandering the woods around his house, and walking Dakota, a nine-year-old Lab-Husky mix. Maple, pine, fir, and spruce trees rise like medieval spires in a land that boasts more moose than people.

"I have the time for self-exploration, meditation, and travel," Frank says, "and I think it's finally paying off. But every day is a struggle to suppress memories and keep anger down."

Viet Nam has left him with a healthy skepticism of the U.S. government, especially its actions abroad. He's not adverse to the occasional conspiracy theory. He makes no bones when it comes to his own country's hypocrisy.

"In America," he pontificates, "everything is backward. The Christians are screaming for war. The priests are molesting the flock. Dissent is an act of cowardice. Conformists call themselves patriots."

But tonight, Frank, who has become a vociferous and passionate political activist in his middle age, lets all that go. Joe has arrived, and the two will spend a quiet night of talking and enjoying their revitalized father-son relationship. Tomorrow, Joe will take Frank to the airport. He'll watch after the dog. Frank will head west to visit his brother and aging mother in New Mexico, as well as an old Army buddy nicknamed "Sarge" in Arizona (Chapter 9). Sarge and Frank plan on heading to Patagonia, a small town in Southern Arizona, for some much-needed R&R. Then Frank will start looking for a place in New Mexico. Maybe. The trip is open-ended. And anything's possible.

"Since Viet Nam, I've just been searching," he says. "The war was my epiphany. I'm just really happy where I'm at now, and where my kids are now."

He's come a long way since saying goodbye to Viet Nam, a long way since the fall of 1979, when a good friend and fellow vet took his own life.

"Frank said many times after the suicide that he felt as though that would be his future, too, if not for the children we had," Jeanne recalls. "He also had difficulty understanding why he did not die in Viet Nam. But he thought there must be something in life he was meant to accomplish."

#

In Salishan, a Native American language family with no recognized phylum, Weatalo means "morning dove."

When she was only sixteen, Morning Dove moved out on her own. She managed to stay in high school. She found a pair of jobs: one selling furniture and the other working at a bagelry. She avoided the common pitfalls – pregnancy, drugs, etc. – that usually entice those entering adulthood before their time.

Now she's finishing her bachelor's degree and eyeing a couple of different graduate schools on the West Coast.

"I don't feel like I got a childhood," she says. "I feel like I had to be more adult than my age. When I look back, I definitely feel like my parents weren't responsible. That's why I moved out when I was young. I felt like I could do a better job than them. Now I'm interested in the whole therapeutic idea of getting back to the innocence of childhood. When I was with my parents, I was struggling so hard just to be a happy person. But when I moved out, it seemed so easy."

If war is a slash-and-burn fire, then it needs fuel to survive. The wind can shift. Depending on the direction it takes, dozens of little spot fires can die to the ground or blaze anew.

Frank puts the issue to rest before flying west.

"My father used to sleep with a bayonet next to his bed," he says. "When he died, that bayonet was given to me. Now I sleep with it next to my bed. And I'm *not* going to pass it on."

He pauses to let the thought sink in.

"I'm a second-generation Purple Heart recipient," he says with conviction. "There won't be a third, I guarantee that. That bayonet's going to be buried with me."

Chapter 7: Suicide
The Rigdon Family

Say what you will
About those who are forced into war.
There is no doubt in my mind that they are forgiven.
If God cannot forgive them their sins,
Then we are all surely damned.

– Mark Donaldson, from a poem dedicated to his half-brother,

James Howard Rigdon

Historians, for the most part, talk about the Viet Nam War in the past tense. For them it's history – something to be chronicled from a safe place; something to be tweezed and parsed, its muddled and disjointed voices sifted through the sieve of objectivity.

Vets and their families know better. Every year the body count grows. But we can't collect our fallen and take them home. They're already home, assuming something like home ever truly existed for them after the shooting stopped. Nor can we survey the battlefield and tally the dead and the missing. No authority, no governmental body is in charge of such an endeavor, assuming it were possible.

The numbers vary widely, depending on the source. According to Pointman International Ministries, as many as 180,000 vets have taken their own lives since the Viet Nam War ended. Other more conservative estimates put the figure closer to 20,000. Everyone agrees that the total is difficult to pin down for a variety of reasons: "accidents" happen, autopsies are fudged to protect the survivors, and many suicides go unreported. It's doubtful we'll ever know exactly how many vets have chosen to end their lives since Viet Nam. All we can say for certain is that suicide, like war, is a family affair.

#

"I was rushing around to go out," Dawn says, recalling May 27, 1994, the night her father took his own life. "He had been in just a foul mood all day. He told my mother he wanted steak and eggs for dinner. The whole time I knew him, he had never asked for steak and eggs. He came out of his room, and it was not cooked like he wanted it. I don't remember if he threw the plate or just dropped it. But he just kind of scoffed at my mom. I was in the bathroom and stuck my head out the door and said, 'Why don't you just leave her alone?' And then I went out for the evening."

While Dawn, then a freshman in college, joined her friends for a few hours, her sister Courtnie stayed at home that evening. When her father asked for a pen and a piece of paper, she complied with little fuss. His request wasn't that unusual; he often jotted things down during the day. And James "Gunny" Rigdon, a former marine whose health had deteriorated steadily since the Viet Nam War, was nearly wheelchair bound. Simply walking the fifty feet to the fishing pond in his back yard left him exhausted and out of breath.

Courtnie gave her father the pen and paper, and he sat down in his chair to write. A few hours later, while Courtnie and her mother tinkered with a new computer in the piano room, he closed himself up in his bedroom. This, too, had become part of the routine over the last several months.

"I got home around eleven or eleven-thirty and walked into our living room," Dawn continues the story. "The hall was right in front of me. I walked down the hall and faced my mother and sister in [the piano room]. On my left I heard the door unlock, and he stepped out of his bedroom. I ignored him. He walked back in, clicked the door, and shot himself. All three of us heard it.

"I said, 'I think Dad's just shot himself.' We all ran to the room. His door was still locked. My mother kicked it down. She's a little lady – maybe five-foot-three – but she broke the doorframe to get into the bedroom. He was kind of slumped in the recliner. He shot himself through the heart. His chest was just covered . . . there was just blood . . ."

Dawn chokes silently as she tries to shake off the image.

"I ran the other way to get to the phone. I passed the phone in the hall and ran to the phone in the kitchen. There's no 9-1-1 in our little town. I had to dial long distance and misdialed like three times. Mom kept yelling, 'Call 9-1-1!' I finally got through to the hospital, which was a good fifteen minutes from us. Mom worked as a nurse through a state agency [Health Department Home Care], and everybody knew us there."

Willacoochee, a tiny rural community in southern Georgia and the only home Dawn had ever known, was closing in on her as every habitual connection – even time itself – gave way to the shockingly surreal fog of the moment.

Back in the bedroom, her father had already breathed his last. He had died instantly. Kellie Ruth Rigdon, his wife of nearly twenty-six years, pulled him to the floor by his legs. She couldn't stand to leave him in the chair, she would say later. She even tried administering CPR, though she knew it was, in her words, "a lost cause."

"It took fifteen minutes for the ambulance to get to us," Dawn continues. "I didn't want to go back there. Courtnie and I stayed in the living room while they worked on him."

After a few minutes the paramedics emerged from the bedroom and slowly walked back to the ambulance. The phone rang in the kitchen, and Dawn answered. The person on the other end of the line asked what county she was in. "Atkinson," she whispered numbly. The person barely waited for her to answer before hanging up. She knew she had just spoken with the coroner's office.

"My mom came in and had [traces of] blood on her hands and on her glasses," she says. "She gave her glasses to Courtnie and asked her to wash them off."

Hoping to spare her children another gruesome image, Kellie Ruth had actually changed clothes and cleaned up before leaving the bedroom. It was all she could do.

But the scene in the bedroom couldn't be washed clean. Her husband had placed his wallet, watch, and glasses neatly on the nightstand. His dress blue uniform hung in the corner of the bedroom, a stark reminder of who he had been and what he had championed. He had shot himself with a .357 magnum revolver. The bullet cleared his body and the recliner he was sitting in, lodging in the wall behind him.

The police collected the revolver and the fatal bullet, which had to be pried from the wall. Before leaving, they found Jim's suicide note. It sat, along with the pen Courtnie had given him earlier, on the table next to his chair in the living room.

#

On June 13, 1948, James Howard Rigdon was born prematurely in Pensacola, Florida. The date was one he would fudge years later when he joined the Marines at age seventeen.

His father, Clinton Rigdon, left when Jim was two years old and his infant brother, Billy, just two months old. His mother, Savannah Rose Swaney-Rigdon, was forced to fend for the two boys on her own. She moved the family to Pendleton, South Carolina, a cotton-mill town, where she could leave her sons with her parents while she worked. William and Lucy Swaney essentially raised Jim and his brother, giving their two grandsons a strong sense of values as well as plenty of love and security.

The ad hoc family thrived until Jim turned ten and his mother remarried. His new stepfather was a marine – and a gruff, unloving man toward Jim and his brother. Years later, Jim would simply refer to him by his last name, Donaldson. The family moved from base to base, never staying anywhere long enough to grow roots, and Rose had three more children, all of whom were doted on by Jim and Billy.

Home eventually became an angry, inhospitable place, and at just thirteen and a half, Jim returned to his grandparents, taking Billy with him. He lived the rest of his childhood with his grandparents, while Billy stayed with his uncle. When money got tight his senior year, Jim dropped out of high school to get a job and help take care of Billy. At least one of the boys would get an education. By then, the war in Viet Nam was kicking into gear, so he registered for the draft, lying about his age in order to become eligible immediately. It didn't take long to receive his draft notice from the Army.

But he joined the Marines instead, a 17-year-old boy looking to do right by his kid brother, his grandparents, and the cotton mills of Pendleton.

#

"I'll always remember when I first met Gunny," Dirty Jack says. "It was like you took him out of the peanut farm and you plunked him down in the middle of the war. He sort of followed me around. I was the old timer there. I was twenty-one."

Jack Arena, who earned the nickname Dirty Jack from his marine buddies in Viet Nam, is a firefighter in Natick, Massachusetts, a modest suburb sixteen miles west of Boston. Divorced, a self-described adrenaline junkie, he reserves for Viet Nam the sort of bittersweet emotions only a soldier can know.

"I was in a Marine reconnaissance unit when I first went to Viet Nam," he recalls. "I picked up a sergeant stripe. But there were too many sergeants in our outfit. I put in a transfer to an Ontos outfit. I had never even seen an Ontos. I became an assistant platoon sergeant. I knew absolutely nothing about a track vehicle. These other fifteen guys just took me aside and schooled me. I brought everybody back; let's put it that way. We saw some of the heaviest fighting of 1967 [including Operation Belt Tight and Operation Buffalo]."

The name Ontos, Greek for "the thing," was given to an eight-and-a-half ton, self-propelled anti-tank vehicle first introduced into service in 1956. The U.S. cranked out 240 of them before realizing that they had two liabilities: soldiers had to reload them from the outside (a risky proposition in sniper-plagued Viet Nam) and they were relatively slow (thirty miles per hour) for such a lightly armored vehicle. Worse still, they were not amphibious, even though they were supposed to provide fire support for amphibious assaults.

They saw their widest use in 1966 and 1967, precisely when Dirty Jack and Gunny were serving their respective tours in Viet Nam.

"I came during monsoon season," Dirty Jack remembers. "Gunny took me out and showed me how to lay out tracks and bore site guns and everything in the rain. I was totally amazed at these 20-year-olds and 19-year-olds who knew these instruments inside and out.

Jim, or Gunny as his fellow marines called him, arrived in Viet Nam in August 1966, a month and a half after his eighteenth birthday. Ironically, he earned the nickname Gunny because his stepfather, whose home he had fled, was a gunnery sergeant when he joined the Marines. Jim and Dirty Jack served with the first platoon, Alpha Company, of the third anti-tank battalion, which was part of an amphibious ready group or special landing force attached to the first battalion, third Marines. In February 1967, the unit was shipped back to Okinawa, where the men regrouped, overhauled their equipment, and were issued new weapons.

They returned to Viet Nam as a special landing force, conducting raids up and down the coast, where they would link up with shore-based units. Once on dry land, they logged plenty of time in the bush, moving from one operation to the next. Jim and Dirty Jack helped make up the platoon's heavy section, which amounted to eight men, with Jack the commander.

"On ships we spent our time cleaning weapons and laying around talking about home," Dirty Jack recalls. "On shore it was all down to business: patrolling, making sure we had proper firing positions at night, taking care of the Ontos, going to staff meetings. I was the highest ranked one at an E5 sergeant and delegated stuff out. I had Gunny going to staff meetings with majors and stuff. People didn't know how to use us. We had to go in and tell them how to use our Ontos unit."

Adds Dirty Jack, "Jimmy Rigdon was a standup kid. He had the driest sense of humor, the absolute driest. It was unbelievable. And he had that long South Carolina drawl."

Pat Canulette, now a retired sheriff who lives with his wife in Slidell, Louisiana, was in Viet Nam for five months before Jim joined the unit. Like everyone else in the platoon, he had a nickname: Frenchy. Like most of the men, he, too, remembers Jim's straight-faced wit.

"We got hit by rocket fire one day," Frenchy recalls, "and we were told to get out and load Ontos while under fire. When everything's over and everyone's shaking and stuff, Gunny says, 'Hell, a fellow could get killed over here.'"

#

A couple months before he left for Viet Nam, Jim married a girl named Peggy, whom he had been dating exclusively. But the marriage never got off the ground. He came back a changed man, haunted by what he had seen and hollowed out by malaria and utter exhaustion. He was, his family insisted, a ghost of his former self. He spent his first few weeks back home in bed, trying in vain to sleep the war off like a bad hangover.

It didn't take long for him to realize that he had little in common with Peggy, whose relatively petty concerns and preoccupations had remained untouched by the war. She couldn't hope to speak to someone who had just walked through fire. The two filed for divorce while Jim resumed the domestic leg of his Marine tour on Paris Island.

Not long after, he met his future wife, then Kellie Ruth Mancil, on a blind date. Kellie Ruth was a nurse at a hospital in Brunswick, Georgia, and lived on nearby St. Simons Island – as she puts it now, "a gorgeous little island nobody knew about."

Kellie Ruth grew up near Willacoochee, where she and Jim would eventually settle down and raise a family. An only child, she spent her youth wandering her parents' farm, where she would run barefoot across freshly plowed fields, the furrowed soil crumbling like sun-baked flour beneath her bare feet. She whiled away lazy summer afternoons with her nose in a book, eagerly greeting each new sunrise with an enthusiasm exclusive to children.

After graduating from high school in 1963, she enrolled in a three-year nursing program at Grady Memorial Hospital in Atlanta. She completed her degree and stayed in Atlanta until the spring of 1967, when she found work and an apartment a block from the beach on St. Simons Island. She had only been there a few months when a coworker at the hospital who knew Jim's mother insisted Kellie Ruth go out with him.

"I worked late and went to the beach afterward and was running late," Kellie Ruth says as she recalls the day she finally gave in and met Jim for a blind date. "He knocked on the door, and I still had my hair in a towel. I didn't even open the door. I told him to come back in fifteen minutes." She laughs, thinking about it. "I wouldn't come back if someone told me that on a blind date. But he did."

Kellie Ruth didn't sense the change in Jim that his family had witnessed. She hadn't known him before Viet Nam. She found in him all the qualities that others had admired before: his quick wit and dry sense of humor, his take-charge attitude, and his tenacity.

The war was with him still, perhaps. But so was youth.

"It was really strange," says Kellie Ruth, who was three and a half years older than her blind date. "When I opened the door, the first thing I saw was that he had a real short military haircut. I looked at him, and I couldn't believe he was so young. I thought, 'This is the guy I'm going to spend the rest of my life with, and he's so young.'"

That was in January 1968. Six months later, the two exchanged wedding vows. And Viet Nam seemed a million miles away.

#

"I guess we had been married two weeks," Kellie Ruth says, trying to draw a line between the way things began and the way they ended two and a half decades later. "I got up in the middle of the night to get a drink of water. I came back to bed and touched him on the shoulder. He was ice cold, dripping in sweat. I thought he was horribly ill, so I shook him and said, 'Jim, wake up!' He jumped up like he had been shot. It scared me to death. And of course it scared him worse."

Post-Traumatic Stress Disorder didn't have a name in 1968. It wouldn't, in fact, for another dozen or so years. But Jim would struggle for the rest of his life with the nightmares, the cold sweats, the anxiety attacks, and the bewildering flashbacks, often feeling alien to everything and everyone, including himself.

Military and hospital officials were uninformed and sometimes unsympathetic to PTSD and the vets and families that struggled with it. Kellie Ruth and her husband were shrugged off. It would pass. Or so said the experts and administrators.

While in the Marines, Jim picked up his GED. He had always wanted to be a dentist, and he applied to Clemson University while still at Paris Island. He was a sergeant when he left the military in January 1968. But he didn't log enough hours as such and was discharged a corporal.

"Before we even got married," Kellie Ruth says, "we talked about what he wanted to do when he got out. He told me, 'Mentally, I don't know if I can survive another tour or go through that again.' If he had stayed in the Marines, he would have had to go back."

Adds Kellie Ruth, "He was coming home on weekends and getting to know his mother. His mother lived with his stepfather at GlynnCo Naval Air Station in Brunswick at the time. But he wanted to go back to South Carolina. It's beautiful country out there. Beautiful lakes. And Pendleton is only a few minutes from Clemson."

The young couple moved to Pendleton, ready to embark on a new adventure.

"It was a few weeks before school was supposed to start, and we went to the registrar's office at Clemson," Kellie Ruth recalls. "I dropped him off and circled the block a couple times looking for a parking spot. When I came back the third time, he was standing in the street where I couldn't miss him. He got in the car. He was pale as a ghost. He couldn't be in the room with all those people. He just couldn't go back there."

A roomful of people felt too much like Viet Nam, where suffocating crowds of peasants blurred the line between friend and enemy, where the poor and the desperate took a people's war directly to the invading army. The old man leading the water buffalo: was he a harmless villager or a Vietcong sympathizer? Was the mother next to him carrying a baby or a bomb or both?

Instead of studying dentistry, Jim learned how to lay bricks with his uncle's construction company. It was physically demanding work. But the job offered plenty of space and fresh air.

Two years later, he started noticing pain in his joints and muscles and realized he needed to find less strenuous work. He and Kellie Ruth moved to Waycross, Georgia, where he attended tech school to study electronics. He went to school during the day and sorted mail at the post office at night.

"He couldn't sleep unless he was so dead tired he couldn't wiggle," Kellie Ruth remembers. "He was basically a workaholic."

The Rigdons moved to Willacoochee a year and a half later and lived in a mobile home on Kellie Ruth's parents' land. Jim got a job at Sears in the TV/electronics repair department. On September 23, 1975, Kellie Ruth gave birth to their first child, Dawn Annette Rigdon.

"We brought Dawn home from the hospital," Kellie Ruth remembers. "It was mid-morning when we got home. He was holding her. I slept for four hours, and he was still there holding her in the same position when I woke up."

#

"Growing up, my mom's favorite excuse was that we never knew Dad when he was healthy," Dawn says, trying to come to grips with her childhood. "And that's basically true. We never had much time with him as a healthy person."

He was, in fact, two men: one whose body was slowly failing him, the other a pale reflection of someone undone by Viet Nam.

The father the family ached to hold onto was an avid outdoorsman who liked to fish and hunt quail. He had a green thumb and could grow pretty much anything. Although he preferred to cultivate things that he could eat, he spent one spring helping Dawn start a rose garden. He was good with his hands and liked tinkering with his 1957 Chevy. He was a perfectionist, a born leader who always knew what to do and didn't mind taking charge. And he had a way of finding the humor in almost anything.

He was a handsome man. He had stunning blue eyes, thick black hair, and, thanks to a trace of Native American blood in his family heritage, olive-toned skin.

He was also a thoughtful man. During both her pregnancies, Kellie Ruth observed to the letter the strict diet her doctor prescribed for her. The discipline involved was sometimes sheer agony for her because she regularly craved hot fudge sundaes, pregnancy or no. After each delivery, Jim brought his wife her favorite dessert.

"It was about the first thing I ate," she recalls. "I didn't ask him to do that. Didn't even think about it. This was just one of the small things he remembered to do."

On his good days, he lavished his two daughters – for whom he had a perpetual soft spot – with affection and praise. He called Courtnie "my squash baby," because he was out in the fields picking squash when Kellie Ruth started having labor pains. And he made Dawn feel like Daddy's little girl, even after he was long gone and she was all grown up.

"Even when he had his bad moments," Dawn says as she fights off tears, "he was never above saying .... He was always very tender with me. After my first breakup, I just cried and cried. And he just rocked me."

Dawn's special relationship with her father came at a price, however.

"He told some gruesome stories," she says. "He would not speak to my mom about the war. He would talk to me. I was maybe thirteen or fourteen. I didn't want any part of it, but I felt kind of trapped."

In fact, Jim did speak with Kellie Ruth about the war, but not in front of the children. He shared some of the same stories with Courtnie as well. For Dawn, though, the point is moot. She felt overwhelmed by – and was too young to hear – the horrors her father shared.

"One of the stories that he would tell over and over again was of being in this vehicle," she says, "and one of the men under his command had his upper body out of the tank. He was shot in the head, and his body fell into the tank. And it was just a mess. Another was about being in the jungle and finding a fellow soldier who had had his testicles removed and put in his mouth."

Another goes like this.

Jim and his unit were assigned the responsibility of protecting an American-friendly village. While there, he befriended a little boy, sharing his C-rations with him and treating him with the kind of affection that often arises spontaneously amidst the chaos and brutality of war. The Americans left the village for three days. When they returned, the boy had been executed by the Vietcong.

\#

One main road runs through Willacoochee. No stop lights. Just country lanes, farmland, and blue-collar homes spread across the rural landscape like cut tobacco on an undulating field. When a little boy died a needless, violent death half a world away, something changed on the horizon. Nobody would ever be the same, least of all one American soldier who could do nothing but rage against innocence lost.

"I remember him in our dining room," Dawn says, recalling an early childhood memory in the family's first home. "We had a piano, and he was sitting on the piano bench weeping, saying we should pray for the people who had died. I was probably five or six. I just knew I wanted out of there. I didn't want anything to do with this. I suspect he was well into his Pabst Blue Ribbon that night."

Long before that night, Viet Nam had wormed its way into Jim's nervous system.

"When he was 'in country,'" Kellie Ruth says, "he was near the DMZ, where they sprayed Agent Orange. He used to talk about how it dripped into their eyes."

Peripheral Neuropathy, one of the myriad symptoms of Agent Orange exposure, is essentially nerve damage. For Jim, it meant chronically aching legs, which put an end to his first job as a mason. The pain got bad enough to warrant a visit to the VA Hospital in Augusta, Georgia. Doctors ran current through his legs until they were jumping. But he felt nothing.

"He had cancerous lesions and polyps on his colon," Dawn says of her father, who received a whopping $250 from the makers of Agent Orange after the class-action settlement in 1984. "A chunk of the top part of his nose was missing where he actually cut it out himself. He pulled a couple of his own teeth once. He was just a mess."

According to Kellie Ruth, a doctor actually removed the pee-sized portion of his nose that had aggravated him for some time. But he did remove the cavity-riddled teeth by himself because he didn't want to go in to the dentist's office.

His health reached a low ebb in 1983 when he suffered a massive heart attack. He had quit his job at Sears; regular contact with the public had become too much. After experimenting with farming for a few years, he had opened his own TV repair shop. The shop had been open a year and was just starting to get out of the red when he had the heart attack.

"It was the day before his thirty-fifth birthday," Kellie Ruth recalls. "It was ironic, because he had always told me he would die when he was thirty-five. He told me this even when we were dating. Anyway, he was sitting on the side of the bed, and he said, 'I think you better call an ambulance.' So I did. They only had one technician who was trained to use the defibrillator. He just happened to be working that night. Jim was still sitting up on the side of the bed when they got there. He slumped down and slid to the floor. The guy defibrillatored him, and he came back instantly. He said, 'Don't let me go because I won't come back.' Later he told me that that was the most peace he had ever experienced, and he was really angry at us for reviving him. He was out less than thirty seconds.

"We took him to the ambulance. I had called my parents to come and stay with the kids, and they showed up. I got in the ambulance with him. One of the EMT's was a young kid I knew from the hospital. I heard someone behind me say, 'It's okay. He's not gonna die now.' I was furious because you're never supposed to say anything like that to the family. I turned around to chew the EMT out, and there was nobody there. They were both up front, and the back doors were closed."

It wasn't the first time Kellie Ruth felt the presence of something or someone divine watching over her shoulder. A devout Southern Methodist, she often prayed to God to look out after her husband. To this day, she's certain it was prayer that delivered him from the clutches of a psychiatric ward at the VA Hospital in Augusta, Georgia. A year before his heart attack, Jim nearly succumbed to PTSD.

"Jim came in one day at lunch," Kellie Ruth remembers. "I was teaching nursing at the college. He came in and said, 'You gotta find a way to take me to the VA tomorrow. Whatever it is, I can't handle it anymore.' I left Dawn with my parents and took Courtnie with us. We went to Augusta to the VA. If they had ever heard of PTSD at that point, no one mentioned it. It was still something nobody knew anything about. Jim saw a psychologist and told him everything. They put him in a locked ward. They assumed he was on drugs. That just about devastated him. He was there a week. It was a miracle he got out. Prayer and God got him out of that ward because the doctors certainly didn't."

Kellie Ruth remembers offering up a desperate prayer just as things seemed too bleak for words.

"He was all drugged up, not even there mentally. But when they brought him the drugs that morning, he said, 'No. It's time to go home.' After that, he said, 'Never, never again. I'm never going back [to the VA].'"

#

Perhaps had Jim suffered only on a physical level, he would still be alive today. That's Kellie Ruth's contention, and it's one that holds up. Simply put: the litany of physical problems combined with his beleaguered state of mind was too much for Jim – or his family – to bear.

"He just had these crazy, crawl-on-the-floor flashbacks," Dawn explains. "I recall one Sunday afternoon he was lying in bed. He would stay in bed for days at a time sometimes. He had a hospital bed at this point because his breathing had gotten really bad. My mom called me and Courtnie in and said, 'Talk to your dad and tell him who you are.' He was sitting up on the side of the bed. He was in a battle. He was calling his men's names, calling for backup. It was very frightening. We couldn't get him out of it. My mom said to us, 'Go to Grandma's.' When we came back, he was okay."

Though Viet Nam was in his rearview mirror, Jim still had his finger on the trigger. He always sat with his back against the wall. His wife and daughters learned never to sneak up on him or surprise him.

"It pretty much ruled him," Dawn says. "Everything with my dad was related back to the war. If we ran out of milk, it was because of Viet Nam. He was just a devout patriot. He was just all about for love of country and the love of the corps."

Like most troubled vets in search of a cure, Jim self-medicated. Alcohol. Prescription drugs. He took what he could to numb his memories.

"It didn't occur to me until after he died that he was an alcoholic," Dawn says. "I remember him phoning me at high school and asking me to bring him home a case of beer for the evening – and a can of worms. We had a little store that would sell to me. He wasn't drunk by the end of the case, so I never thought he had a drinking problem. His drinking would always begin in the evening and go way into the late hours. And he would be taking Valium with it. By the time he died, he was up to [several] pills a day. Some of it was legitimate; some of it was not. But I had no idea at the time. I just thought it was all very normal. He once had me borrow some money from the school office to get him some beer and bait and cigarettes."

Adds Dawn, "It's really hard for me to think about now because everything just revolved around feeding his illness. Sometimes I wonder what was legitimate. We were enablers – the world's best. I knew something was weird. I just couldn't qualify how weird it was or why it was weird. I don't remember at what age I just stopped having people over. I was about fourteen or fifteen, and I thought, 'I don't wanna have to explain all this shit.' He would usually suck it up for me to bring home a date or something. But my girlfriends and I rarely came over. And then he would complain, 'You're never at home.'"

For her part, Kellie Ruth has a different take. She insists Jim never abused drugs, although he was taking several prescriptions before he died, both for PTSD-related symptoms and his heart. He was, she says, adamantly against drug use, which was rampant at the time.

"Jim will come back to haunt all of us if he is portrayed as a drug addict," she says.

Kellie Ruth also objects to her daughter's use of the word *enablers.*

"Dawn's degree is in psychology," she says. "And I have had the same courses. But there is something about the term *enablers* that conjures up the wrong meaning when applied to PTSD. To enable implies the person you are enabling has a choice in the matter, that given the correct motivation that person could choose to stop the behavior. That doesn't apply to PTSD. It does to drugs, alcohol, cigarettes, etc. But the root problem was PTSD. If I had chosen not to enable Jim, I think he would have died years before he did. I think, and he said so many times, that his family was all that kept him from dying years before he did."

Memory is a funny thing. The same event or series of events typically means different things to different people. Facts, too, get fuzzy as the years separate individuals from a moment in time. But one thing Kellie Ruth and Dawn can wholeheartedly agree on is that, for a brief period, there existed a sliver of hope.

#

"Jim had a lot of massive damage in the large muscle of his heart," Kellie Ruth recalls. "The doctor told him, 'Don't do this; don't do that.' And of course he kept on trying to work. But he just didn't have enough heart muscle to sustain that. After about six or eight months, he got into the VA medical system in Gainesville, Florida. At some point there they recognized the PTSD. They got him into a PTSD group. It was really a relief to find out what was going on all those years.

"Earlier, when he woke up in ICU from the heart attack, the first thing he thought of was, 'I can't die until I have a house for the family.' He built a house from scratch. Worked on it for three or four years. Courtnie, who had the same dry sense of humor, asked, 'Are we ever going to be able to afford pizza again?'"

Jim joined a PTSD group, which met for eight weeks at a time at the Augusta VA. Each time, he would return home refreshed and upbeat. The treatment and counseling seemed to offer the ever-elusive redemption he had been seeking.

"If he had just had the physical problems to contend with or just the PTSD problems," Kellie Ruth says. "The group did help. But by then he had had it for almost twenty years. A lot of the things they did for the PTSD group were demanding. And we're talking about a guy who had such a small percentage of heart muscle left. The worse the heart got, the worse the legs got, and the worse the PTSD got. That's what the kids remember most: PTSD rages. They remember going to a hotel and spending the night. I'd just take them out of the house and let it take its course. Once you know what's going on, then you know what to do about it."

Eventually, Jim could no longer attend the PTSD group. He simply couldn't muster the energy. He worked less and less. His activities dwindled. He gained weight. He started retaining fluid – a sign of congestive heart failure. He was by this time rated by the VA one hundred percent permanently and totally disabled because of PTSD and was receiving disability compensation.

In 1993 he had a slight stroke. It was enough to affect his speech and memory ever so slightly. Those who knew him could detect the deterioration. It eventually put an end to his enrollment in the PTSD group, just when the counseling was starting to do him some good.

#

"My father was a very generous, funny, smart man who, on his good days, spoiled us," Dawn says. "He really overcompensated for his bad behavior. He was getting a [disability] pension from the government. Plus, my mom has always had a great job as a nurse. He'd buy us what we wanted or slip us a twenty-dollar bill here and there. He was great when he was great, when things were going his way. But the last year of his life, it was just rotten to be around him."

There had been a brief period after his heart attack when he had quit smoking and drinking. But that time was a distant memory now.

"Every day when I came home from school and put the key in the door, I never knew what I would find," Dawn remembers. "You could cut the tension with a knife. He was not above flipping furniture or throwing things or saying just cruel, hurtful things. But those things were directed more at my mom and my little sister. They got the brunt of it. I heard him confess one day to someone on the phone that he hit my mother, but I never saw it. But he wasn't above exaggeration. The more sick he got and the more needy he became, the more codependent we all became. He would say some pretty outrageous things.

"He would go from being addicted to food to cigarettes to beer to whatever, just trying to fill that void or whatever it was. He was pretty hardcore. He didn't do much half-assed when it came to addiction. Again, it was all just normal behavior in our house."

Kellie Ruth confirms that Jim never hit her. Despite how much she loved him, she would have left him, she says, had he resorted to any sort of abuse. But she felt the same tension that her daughters struggled to escape. And she, too, suffered its toll.

"I always remember the strain in her voice, like she was about to crack," Dawn says. "She tried to buffer it as best as she could, but I think she just kind of gave up the last two or three years of his life.

"They would go days without speaking, especially near the end. Practically the last six months of his life he spent his time in their bedroom with the door shut. He would lock her out."

"I have no idea why Dawn thinks this," Kellie Ruth counters. "We talked daily. I left for work early, while Jim was asleep, but he was always awake when I came home, and we talked. Dawn was usually not home until later in the evening. By the time she was home, Jim and I were usually talked out and ready for bed. The last six months of his life he had to spend most of the time in bed, due to weakness, edema, etc. But he did not 'lock me out.'"

Either way, the signs were all there that Jim was ready to resort to something drastic. He spoke frequently of death. He obsessed on the war and the horrific images in his head. He had even made one aborted attempt at suicide years earlier, slitting his wrists before waking Courtnie up and asking for help.

"I think of that as a very malicious act," Dawn says. "But we were so encapsulated in this world of ours that we didn't think it was strange. We didn't think he would do it again."

In fact, he had told Kellie Ruth that he would never take his life, that he couldn't do that to her or the kids. She often spoke with her daughters to prepare them for his eventual death because his health was so poor. But she never expected he'd hasten its arrival in such deliberate fashion. In retrospect, she can see the signs now. A week before he committed suicide, he visited the doctor but would not let Kellie Ruth sit in on their conversation. Later, he asked her while the two were sitting on the porch if she and the kids could get on without him. At the time, she thought he was simply referring to his poor health and assured him they would be okay.

"He woke up in just a foul mood, which was unusual for him," Kellie Ruth says of the day he took his own life. "But he had been irritable all day. Now I know he was just trying to cut the ties. He knew what he was going to do and was trying to distance himself from us."

When she pointed out that it was Memorial Day weekend, she got a chilling response.

"Yup," he said cryptically, "this is gonna be a hell of a weekend."

#

Suicide is many things. One thing it is not is selfless. The decision isn't made in a vacuum, regardless of how consumed with one's own affairs the person who makes the decision is. In the end, it is a desperate act that leaves a legacy of grief, bitterness, and confusion. Those left in its wake will never be able to answer the basic question of *why* with any sort of satisfaction. All they can truly know is what they are left with: bittersweet memories and a dull ache that can't be assuaged.

Memorial Day weekend has never been the same for the Rigdon family. Jim served up a bitter twist of fate whose irony was lost on no one.

"I'd like to think he wasn't thinking about that, but he was too smart for that," Dawn says of her father's timing. "It was kind of mean what he did. Three or four more days would have been their anniversary."

Dawn wonders, too, why her father peeked his head out of the bedroom when she came home, only to close himself in his room and pull the trigger. Was he simply making sure his oldest daughter had come home safely for the night? Was this one last gesture of concern before he moved on to the next life? She hopes so.

The next few days passed like years for Kellie Ruth and her two daughters. Friends and family came to console them. A beautiful memorial service formalized Jim's death. And the room where he took his own life was attended to, the carpet pulled out and the chair hauled away.

"The first six months I truly didn't think I was gonna live," Kellie Ruth remembers. "It was horrible. When Jim and I got married, I never conceived of living without him. Just the tightness between us ...."

Frightened and alone, she did all she could to face the burden of taking care of her family by herself.

"I just put one foot in front of the other and got through one day and then another day," she says. "I tried to not let them know how desperate I felt at times. I was looking at some records at work. I went back to work on June 13. I thought, 'My word, that wasn't long at all. But it felt like two months.'

"At one point, I think it was about nine months after, I knew I had to make a choice. I could either stay in this house and make it a shrine and totally live in the past; or know that it was a great past, that I loved a fantastic guy and he loved me, and I could go on from there. I knew what Jim would say. He'd say you're a fool if you live in the past.

"The first couple months, I honestly was just living from one day to the next. I couldn't let myself feel too much, because the few times I did I was just overwhelmed with feelings. It finally got to the point where I got up one Sunday morning and was completely drained. I just thought there was no way I could make it. I got in the shower. I turned on the water and said, 'Okay, God, I give up. There's nothing else I can do. I quit. If you can make things better, please do, because I can't.'

"Before I got out of the shower I just started feeling light. Physically, I felt light all over. I got out of the shower and felt good for the first time in years. I just felt happy. And I was smiling. It was so amazing. I felt like I was walking a foot off the ground. I went to church, and I told the Sunday school teacher, 'Someday I'll have to tell you what happened.' He told me, 'I can see it.' That feeling stayed with me about two days. I could tell when it started to go away. I could feel it kind of ooze away. Once it was totally gone, I felt healed. I knew I could go on, that life will go on."

Dawn, meanwhile, left for school in September. She had already planned to transfer to the University of West Georgia in Carollton for her sophomore year.

"On a rational level I knew my father was responsible, but that's not how we operate all the time," Dawn says. "I was eighteen. Girls are strange at eighteen. I was getting ready to move. I was just going to go to school no matter what. I moved. I think that's what kept me sane. A five-hour car ride from home – to me that was a big deal. I moved to this place where I knew two people. When I got down there, I just went a little nuts. Floated for a while. Tried pretty much everything at least once. I was pretty miserable. I didn't know what to do. I got involved with a private organization that helped families of Viet Nam vets."

Bill McBride joined the Marine Corps on his seventeenth birthday in March of 1958. He retired a lieutenant colonel in 1983, eventually landing a job as an engineer with Southwest Research Institute. Part of his record included a thirteen-month tour of Viet Nam from June 1967 to July of 1968. For six months, he led patrols and was a company executive officer. He sustained minor injuries and lost half a patrol three months into his stint. The bodies of the four men who didn't make it home were finally recovered in 2002.

Bill knew Viet Nam firsthand, and his experiences informed him in 1993 as he helped set up a web site for the Viet Namese Memorial Association, an organization dedicated to building schools in Viet Nam. The web site eventually morphed into an online support group for vets and their families, which is how

Dawn discovered Bill and his organization. Her heartbreaking narrative of the night her father took his life helps make up the personal testimonies at www.vietvet.org.

"The inability of many veterans to communicate their feelings and experiences in Viet Nam to close family members and friends is a very serious problem, as Dawn knows," Bill maintains. "I see this mentioned repeatedly on our forum. Many vets can talk easier to strangers than they can to their loved ones."

Bill helped Dawn put her father's life in perspective, often simply acting as a sounding board.

"I think that having other veterans available to family members, especially the children, is very important," he says, "if they want it."

When Dawn graduated from the University of West Georgia in 1998 with a bachelor's degree in psychology, one marine was there to congratulate her.

"I don't know for sure when I decided to go," Bill says. "Probably a few months before. It's hard to explain to someone who was not a marine, but it is the marine kind of thing to do. I felt her old man would have approved. I feel very close to her dad, even though I didn't know him personally. During my early years in the Marines, I was billeted next to the Ontos battalion and had a few friends in that outfit. In Viet Nam, late '67, the third anti-tank battalion was disbanded and many of the marines from that outfit were transferred to mine.

"Anyhow, by the time she sent me the graduation invitation, my mind was made up to go. This trip was in collusion with Nancy Ralph, a lady who had been helping on the Viet Nam vets home page and who was living in Atlanta at the time. We agreed to meet up at the graduation hall."

So Bill made the trip from San Antonio to Carollton, driving a day and a half straight and arriving at the college in the early afternoon, just in time to pick up some flowers for Dawn and meet up with Nancy.

He surprised Dawn on the floor of the auditorium as the graduates were lining up for the ceremony.

"That meant the world to me," Dawn says.

"It was a nice feeling to be there," Bill recalls. "The next day I headed back to San Antonio. I heard her dad say, '*semper fi*,' somewhere along the way."

#

For Dawn, the only way to move forward with her life was to take an unflinching look at the past.

"Bill and the people from his organization are really good people," she explains. "They're very supportive. They wanted me to go to the Wall. And I was invited to go speak on Veteran's Day in 1997. I spoke at the Wall, and then my story was published online and then picked up by a few different publications, including *The Atlanta Journal Constitution*. A lot of people saw it there. I was contacted by the Friends of Viet Nam Veterans Memorial [now defunct]. They did a program every year. They wanted me to talk about my dad. We all went up there. My mom was miserable the whole time, but it was very cathartic for me."

Kellie Ruth, meanwhile, remembers the visit differently and says that she was very proud of her daughter's speech at the Wall.

Dawn continues, "The following year, I went to an elementary school where my friend taught and talked to different classes and spoke with kids. If there's a charity I give to, that's it. That's where my donations go. But after the Wall and stuff, I was able to sort it out in my head and put some of that stuff to bed. When I met my husband, he was just great. He listens and has patience and has helped me work it out."

A diehard Elvis Presley fan from Oswego, Illinois, Darren Birr is a plant molecular biologist with a sharp wit and a playful sense of humor. He met Dawn in Atlanta in October

1999 and married her four months later. It was love at first sight for Dawn, who barely knew a soul in Atlanta, where she had found a job in the Georgia Mental Health system. They met through a longtime friend of Dawn's and soon discovered a special bond.

"I called Dawn to tell her that I was going home for Thanksgiving and that I had a pretty sick feeling about it," recalls Darren. "My youngest sister, Kristine, committed suicide in November of 1994, and I haven't spent much time at home since. Kris was twenty-one at the time, and I was nineteen and living about a thousand miles away from home. The guilt still tears me up. So I talked about Kris and why I really feel no comfort being back home. Dawn was really shocked. Dawn then told me about her father, and, while the situations are different, she still knew what I was going through and we talked a long while about it. It was quite a moment."

Not long after getting married, Dawn and Darren both found work in Connecticut. These days, he's a plant molecular biology research associate and she's a product manager at Neumann USA, a maker of top-of-the-line microphones and recording studio gear. Groton, Connecticut, has been good to both of them. Jim's suicide, though still a powerful issue in Dawn's life, is no longer center stage.

"Early in our marriage," Darren explains, "I think it was a bigger issue. Sometimes I did need to reassure Dawn that I wasn't going anywhere. I had to remind her every so often that I am not her father. Dawn's family was fond of giving someone the silent treatment if they weren't happy, and that's just something I would never do. Also, Dawn used to wake me up from fifteen feet away, just in case I was having a flashback or nightmare. But it really disturbed me having someone watch me from fifteen feet away and saying my name over and over till I woke. I would be really confused, and Dawn would appear all timid, so I would think that something horrible just happened. It really wasn't a huge issue or anything. It just kind of illustrates that whole thing of Dawn adjusting to living with someone not dealing with shellshock.

"My own personal feelings toward James are quite polar. I'm pretty protective of Dawn, and anything that causes her pain or sorrow really makes me angry. But this is quite different. It's her daddy. I have no idea what James was going through, but I could never see leaving Dawn by choice. It's just something that I can't even fathom."

#

A little more than a year after Jim died, Kellie Ruth met a retired marine and struck up a friendship. They eventually began dating and got married in July 2002. Though they still live in the house where Jim died, they've tried to create their own history there.

"I try not to live in the past or dwell on the memories," says Kellie Ruth, who did quite a bit of reading and research on Jim's tour in Viet Nam before putting the topic to rest. "You can't do that, not if you're going to continue living. I made that choice real early. I knew if I stayed in this house, I was going to have to start again from that day forward. The girls will have to start over as well."

What of Courtnie? Her father took his first suicide attempt to her. Before he finally succeeded, he asked her for the pen and paper to write his suicide note. And after he put a bullet through his heart, she cleaned the blood from her mother's glasses as the family reeled in shock.

Her healing will remain private.

#

While trying to make sense of the way he ended his life, it's easy to forget who Jim was while he lived it. It's easy, too, to forget the little things, the day-to-day moments that helped comprise the life of one man. But certain memories don't go down without a fight.

"It was my first prom," Dawn says, recalling her sophomore year in high school, "and I was asked to go. I was so excited and set to buy a prom dress, and I dragged my mom to the nearest town of any size to try dresses on. I found this dark green sequined affair that I just fell in love with and wanted to leave with. It was very expensive, and Mom suggested we wait, try on some others in other stores, and maybe find one in our price range."

Dawn was disappointed, but she heeded her mother's wisdom and vainly searched for another dress and a better deal. She came home empty-handed and recounted the trip to her father.

"The following Monday I was called quite unexpectedly from the school's office to find Daddy in the lobby waiting on me. He wouldn't tell me where we were going, but about halfway there he said we were going to buy my dress! So we got there, he gave me his wallet, and he told me to go in and get the dress. He waited in the truck patiently, and I got the dress. We had just enough cash left over for hamburgers on the way back to school. I will never forget that – or how much he loved us."

He was more than a combat veteran. More, even, than a former marine. He knew tenderness. He knew how to laugh. He knew how to make his wife and daughters smile. He watched *Days of our Lives* every summer with Courtnie. He taught her how to fish and how to fly a kite on the beach. He taught both of his daughters how to drive a stick shift long before they had earned their driver's licenses.

He liked bacon-cheeseburgers and cooked roast beef to perfection. He built a kitchen for his mother-in-law. He showed Courtnie and her friends how to make tea so sweet that Dawn called it "diabetic tea." And he reveled in the throw-up sounds his daughters made while he kissed their mother in the kitchen.

Even toward the end of his life, when his health had plummeted to new depths, he found a way to be there for his family.

"Just the year before he died, my senior year, he let me take him to the nearest men's clothing store and pick out a suit," Dawn remembers, pointing out that she'd never seen him in a tie before that moment. "And he walked me on homecoming court. He was in pain, swollen. But he looked great. That took a lot from him. By then, the PTSD was in control in a big way. His hate and fear of crowds and people were really a problem. His legs were in terrible pain. In the photo, he's obviously swollen. But he sucked it up just for me."

#

James Howard Rigdon never had much patience. He was born too soon. He joined the fight too soon. And, at least from the perspective of those who lived and served with him, he died too soon.

"I just couldn't fathom Jimmy Rigdon doing that," Dirty Jack says, recalling the day he found out Jim committed suicide. "To this day, I can't imagine it. I couldn't believe the war had affected him that way. There was never any sign of depression. We always released it. We always let it go. Every time we went into a landing, we went in with a nasty attitude that we were gonna come back.

"I know in my own personal life I just have kind of a non-caring attitude, like, what could be worse than what I've seen? I've gone through life that way. I know deep inside that there will be one thing that's gonna trip my trigger and I'm gonna be bawling like a baby. I suppose that's the same demon Gunny was fighting. It still boggles my mind. He was the quietest guy. If he said anything at all, it would be one of the driest jokes you'd ever wanna hear. But you could always depend on him. He'd do everything to the utmost of his ability. He'd never let you down."

Frenchy, too, struggles with disbelief.

How? he asks. *Why?*

"I know he was depressed," he reflects. "Some of it was because of the war. I don't know if all of it was because of the war. But I do know that he loved his wife and children. He worshipped them. On several occasions, he asked me to speak to the girls. On one occasion, he asked me to write Courtnie and explain to her why he was different from the other dads. And I tried. But what do I know? I think when he got to where he couldn't go and do things, then the more time he had to sit around and reflect on Viet Nam.

"Right at first, I was angry with him. But I can't judge him. I loved him too much to judge him. I don't know what went through his mind. My anger has subsided. It was very painful to lose a friend in Viet Nam, and it was very painful to lose a guy who you shared what we shared there. When we saw each other at the reunion, we hadn't seen each other for twenty-two years. But it was like no time had gone by. We loved each other dearly, and we still do, and there's no doubt in my mind that I couldn't call one of them and ask for anything.

"I'm absolutely brokenhearted that he did what he did. I was crushed. He was the best-loved guy in the whole outfit. I can't answer why he did what he did. But I know this: I wasn't responsible, and neither was his wife or his two daughters."

Jim's suicide note didn't say much about his family. Most of it was aimed at a country that he felt had fallen far short in its treatment of the men and women who had served it. If his death was a tragedy, it was a tragedy the government shared. Angry and at times incoherent, the note provided little comfort to his family.

Shortly before he committed suicide, however, he made an entry in his makeshift journal, describing the fear and shame he faced on a daily basis. In the entry, he promised never to mention Viet Nam or the war to his family again, especially his oldest daughter. But it was a promise he knew he couldn't keep.

When you lose a man to a mine and you are section or squad leader, your men get to show some emotion, he wrote. *Then you get them the hell out of there! You get them the hell on the move before it sinks in too deep. I am the leader, and I get to show no emotion. If the battle is not so severe that I must move with the troops, I stay behind, picking up what parts of the body I can find while I wait on the medevac. I put the body parts in the body bag while listening to the wounded cry and scream for help. All I can do is try to comfort them, taking the names of their wives, mothers, children, and girlfriends, and promising to write a personal letter if they don't make it.*

Earlier in the entry, he calls himself the *most chicken shit marine in Viet Nam.* And he signs off prophetically, *Fear will not kill you, but the fear of fear will.*

#

Was he a coward? Had he disgraced himself on the battlefield and then years later on the home front? In his weaker moments, perhaps Jim thought so. But if he did, he was the only one. To those around him, he was the personification of the human will. He had guts. He had gumption. He had a gruff, gritty desire to do right by those he loved, even when wracked by pain and tortured by fear.

"Jim was a very brave person, period," Kellie Ruth says. "I think it was because he had to make so many hard choices when he was young."

Dirty Jack is equally adamant. "I never once doubted his competence or his judgment," he says. "I made him an Ontos commander."

Frenchy puts the question to rest. "Jimmy was the best-liked guy in the platoon, bar none," he insists. "The whole time I was with him, he never did anything to embarrass himself. The only thing I can think is that he didn't feel he did enough. A lot of guys had a guilt complex for making it home alive. But he went from loader to driver to commander. He went from the lowest job to the top job, and he did it in style and he did it right. He was recognized for that at eighteen years old. He had guts."

So does Frenchy. The conversation is tough for him, bringing forth painful memories that he'd rather leave buried in the past. He wouldn't be talking, he insists, if it wasn't for Dawn, whose father was a marine he loved and whose wishes he feels duty bound to honor.

"All casualties of war don't come home wrapped in a flag," he says, his voice cracking. "A lot of guys suffer the rest of their lives for it. Every man who was there will tell you he was affected by it."

PART III:
FROM THE ASHES

Certain rumors have an inexhaustible shelf life in the military. They are passed on from one generation to the next, without anyone pausing to take note. Painful but potentially instructive lessons are routinely forgotten, only to be relearned again and again by a fresh set of naïve recruits.

Take, for example, the old barracks rumor from my day that less-than-honorable discharges were automatically upgraded within six months of a soldier's termination of duty. The fallacy was so deeply embedded in our collective psyche that it took a signed letter from H. J. McIntyre of the Department of Defense to convince a recently retired Navy chaplain in Olney, Illinois, otherwise. The chaplain hasn't spoken to me since I handed him a copy of the letter in a local restaurant we both haunt. Evidently, I ruined his appetite.

But the chaplain wasn't the only one working from false assumptions. The farce persists to this day.

"I find that guys who are being separated out are constantly told that a less-than-honorable discharge is no big deal because they can get it automatically upgraded in six months," says William Cassara, an attorney in Augusta, Georgia, who specializes in military law. "They are told this by their commanders in order to get them out quickly; their lawyers, who should know better; and their enlisted chain of command."

Although he gets countless calls on the subject, Cassara says he has only helped a handful of vets upgrade their discharge status. So many obstacles face vets hoping for redress that few go through the trouble of bringing their case before a discharge review board. Viet Nam vets, in particular, have a challenging road ahead of them.

"Generally, since they have been discharged longer than fifteen years," Cassara says, "the remedy lies with the Board for Correction of Military Records for that particular service. Probably the biggest obstacle they find is that their records no longer exist, and they have to try and recompile them."

While dishonorable discharges are linked to court-martialable offenses like desertion and murder, less-than-honorable discharges are administrative discharges handed out for smaller offenses like theft, minor drug use, and AWOL episodes.

Dave Barker, a Veterans Service officer at the VA Medical Center in Chillicothe, Ohio, has been working with vets since 1977. He can only hazard a guess, but he estimates that he's helped between 200 and 500 vets upgrade their discharge status over the years, although he no longer offers such services since taking up a new position with AMVETS (American Veterans).

"Of those discharges and corrections to records, I would guess about forty percent [were successful]," he says. "That would be the Army and Air Force higher and the Navy and Marine Corps very limited. I doubt if more than three or four Naval Review Board issues were resolved in favor of the veteran."

For those whose records remain tarnished, Barker says the ramifications are devastating. They include, "loss of VA benefits, loss of employment in some agencies and even private companies, loss of fellowship with most veteran organizations, and loss of social status."

Voting rights, too, can be stripped away. When vets are sent packing with a dishonorable or bad-conduct discharge, a court-martial is usually involved. If the court-martial is based on a felony conviction (as opposed to a misdemeanor), the vet usually loses his or her right to vote.

Overall, vets with poor discharge status often find themselves caught in a Catch 22. On the one hand, it's wise not to mention the terms of their discharge. On the other hand, if prompted, a vet must tell the truth; lying on an application or during an interview is grounds for immediate dismissal.

Contradicting – or at least convoluting – Cassara's earlier statements, Barker says, "It is extremely important to know that the military services warn people about the severity of a bad discharge prior to action being taken. Most of the time the service member is given options to abide by regulations, prior to the decision for a bad discharge. The service member is protected by the Uniform Code of Military Justice. The service member is provided free attorney service or allowed to hire a private attorney. Most just want out and forfeit those rights – permanently."

Maybe. Or maybe they just think they'll get an automatic upgrade in six months. If so, such vets will learn the hard way the difference between salesmanship and policy.

In 1977, President Carter issued a Pardon to selected draft dodgers and deserters from the Viet Nam era. Is it possible that a president and Congress will someday issue an amnesty for those who mistakenly accepted a less-than-honorable discharge – thus being stigmatized for life while only a youth?

When these youth were stigmatized, the whole family became life-long victims of events far beyond their control.

"Perhaps there will be an amnesty," says Cassara. "But that seems a stretch."

During the Carter Administration, the Defense Department created the short-lived SDRP, or Special Discharge Review Program, on March 28, 1977. Designed to upgrade undesirable discharges to at least general, the program could have redeemed nearly a half million young boys before they died in desperation.

SDRP, coming on the heels of Carter's pardon to draft dodgers, offered vets a shot at restoring their discharge status, their public honor, and their personal dignity. But conservative Republicans in the House and Senate had other ideas. They put together their own amendment, a vindictive and, according to some of Carter's aides, unconstitutional provision that emasculated SDRP. Carter grudgingly signed it, promising to redress its flaws in the future. That never happened.

Before the conservative Republicans could sink SDRP, 1,682 vets managed to get their discharge status upgraded from undesirable to honorable. As for SDRP, the ill-fated program is still listed at the Department of Defense's Forms Inventory web site. The form, of course, is no longer available. It was officially canceled on November 9, 1984.

In spite of my intense efforts during the 1970s, and having been in communication with congressmen, senators, bureaucrats, and quasi-military, I was basically unaware of this late-1970s action except for the brief controversial announcement in newspapers surrounding President Carter's Pardon. How would the average parent of a troubled Viet Nam victim know of this action or what they could do? There was absolutely no community of quasi-military support for Carter's action.

I wrote to all the various services, Army, Navy, Air Force, Marines, and Coast Guard for information on the numbers of less-than-honorable discharges. I was sarcastically told by each service, "The information is not available." One service said that to get a statistical report of the discharges would cost $13 million to reimburse them for personnel costs. Even at that, they would not guarantee accuracy. Another agency told me, "If you will send a money order for $17,000, we'll start the process."

In short, the nation that created these victims of war cannot provide a statistical accounting of our young men. Yet one can check the Internet and discover within minutes how many people were killed in automobile accidents in a given year, and how many nonfatal crashes there were, and how much was lost to property damage caused by automobile accidents.

Ironic, to say the least.

Chapter 8: Outcasts
The Cantrell Family

Would he go again?

Don Cantrell chews on the question for a second, putting the war – and his sacrifice – into perspective. He answers with a couplet from one of his poems.

"Would I go again if I was called to war?" He lets the question hang in the air like an illumination round, its eerie glow turning utter darkness into a surreal and frightening landscape. "Not until the enemy is at my door!"

Cantrell is, without a doubt, bitter. But he has earned that right. He is deeply suspicious of the U.S. government because he is one of its discarded tools. He knows only cynicism when it comes to U.S. foreign policy – whether overt, covert, or a seemingly incoherent mix of the two – because he lived on the edge of the sword for three terrifying months not so long ago. The blade, he found, is razor sharp. And it cuts both ways.

"Knowing what I know now – and finding out what I found out after I was there for a little while – I wasn't serving my country," he says. "The war in Viet Nam didn't have anything to do with the welfare of this country. As far as I'm concerned, it was nothing short of murder."

Cantrell, it should be pointed out, is anything but a bleeding-heart liberal. Rather, he is a typical American in many ways:

inherently suspicious of foreign alliances and entanglements, unabashedly proud of his Oklahoman roots, and unafraid to wax nostalgic about the good old days. A jack-of-all-trades who's equally at home on an oil field or under the hood of an old American-made car, he chooses his words carefully and eloquently, his Southern drawl evincing a sort of down-home, congenial pride. He still uses the word "gook" to describe his former enemy, but he does so without malice. As far as he's concerned, it's a technical term he learned in the bush – and one he uses to describe NVA regulars, Montagnard tribesmen, and Vietcong sympathizers alike.

Cantrell personifies the rugged individualism and hard-working ethos of the American heartland. Which makes his story that much more damning.

#

Born October 7, 1947, in Tulsa, Oklahoma, Donald James Cantrell grew up a couple hours south of there, just outside Wetumka, a rural town of about 1,500 people. Everybody knew everybody, and every family had a cellar, just in case the *Big One* touched down in the back yard between the clothesline and the vegetable garden.

Tornadoes, though, came and went. Not so for the community's work ethic, which practically sprung up from the soil, its roots as deep as the earth that fed it.

"We were raised on a farm out in the country," says Don, who grew up alongside two sisters and a brother. "It was a typical farm life: slop the hogs and feed the chickens. It was called a *truck farm*. We had five acres of okra, five acres of cucumbers, and three acres of tomatoes. We had our own market. We would take the cucumbers south to Calvin, where they had a pickle factory."

Wetumka, which means *still water* in the Creek Indian dialect, is sandwiched between Wewoka Creek and the North

Canadian River. When Don wasn't working in his parents' fields, he was passing lazy summer afternoons at river's edge, having traded his hoe for a fishing rod.

"I've always told everybody I was conceived on the river bank," he quips. "All the time growing up as kids, if we weren't working on the farm, we was fishing. It stuck."

So did his first romance.

He met Tearesa Kay Mead when the two were in grade school. Her grandparents lived in Wetumka, and one weekend Tearesa's and Don's paths crossed at the home of mutual friends of the Mead and Cantrell families.

"I thought she was gonna be my woman right there," Don says affectionately of his wife of nearly forty years. "We started puppy-loving, and it just kept growing."

Says Tearesa, "It was love at first sight. Just a little dabbling here and there along the way, but we always came back to each other."

Tearesa, who hailed from nearby Weleetka, had lived in the same house since she was born. She left it when she was sixteen, the beautiful young bride of her childhood sweetheart. Don was three months shy of eighteen. They exchanged wedding vows two days after Independence Day, 1965.

The two settled down in Weleetka, which, as opposed to Wetumka (still water), means *running water* in Creek Indian.

"I'd go to Tulsa or Oklahoma City for work," Don says, "and we'd go stay a while. But we'd always come back."

They had their first child, Donny Ray, over a year and a half later on March 28, 1967. Young and impetuous, they had barely adjusted to parenthood when the wind shifted.

#

In February 1969, with his son not quite two years old, Don volunteered for the U.S. Army. He was only twenty-one.

"Everybody around me was going," he remembers. "At that time, as young and dumb as I was, it felt like it was the thing to do."

He left for Fort Polk, Louisiana, where he completed fourteen weeks of basic training, including a stint as a squad leader in advanced infantry training. He eventually traveled to Fort Benning, Georgia, for NCO (Noncommissioned Officer) School.

"Because of a hardship in the family," he says, "I left NCO School before finishing. My wife was having a hard time. I just wanted to keep progressing forward and get the thing over with, instead of stringing it out."

Though they visited him regularly at the fort, Tearesa and little Donny were still living in Weleetka. Tearesa worked when she could, and her grandmother looked after Donny whenever she was away.

"At the time, I was so young and immature that I really didn't even know what was going on [in Viet Nam]," says Tearesa, who had barely turned twenty when her husband left for boot camp. "The people being killed were other than someone around me. Of course, I had the fear that he might be killed. But it wasn't something I could deal with at that point in my life."

She had more immediate concerns. Donny was a busy baby – a handful. And Tearesa couldn't help but feel abandoned by the boy's father.

"It was like he was saying, 'I would rather be in a jungle fighting for my life than to be with you and this two-year-old child,'" she explains. "It always kind of made me feel bad. But we worked through it, as we have so many things. We were both so immature. He didn't have an inkling of what he was getting into."

#

"The regulars were usually village people," Don says, dispensing a lesson he learned early on in Viet Nam. "They would sell us pop and drinks. They would even give us haircuts during the day. But at night, we would sometimes fight them. Our objective was to starve the NVA [North Viet Namese Army] and the Mountain Yards [Montagnard tribesmen], to keep them from coming into the villages for rice. But at night, some of the village people would smuggle rice out to the enemy, and we would fight them – some of the very same people we would do business with during the day.

"We couldn't fire on anyone during the day unless we were fired upon first. But after five o'clock, the village people were not supposed to be in the jungle. Anyone there after 5:00 p.m. was free meat."

Don flew into Long Bhin in October 1969. He was assigned to the 101st Airborne and teamed with a Viet Namese scout. The two men trained together for two weeks before joining Echo Company, a seven-man unit, on patrols in the jungle. Don walked point with the scout, a former NVA regular who had surrendered to the Americans. The company chopped LZ's (cleared landing zones), pulled recon, and set up ambushes.

"It was kind of shaky at first," admits Don, who wasn't sure he could trust the scout. "But he saved my bacon once. We had gotten into a firefight in this big gully where they were coming out of the mountains to split up into teams and get rice. We went there one night before dark to set up an ambush, but they got there at the same time as we did. We didn't have time to set up our claymores, so we got into a pretty good firefight. Had to call in the Cobras for air support. The next morning, we pulled a little recon down the gully. I was walking point at the time, and he was right behind me. He noticed a trip wire and jerked me backward to keep me from hitting it. It was an 80mm mortar round. I was just fixing to hit it, and he seen it and jerked me backwards. I felt a little better about him after that. I could sleep a little better . . . when we did get some sleep."

The absurdities and paradoxes of the United States' military strategy in Viet Nam are well documented today. At the time, Don found the sheer waste shocking.

"We'd send teams out to take positions, and the VC would be really dug in," he recalls. "We'd lose a lot of men to take the positions, and then they'd pull us back. Then three or four days later, the VC'd be dug in again, and we'd do it all over again. It was like they were just trying to get you killed. There was so much unnecessary death over there. It was unreal. It was pitiful. It made you feel like they had you there to get rid of you."

After three months of combat, Don's unit returned to base camp for a routine medical checkup. Unbeknownst to Don, his tour in Viet Nam was about to be cut short – effective immediately.

"The doctor said some of the guys who came in before me were complaining about my breathing," he explains. "He checked me for it and said, 'I gotta get you out of here.' The next day I was on a plane to Japan."

Don had bronchial asthma. He had actually had it, plus rheumatoid arthritis, since he was a young boy. He had almost died of the former as a small child. He was diagnosed with both in Japan and given a permanent profile, his combat career over.

A few nights earlier, Don and his tiny seven-man unit had set up an ambush in the jungle. They held their fire as 270 NVA regulars walked by within an arm's length. Don figures that's when his fellow soldiers started to worry about his breathing.

"I had grown accustomed to it," he says, "so I didn't notice it when I was asleep. But I would notice it when I was awake, and I tried to control it."

In the ninth grade, Don didn't make the football team because of his asthma and arthritis. Somehow, though, he had qualified to fight in the sweltering heat of Viet Nam.

He spent a month in the hospital in Japan while doctors ran tests and treated his conditions. He waited another month for the Army to cut him his orders and then was shipped stateside. His first stop on the long journey home: Hawaii.

"While I was in the airport awaiting a layover, I went into the airport bar to have a beer and kill some time. Another soldier on his way home came in, and we got to talking about our stay in Nam. He told me what outfit he was with, and I told him mine. When he heard which unit I was with, he told me they were caught in an ambush and killed not long before his departure. He told me I got out just in the nick of time."

#

Don was lucky to be alive. But fate wasn't done with him yet. He was assigned to finish out the rest of his tour at Fort Riley, Kansas. His health, already precarious, had taken a turn for the worse.

"At that time, the arthritis was so bad I couldn't even lay down in a bed and sleep," he remembers. "I had to sleep on the side of the bed with my arms hanging straight down. It was the only way I could get any relief from the pain. My knee was all swollen up. We were living off base. I couldn't even drive a car. My wife had to drive me to the base. That's when they assigned me guard duty."

Don told his CO that he couldn't stand for long hours at a time, or walk back and forth, for that matter. But he was willing to pull guard duty from a chair. When his CO balked, Don contacted the inspecting general.

"My CO got mad," Don recalls. "He said, 'If you're that sick, you need to be in a hospital.' That's when they cut my pay.

"I went back into the hospital, by his request, and my pay immediately stopped, along with my wife and son's allotment pay. My CO would personally bring my pay vouchers to the hospital for me to sign. They would be zero. I asked him why I was not being paid, and he said he would straighten it out when I was released."

Don spent several weeks in the hospital while doctors alternated between administering ice and heating pad treatments. Finally, a pair of cortisone shots in his shoulders helped ease the pain, and he was released on convalescent leave.

"I immediately went to Finance, where I tried to find out why my family and I were not getting paid," he says, resuming the narrative. "They would only tell me that I owed them a bunch of money. But they wouldn't tell me how much or why."

He had never borrowed money or damaged any equipment, so the assertion that he owed the Army money baffled Don. When he realized he was butting his head against a brick wall, he gave up.

"I told them that I was going to go home and get a job and take care of my family," he says. "I also told them when they wanted to get this straightened out to let me know, and I would come back.

"I left Fort Riley to go home with no car or money in mid-February. All the clothes I had were my boots, pants, and a T-shirt. My wife had no money to send me or to come and get me with. I hitchhiked and finally caught a ride with a trucker to Wichita. That was his destination. When he let me out, he gave me a jacket and a couple of dollars to get a cup of coffee and a bite to eat. A policeman saw him drop me off. As soon as the truck pulled off, the policeman stopped me and asked me if I had any money. I told him what I had and my story and showed him my military I.D. He said, 'Do you see that café across the street?' I said, "Yes, sir!' He said, 'Get in there and don't come out until someone picks you up.' He sat across the street and watched me.

"I went into the café and ordered a cup of coffee. When the waitress brought the coffee, she asked what was going on. I told her the story, and she fed me so I could use my money to call my wife. I called, and my wife finally found a cousin to bring her to pick me up."

Back in Oklahoma, Don found a job doing carpentry work. He wrote the base in Fort Riley, plus several politicians, including President Nixon. The base never wrote him back, but the politicians (or their aides) all told him the same thing: "Go back to your unit, and we'll help you straighten this out."

The dance went on for three years.

"While I was in Viet Nam, my wife felt like I had abandoned her," Don says. "During my AWOL experience, she was a nervous wreck. We both lived in daily torment."

While Don was still in the hospital back in Fort Riley and the Army had cut his pay, Tearesa had been getting by as best she could. At times, she lived with her mother, the main breadwinner in her family, who gave what little she could spare to Tearesa and Donny. She also turned to the Red Cross, explaining her family's misfortune. But they wouldn't help.

Although Don was able to provide for the family when he returned, his AWOL status didn't exactly alleviate the stress the family had already been enduring.

"I was fearful every day and every night, thinking they were gonna come and put him in jail," Tearesa remembers. "Just watching and waiting every day and every night. Every night when I went to bed, I thought about it. Finally, we thought, 'We can't live this way. We've got to get this straightened out.'"

#

After three years of insecurity, Don returned to Fort Riley, not knowing what to expect but hoping for a positive resolution.

"When I reported to the hospital, they called the Military Police," he remembers. "They took me to MP Headquarters, where they couldn't find any record of me. I had to find my own records before they would take me! After I proved that I belonged there, they put me in a holding company. There I pulled details. All the while I was under medical treatment. Finally, they took me in front of some colonel who determined what type of discharge I was to receive: other than honorable.

"Before they released me, they did stomach surgery on me [for a fissure in his colon] and then let me out. I never did hear from any of the people that said they would help me. I never did get the pay situation straightened out. I never received any of the money me and my family was supposed to get before I left Fort Riley or after I went back. When I was in Viet Nam, I put part of my pay in the Wells Fargo Bank. When they flew me out, they took me by ambulance to the plane, and I never had a chance to get my money from over there, either."

Three months after returning home, Don received mail from St. Louis, Missouri. He opened the envelope and found a letter from the government stating that he owed the Army a truckload of money.

"I wrote back and asked them why I owed them money, and they wouldn't tell me," he says. "After I wrote the next letter, I never heard from them again."

#

"The discharge was a bit of a relief in a way," Tearesa says, recalling the day her husband's military career came to an official end. "We were so young. We felt like, now it's over, it's behind us, and we've got it all straightened out. Three years is a long time. It was like we were fugitives."

Finally, the drama was over. And the Cantrells, now a family of four, could move on. Unfortunately, they would soon find out that fear and uncertainty were in some ways better than what lay ahead of them: a slow grind they would largely face on their own.

"You have to understand," Don says, "when we were raised, we were taught to respect our elders, law enforcement, any government agency, and so forth. When the military shafted us like they did, it made us feel like we were rejected by our country. We felt like we were beneath everyone else, and still do."

He had fought for his country. He had put himself in harm's way. He had done everything asked of him, joining his generation's call to serve the collective good. But his sacrifice wasn't enough, apparently.

His discharge status mattered more. To friends and family. To prospective employers. To the community at large.

"It's a two-fold deal in this community," Don explains. "There's not much to do anyway. Everybody knows your business. You can't sneeze without someone else knowing about it on the other side of town. Banks know it, so it doesn't help with getting a loan or starting a business. It follows you all through your life.

"You wind up doing a lot of things over the years. There are no major companies here. I've spent a lot of time off working on pipelines and building drill rigs. There were many jobs that I couldn't get because of my discharge status. It's caused me to have to take jobs that had no future, retirements, or benefits. And some in my family looked upon me as a failure, like I couldn't finish what I started."

Adds Don, "Some family stood by us. If they hadn't, we wouldn't have made it!"

#

The Cantrells learned self-reliance the hard way. They also learned not to take anything for granted.

For his part, Don, like most vets with combat experience, would need the next several years of his life to purge Viet Nam from his system.

"It's really odd," Tearesa says, "but he has never really talked about the war. And he talks about a lot of things. But it seemed like he kept so much inside about what he saw. I don't know if he was trying to protect me from knowing what happened, but he's rarely talked about it. Usually, every experience he has he can go on and on and on about it. But this he just couldn't.

"He's a pretty strong person, but there were some times – and they were quite often back then – I'd wake up and he might be popp'n me. But it went away."

Says Don, "I still have nightmares, but not as often as in the past. I have learned to live with them. I had anger problems, also. If I heard anything on the news about Nam, it would trigger my anger. When I would hear of other vets being dumped on and treated badly, it would trigger my anger. And in my youth, I would take it out on my family.

"Church and the Bible helped me to be able to cope with my problems. Also, time and age seems to temper a person's emotions."

The Cantrells' two children, Donny and Dana, were too young to sense the psychological battles being waged in their home. In fact, Donny, a 35-year-old father of two, is amazed that his father escaped Viet Nam relatively unscathed.

"I think it shaped him pretty good," Donny says of Viet Nam. "I think it's made him a lot stronger. Probably like any experience like that, it makes you evaluate life."

#

Don Cantrell is an average guy. He's a little over five-foot-ten. Neither overweight nor thin. Bit of a belly – the kind most folks acquire with middle age. Some male-pattern baldness.

"He's outgoing," his son says. "True. Unique. He's very honest. He's a straight-up guy."

He's also still waiting. Still waiting for redress. Still waiting for vindication. Still waiting to be thanked, instead of shunned, for his part in a war nobody but the politicians wanted.

More than thirty years have passed since he left the jungle. His asthma and arthritis are worse, not better. The joints that swelled in the heat of Viet Nam still give him fits in Weleetka.

And still he waits.

"I really get worried a lot because he is so anti-government," his wife says. "Sometimes it seems to rule his life. That's all he can think about. That's all he can be interested in. Sometimes it just goes on and on and on, and it all stems from his experience in Viet Nam. I don't think anything could help put that behind him. He thought he was fighting for this country. He put his life on the line. And he was treated like dirt by the same people who took him, shaped him to go there, and sent him."

She pauses a moment to consider the war's legacy in her own home.

"It was really bad for me," she says. "I've tried to put it all behind me. But the worst part of it to me is that it's made him be able to see all of the bad but none of the good."

Don has been in the oil and gas business now for the last twenty years. The work is somewhat regular and "the only thing here," in his words, "you can rely on."

He's fifty-five and a chain-smoker. He's on medication for sky-high blood pressure and arthritis. His blood sugar levels, too, are off the charts. He still passes blood on occasion, just as he did before the Army operated on his colon. And the asthma is still a big problem, complicated, no doubt, by his addiction to cigarettes.

He can't afford insurance. So he pays cash, when he can afford to see a doctor at all, for his medical care.

"I've fought this health deal about as long as I can," he says. "I just need a little help. I'm thinking the VA would be the way to do it. I would think, God, after all these years, surely they would be able to straighten it out."

Don has contacted a few different officials recently, hoping for help. But no luck so far. Dave Barker, a Veterans Service officer at the VA Medical Center in Chillicothe, Ohio, and the only one of those Don contacted who could be reached, has no record of ever corresponding with Don. His advice for Don, though, is simple.

"He needs to go to a [Veterans Service officer] who does discharge upgrades," Barker says, "like his county Veterans Service Office."

Meanwhile, as Don waits for redress, his discharge status festers. Hope remains elusive. From the beginning, Don's quest has seemed impossible.

"I contacted President Nixon, Speaker of the House Carl Albert, a prominent lawyer named Gene Stipe," Don says of his initial efforts at seeking redress. "An aid for President Nixon contacted me and told me they would help me get it straightened out, but they did not help. Also, Carl Albert's office, along with Mr. Stipe's, said the same thing. No one helped me.

"Over the years, I became good friends with the commander of the American Legion in Henryetta. They asked me about my military status and wanted me to join the Legion. When they found out I had a bad discharge, they just gave me a guest card so I could get into the Legion. They did not offer to help get my discharge overturned, so I didn't mention it any further. I wasn't going to ask because they showed no interest.

"I was and still am beat down as far as asking for any kind of help. When the President and the Speaker of the House lie to you, why go any further?"

His sense of futility, unfortunately, is reinforced every day. Don has been barred from over 40% of all American jobs, i.e., county, city, state, federal, and defense. Less than 2% of these discharges ever get upgraded. "My mom and dad are on a very limited income," explains Dana, who was born while her father was AWOL. "He can't afford treatments he needs. So it's just another reminder – a constant reminder – that he didn't get treated right by the government."

Dana Britt lives nearby in Dewar, Oklahoma. She works at an auto parts store and is the mother of two, with another one on the way. She can't stand to watch as the war eats away at her hero.

"He's just a really super person, despite everything that has happened to him," she says of her father. "He has a good heart. He's very passionate for anything he gets involved in."

Including his childhood hobby.

"He'd rather fish than breathe," Dana says. "I used to go with him when I was younger. I haven't been in a while. I don't get a lot of time off from work, and we live away a little bit. When I get time off, we go over and have dinner with him. He's a good grandfather."

#

Two disparate memories. Both in the jungle.

"One night we were in a firefight with the gooks during the monsoons," Don recalls. "It had been raining for days. We were in between two rivers, and a flash flood came, and the rivers came together. We kept going for higher ground until there was no high ground and we were trapped with the gooks. Neither side could fight for hanging onto the trees.

"We stayed there all night, holding onto trees and holding onto a buddy while he slept. Then we would trade. He would hold me while I slept. We did that all night. The next morning choppers came in and lifted us out. When we got out of there, we looked like prunes and had jungle rot. A buddy took eighty-seven water leeches off me that morning. That was a very bad night."

The other memory stands out just as distinctly in Don's mind.

"A strange thing happened while I was in Nam," he says. "While in the field, we had mail call, and I received two letters from the stock market. I opened one up, and it was a check for $12,000. I opened the other one up, and it was a check for almost $12,000. Both were made out to me. I knew I didn't have any stocks, so I put them in an envelope and mailed 'em back. And I never heard anything more about that."

To this day, Don wonders if the un-cashed stocks had anything to do with the money the government said he owed them. He also wonders what sort of long-term effects his own story will have on his children. And their children.

"They're not very fond of the Army or the government, either," he says of his son and daughter. "It's affected all of us. My kids look back and see what we've had to go through. They're old enough now and have their own families. They can fill out job applications and don't have that hanging over them."

Tearesa, too, worries about her family's outlook.

"Our son now is grown," she says, "and he thinks exactly like his dad does. He's heard all this, and sometimes it's hard for me because, well, it's like the war in Iraq now and all the contention here in the U.S. over it. He's all up in arms about stuff, and he sounds just like his dad. Whereas, he hasn't had any kind of experience with any of it. Our daughter, her interests have been elsewhere, and she kind of escaped all of it."

Donny maintains that he has come to his opinions on his own and that he doesn't always agree with his father. But he admits the apple hasn't fallen far from the tree, especially where war and politics are concerned.

"If someone was attacking our country and our freedom directly, I would go to war," he says, answering the same question posed earlier to his father and echoing his sentiments. "But I would go to fight for myself and my family and my freedom, not for the government."

Dana, meanwhile, has a different focus.

"I don't really care a whole lot about the government," she says. "My dad did what he needed to do for the government and then . . . I really don't have a whole lot of thoughts about the government."

Adds Dana, "I just listen to him. He will go on forever, and listening to him helps him because he can get it all out."

Catharsis is, of course, problematic. It's not exactly permanent. The war and the government come shrieking back.

"It's something that will always haunt him," Dana says.

Her mother takes it one step further, saying, "It's something that's always in the back of your mind, no matter what."

When it comes to the Cantrells, one thing is clear: the U.S. Army didn't just strip away one man's discharge status. He had a family, too.

Chapter 9: Homeless
The Lintecum Family

What do you get when you turn a born lover into a trained killer?

You take a young man with the gift of poetry and music, and you place a rifle in his hands. You point toward the enemy. And you tell him to shoot. *Kill.*

What do you get?

You pluck a gangly 19-year-old kid from Emmerich Manual High School in Indianapolis and drop him into the jungles of Viet Nam, where men are made into pulp by bouncing betties, wooden spikes, and jellied Napalm. Where an impenetrable canopy of trees reduces day to night and night to utter blackness. Where body counts take on the sanctity of the sacraments. Where asking questions is apostasy and refusing to kill the old woman stumbling away from you is nothing short of heresy.

What do you get?

His third and final tour comes to an end, and you send him home. His family no longer recognizes him. His peers spit on him. And the government that hired him to kill strangers in a strange land has no more use for him. He is told by everyone to simply get on with it. Get on with finding a job. Get on with raising a family. Get on with being a productive member of society.

His wife loves him, even if she can't see the trip flare lighting up the night sky or hear the incoming mortar rounds. His children feel the tension, even if their father can't elucidate its source. Everyone sees the river of hurt in his eyes, even if they can't navigate it.

What do you get?

The poet speaks:

> *I was brought up to be just a big puppy,*
> *Then they trained me to be an attack dog.*
> *After my career as an attack dog*
> *They said I didn't fit into the pack any more.*
> *And they wanted to have me put to sleep,*
> *So I ran away and become a stray dog,*
> *Looking for a kind handout, but expecting a kick.*
> *I tried to get a job as a guard dog.*
> *But after a few days*
> *I wouldn't even let the owner in.*
> *Being a stray dog is no picnic,*
> *But being old and a stray*
> *Is a bitter fate for any dog,*
> *Especially since I'm not a dog at all;*
> *I'm an American veteran.*
>
> – From "Street Dog" © 1997 Sarge Lintecum

The statistics from the Department of Veteran Affairs are as grisly as the wounds inflicted a half a world away. On any given night, more than 275,000 vets spend the night on the streets, under bridges, and in makeshift cardboard shelters, among other places. In any given year, the number of vets who spend at least one night homeless tops a half million. Forty-seven percent of those homeless vets served during the Viet Nam era.

Alcohol. Drugs. Post-Traumatic Stress Disorder. To escape the world of the homeless vet and the conditions that accompany it requires community support – and a Herculean effort on the part of the vet, who must overcome every kind of inertia, some of it his, and some of it ours. All of which makes the story of Sarge, as he is now called, and his family truly inspiring.

Here is one vet who fell into the abyss – seemingly lost in the torturous depths of the Viet Nam War and its aftermath – and emerged to wax poetic. Here is one family that took that same journey, following the descent as deep as it plunged and climbing the ascent as high as their collective muse would take them.

#

His name is Russell Wayne Lintecum, but everybody calls him Sarge, a nickname he adopted several years after returning home from the war. He was born on June 8, 1946, in Indianapolis, Indiana. He dropped out of Emmerich Manual High School when he was nineteen years old to join the military and fight in Viet Nam, where the war had become, in his words, "a daily occurrence on television." He felt compelled to answer his country's call to arms. He was also driven by youthful zeal – and an ever-gnawing quest for adventure.

"Here I am a goofy 19-year-old white kid," he recalls, "and how do you transform yourself from this stumbling-over-your-own-feet, gawky dude to a respectable person that society would recognize? The only way to do that was to be all I could be. It was quite a letdown to get home after all that and find out that I was two steps below drunk and crazed bikers on the socially acceptable list."

Sarge volunteered for the U.S. Army and was sent to Fort Knox, Kentucky, for boot camp. He wanted to be a paratrooper, which meant that everything from basic training to jump school would be physically and mentally demanding. At jump school in Fort Benning, Georgia, he successfully completed five parachute jumps, though he would only have to make one jump in Viet Nam.

"I met Sarge at Fort Benning," says Frank Hayes (Chapter 6), who served with Sarge during his first tour in Viet Nam with the 101st Airborne Tiger Force. "We were all just coming off leave, and we got into Fort Benning and went to our assigned barracks. Somebody started singing a song. I grabbed a cigarette butt can and started beating on it. And Sarge came in and started singing. We've been close ever since."

Not long after arriving in Viet Nam together, Sarge and Frank were split up, with Frank joining a reconnaissance team and Sarge picking up with a rifle company. While Frank explored the jungle trails with an eight-man team whose chief goal was to track the enemy but not engage it, Sarge went on patrols that were itching for a fight. In the end, both ended up earning a Purple Heart. Both saw more than enough combat. Sarge, meanwhile, was forever changed by his encounters with the enemy who, more often than not, looked less like soldiers and more like young boys or, conversely, old villagers just trying to scratch out a living.

"Nothing counted but the body count," Sarge recalls. "My first tour in the jungle was more tortuous than frightening, and it was plenty frightening. Just to put an eighty-pound backpack on – that was before they redesigned the backpack to put the weight on your hips – all the weight was on your shoulders."

Sarge still has an old photo of himself in the jungle looking lean and tough. Gritty. A survivor. He's smoking a bamboo pipe and wearing Italian wraparound sunglasses.

"We went on search and destroy patrols," he says. "When you'd walk down the trail, there'd be one set of footprints. They'd be kind of big and smeared, but that's where everyone stepped. If there was anything laying across the path – a root, a stick, anything – you wouldn't touch it.

"I remember one time I got so jealous of this guy. He had just gotten there a few days before. He sets off this bouncing betty mine, which blows up with the first explosion and down with the second, and it shoots a piece of shrapnel through his arm and breaks both bones, which is a million-dollar wound. It can be repaired completely, but you have to be sent home. I was shocked at how enraged I was at this guy. I was jealous of some guy for getting blown up. But things were strange out there. You're scraping green slime from some puddle in the jungle, clenching your teeth as tight as you can to avoid leeches, and that's like a blessing straight from God – the best drink of water I ever got."

Strange indeed. Mortal combat does uncanny things to people. But when the smoke clears, fierce, hand-to-hand encounters with men as young and desperate as you can only end one way. One man dies a savage death. The other walks, limps, or crawls away, forever changed.

"The killing sticks with me the most," Sarge says. "When you violate your true nature, you put your mind on a self-destruct mode."

Sarge finished his tour in 1967. But he stayed on for two more.

"I kept asking myself, 'Why are you extending?'" he recalls. "'Why are you going back to hell?' Well, I was trying to get myself killed. I didn't think you were supposed to go home alive. I kept telling myself it was because my brother Dave can't be sent here as long as I'm here [U.S. law ruled out the possibility of losing all the sons from one family to the war]. The guys I'd seen die – I couldn't think of one that was less worthy of being alive than me."

Despite whatever unconscious objectives Sarge might have had, his second and third tours of duty, though still relatively dangerous, placed him closer to the rear of the fighting, if there was a rear in Viet Nam. For his second tour, he served as a perimeter guard at Phan Rang Air Base. For his third and final tour, he swapped the jungle of towering trees and wait-a-minute vines for the urban jungle of Saigon, where he served with an elite troop as a machine gunner on a gun jeep.

"Sarge and I met the first time on the gun jeeps," says Greg Bowles, then a driver for the 52nd infantry security guards. "They put us together, probably because we act a lot alike. We were rebellious and did our own thing. There was a connection there. It's critical to have that kind of relationship between a gun jeep driver and the gunner.

"We got into a couple firefights, but mostly we came to assist. We were still cleaning up the Tet Offensive. It was still messy. And there were still some hot spots. The biggest problem we had were what we called 'the cowboys.' They'd break into the commissaries, steal TV's and cigarettes, and get on these little Honda motorcycles with the driver facing forward and the other guy strapped to him and facing backwards. We used to chase 'em and make 'em crash. The Saigon police would take over and arrest the kids. It was just little petty crap like that. They would lure you, too, sometimes, and pull you into an area where you'd be trapped. The alleys were only ten feet wide."

Sarge and Greg worked hard at night and then relaxed during the days, typically heading down to the Chinese sector on the Saigon River.

"We got to know the people," Greg recalls, "got food, mingled with the culture, partied with them. The river was funky. You got the humidity and the heat, plus these two-cycle engines that burn oil and gas. I took that smell home with me in a duffel bag. When I get it out for other vets, they all say the same thing: it still smells like the city."

Greg maintains that Sarge, other than growing his hair and beard long, hasn't changed since the war. Frank Hayes, Sarge's buddy from his first tour, agrees.

"Sarge was a good singer even then," he says. "He and I used to harmonize and sing together. He was an upbeat guy who liked to be happy. He was the type of guy who, when we're taking our first jumps out of the plane at 3,000 feet [at Fort Benning], he's got his camera out. The rest of us are scared to death and just waiting for our chutes to open up, and he's taking pictures."

During his first tour, Sarge often met Frank at base camp in between missions for much needed R&R.

"Instead of getting drunk in town like most guys," Frank explains, "we'd sit around a watering hole and watch the kids with the water buffaloes. We'd just smoke a couple joints and watch the kids. Whenever we had the opportunity, we just tried to have a cultural experience."

Even then, amidst the brutality, Sarge was just looking for some peace. He didn't find any. What he did find – the truly monstrous horror of war – is locked away somewhere deep inside. Though he's candid and forthcoming when it comes to talking about the war and its overall meaning, he's reticent to recount – or relive – the fighting.

Those moments he left behind when he finally went home.

#

After surviving three tours of Viet Nam, three bouts with malaria, jungle rot, immersion foot, intestinal parasites, a shrapnel wound in his leg, and exposure to Agent Orange, Sarge went home to Indianapolis.

"I knew there would be protests at the airport," he recalls, "so when I got on the plane to go home, I went into the bathroom and changed into civvies, thinking I could sneak off the plane at the other end. It didn't work.

"I got spit on. I just tried to get through there. I just felt, you know, just get away."

While U.S. citizens took their collective anger out on the soldiers fighting a dirty war perpetuated by politicians, the government did nothing to ameliorate the circumstances.

"You went from your unit to an airfield to a plane," explains Professor Ed Moise, Ph.D., who teaches history at Clemson University. "It could be very fast. There was no effort to sort of . . . put you with people."

No counseling. No reprogramming. No preparation for what awaited you on the home front.

"You know how you look forward to something so much for so long that it can't sink in when it finally happens?" Sarge asks. "That's how I was feeling when I came home. I felt like, jeez, I still don't feel like I'm home. I was looking for that feeling for so long, and it wasn't there. Then my mom took me to the VA hospital, and she said to them, 'This isn't the boy we sent.' And I knew I'd never have that feeling. I made it home alive, but my mother's son didn't."

The transition from the wild man's world of war and terror to the civilized man's world of clean sheets and indoor plumbing proved difficult, to say the least. Sarge found the world he had longed to return to no longer wanted him. And those who had waited for him to come home wondered if he truly had.

When his mother tried to wake him after one typically fitful night of sleep, Sarge responded instinctively, proving that the scars from Viet Nam ran deep.

"I knocked her clear across the room," he remembers. "They wouldn't wake me up after that. They'd stand at the bottom of the stairs to try to wake me up. They were afraid of me. All my friends were afraid of me. They all thought it's normal for Viet Nam vets to *seem* normal, but soon as something goes wrong, he's gonna pull out his M-16 and level us all. I was totally isolated. I'd come home to a life of exile."

#

So he floated.

He walked away from the job that had waited for him for three years: driving a forklift. He says he couldn't risk breaking down in front of a group of men; he was, after all, the only one with a body count. He left home, saying goodbye to his mother, brother, and two sisters (his dad had already passed away). He moved to Tempe, Arizona, where the warm climate seemed more suited to someone who had contracted malaria three times.

"Here I am, totally PTSD'd out," he says, "living in a back yard of a commune that was too full to accommodate me. I'm living under a grapefruit tree, blissfully happy. I'm hanging out at Perry's Bar, which was a rowdy scene. Almost nightly a fight would be broken up. The owner would pull out this huge long-barreled pistol and start shooting at the ceilings, which were very high, and work his way down the wall. That's how he broke up a fight."

Sarge earned a living by picking up change off the floor and bringing glasses to the bar. He collected cans and bottles to make enough to pay for a meal every day.

At an arcade across from Perry's on Mill Avenue, he met an 18-year-old girl named Leslie. Wide-eyed and innocent, she was also fearless.

"I would tell people within the first sentence of meeting them that I was a Viet Nam veteran," Sarge says, "because I had to know if they would make me a hero or a baby killer in their mind. It seemed to be one or the other. Leslie made me a hero.

"She moved in with me, under the grapefruit tree, just laying on the ground. We were there for about six weeks. I had been sleeping under the Tempe Bridge, but this guy warned me about flash flooding. I was scared to sleep there. So he told me about his commune. I moved into his back yard. I had only been there a week when I woke up to eight inches of irrigation water. His back yard had flooded.

"When Leslie moved in with me, she would sleep at the bottom of the tree. I would spend the night up in the tree in this indescribable animal state of awareness that we were trained to use in Viet Nam. Just total full alert. Only, I was in heaven! I was guarding Leslie like some pit bull with a bone. I just got such a feeling of joy from having her down there and knowing she was safe. I mean, a SWAT team could have come in, and they would have never gotten to her."

At the time, Leslie was living with her mom in an apartment in Scottsdale, where she worked at an electronics company.

"Sarge was on the streets, basically," she remembers. "He needed a lot of adrenaline rushes. When I met him, I almost fell off my seat. I was always a person who thought I wasn't born to be bored. I knew Sarge wasn't a nine-to-five guy. I came from a blue-collar family. I didn't grow up getting everything I wanted; I was brought up with a very strong work ethic, just like Sarge before he went to Viet Nam.

"Anyway, when I first saw him, I was very attracted to those types [hippies], more so than anyone in the military. So I thought it was so cool that he was a hippie hanging out on the street. Truthfully, he was a homeless vet living under a bridge. This man had been to hell and back three times. When I first met him, his hair was already growing out, shoulder length. When I found out he had been to Viet Nam, I almost fell off my seat because he looked so young. He was so sweet. I remember seeing him across the room at a pinball joint across from Perry's Bar and just seeing the cutest smile I had ever seen in my life. We walked back to Perry's Bar, and he sat down next to me and started talking. I asked a really naïve question: 'Did you have to kill anybody?' Within two minutes his watch alarm went off and he had to go somewhere. I learned later that he would set it whenever he felt uncomfortable.

"I would go to work, and all I could see was his face in my head. I didn't have a car at the time, so I'd hitchhike into Tempe from Scottsdale to go see Sarge. I'd buy him some

Captain Crunch and take him back to my mom's apartment, or I'd take him to Jack in the Box. But he never imposed on anybody or asked for help."

For their first official date, Sarge and Leslie hitchhiked to the airport and caught a plane to Los Angeles. Upon arrival, they fell asleep at Griffith Park. The next morning they awoke to a "love in," with several drummers and percussionists holding an impromptu jam.

"We got an apartment for a while," Sarge remembers. "She would work, and I would bake a chicken for when she got home. We were homeless off and on. I must have done a hundred jobs, but I couldn't get by with my memory loss. If you tell me three things, I remember one and erase the other two from my mind."

Three bouts with malaria had literally fried parts of Sarge's brain. Leslie, in effect, became his memory.

They hitchhiked back to Indianapolis for the Indy 500 and, more importantly, for Leslie to meet Sarge's mom. Leslie, though, failed to tell her own mom where she was going. In fact, she had essentially been MIA since the young couple flew to Los Angeles for their first date three months earlier. She finally wrote a letter to her grandmother just to let her know she was okay. She received a reply that her grandfather was sick (a slight exaggeration), and eventually went back.

Before returning home, though, Leslie got to know Sarge's family.

"His mom had a really hard time," Leslie says, "because she just did not understand why Sarge couldn't go get a job. He had never been like that. Nobody understood or even knew the term Post-Traumatic Stress Disorder. We went to a picnic, and one of his aunts said, 'Gee, can't we check you into a hospital?' We were at that reunion for about five minutes.

"They take these guys right out of combat and expect them to work nine to five. The government knew this would happen, but they didn't prepare the soldiers' families. So many vets ended up homeless or dead, and their families didn't understand why they weren't the people they had sent over there. You take a young man who works and goes to school and gives all his money to his mom, and now he can't even hold a job for three weeks? PTSD shouldn't have been a big surprise. There was shell shock and battle fatigue. When you have someone in combat, especially that long, you don't just send them back to their job and their families and expect them to be able to deal with it."

Sarge's memory was essentially toast. He had trouble sleeping. He felt abandoned, in many ways, by his family, his peers, and his country. But he was in love.

On December 28, 1969, Sarge and Leslie wed.

"It was very, very basic," Leslie recalls of the wedding. "Just me, my mom, my grandparents, and Sarge. My mom had a big, roomy Oldsmobile. We all went from Phoenix, where we had been staying with my grandparents, to Winterhaven, California, just across the border. We got our marriage license at one of those places where you can get a license quickly. We were married at a little chapel by a Protestant minister. I wore a simple white shirt and a purple mini-skirt. Sarge had some jeans, shirt, and shoes. It cost forty-five dollars. My mom then drove us back. We went back to my grandparents and had Kentucky Fried Chicken. Some friends in Indianapolis gave us airline tickets back there as a wedding gift. We stayed until April and then moved back to Mesa, Arizona."

For the next few years, Leslie and Sarge got by the best they could. Occasionally they would rent a small cottage. Other times they'd set up a trailer or two on a friend's property. They even built a nursery in the back of a 1958 Volkswagen bus for their first child, Colton Dane Lintecum, who was born on August 11, 1971.

"Sarge and I picked an unorthodox, different kind of lifestyle," Leslie says. "So when we ran into serious financial binds, which can happen regularly, we never went to family for help. We just did it on our own. A lot of that was because I thought we picked this lifestyle.

"To most people, it doesn't sound typical to be sleeping in someone's back yard. I loved it. As much as Sarge tried to protect me, do you think I felt special? Sarge for decades couldn't sleep until daylight. It wasn't just PTSD; it was being disenfranchised from society. He just saw so much cold treatment. He joined the Army; he didn't get drafted. He went with all honorable intentions and put his life on the line."

Leslie and Sarge recognize that their homeless years weren't literally and entirely "homeless." They usually had a roof of some kind over their heads, even if it was made of canvas and leaked like a sieve. Compared to the experiences of most homeless vets, theirs were ideal. Romantic even. They spent much of their time in a rural setting or in the woods. By contrast, most homeless vets today –seventy-nine percent, in fact – live out marginal existences on city streets. In San Francisco alone, 2,400 homeless vets will sleep outside tonight, according to Swords to Plowshares, a homeless agency.

"It's all been exciting," Leslie says, "even the terrible times. I feel more blessed to have experienced the really rough times than if I had just lived a cushiony life my whole life, because that's when you really experience the miracles of life. I remember one day thinking we could really use a couch. Within a few hours some friends of mine called me saying they had a couch they needed to get rid of. Those things to me are the real thrill in life. Everything points to the fact that nothing is an accident and you are in the exact place you need to be every moment of your life.

"A lot of it was pure fun. Do you think we were one of the coolest couples in the scene back then? Of course!"

#

Not quite two years after Colt's arrival, Leslie gave birth to their first daughter, Brandy, on May 4, 1973. A family of four now, the Lintecums lived a precarious life. The kids were home schooled, and the family lived from disability check to disability check. But the kids got plenty of one-on-one attention from their parents.

"Most of my friends are envious of my upbringing," says Brandy, a 30-year-old slam poet who performs nationally like her father.

Indeed, despite their circumstances, the Lintecums shared intimate moments while overcoming daily hardships.

"When I was about eleven," Colt remembers, "we moved to Patagonia, Arizona. My parents had some friends there. We stayed with them for a while. I wasn't a big fan of the whole idea because I was used to Phoenix, and I loved the big city. We ended up going a few miles out of town, and my dad set up an official mining claim to claim some land. We put three-foot rock towers on the corners of the property and met all these different regulations. My dad's feeling was that he would find a way to provide property for us to live on regardless of what the government or the local authorities thought about it.

"Then we actually ended up camping. We were probably only going to town once every couple of weeks. We had a big ugly green International truck – it was bizarre looking. We had a little room in there, and then we had tents. It was like *Survivor* to an extent. My mom would cook over the campfire. We didn't have any luxuries out there, obviously. They were hard times, but I remember we made the most of it. We had a blast. We'd do all sorts of activities during the day. We made bows and arrows. We'd go exploring to see the wildlife. It was really like an extended camping trip, but there was the underlying stress that we weren't camping. At that time, my dad was only getting about four hundred dollars a month from the VA because he was only considered fifty percent disabled [his status has since been upgraded to one hundred percent by the VA]. So there was barely enough money to survive."

Things finally came to a head when a flood threatened to sweep the family and their homestead away. Locals warned them of the danger and helped them evacuate in time.

"I was three months pregnant at the time [with Carrie]," Leslie recalls. "I was going up hills to throw up. You really have to prove to your Viet Nam vet husband that you are one hell of a trooper. Brandy and Colt really helped out. But there were a lot of days when I wondered where our next meal was coming from. But they always came. We had faith. I think I really know the meaning of the word *faith*.

"Still, it was heaven compared to what you go through in the city if you're homeless. It's so degrading, and it can be such a downward spiral. I remember getting food stamps, and you just don't feel good. People look at you in such a bad way. But it would really put a grind on our relationship when I tried to go out and work. Sarge didn't want me to leave.

"When I was sick, he'd push me away. He couldn't bear to see a loved one sick. And he saw so many guys get Dear John letters that it took him a long time to realize I really, really loved him. Though I couldn't understand what he did in Viet Nam, I still loved him."

Years later, Sarge read his poem, *The Flood of '83*, at a book signing that Leslie's mom attended. She cried. She never knew her daughter and son-in-law had been homeless.

#

Leslie maintains she and Sarge chose their lifestyle, and that they took responsibility for that choice. It could be argued, however, that a life without roots chose them.

Sarge came home from Viet Nam a shell of his former self. Optimism was replaced by fear. Idealism gave way to shame. The dreams of youth were shattered by nightmares on the wire. Where do you go after you've killed a man with your own hands? How do you shed the training that has become instinct, the blood-soaked memories that leave no room for the future?

When does the fighting stop?

"I couldn't tell Leslie, especially, about what I'd done," Sarge says. "The loved ones you have afterwards are all you've got. What if they see you as an evil person? If you want to hurt a Viet Nam veteran, what do you call them?"

Baby killer.

"My weapon was a grenade launcher," Sarge continues. "One bullet weighed half a pound. It spins two hundred and fifty revolutions and then arms itself. When it hits something solid, it explodes. They would always call me up and say, 'We have a sniper in that hootch.' I'd put one through the window, and then I'd have to go look at what was in there. It wasn't always a sniper. That's why I wanted to kill myself for so long and didn't even know it.

"The poor villagers – if they gave any sign that they were helping the Vietcong or were the Vietcong, we killed them all. If the Vietcong came through and saw any signs that they were pro-American, *they* killed them all. So how do you survive as a villager? I'd say the first thing you have to get rid of is loyalty. You have to be loyal to whoever's in your face, and they have to believe you. Otherwise, you're dead."

When Sarge came home, he desperately needed intimacy, understanding – forgiveness. But he couldn't ask for it. He didn't think he deserved it.

"The war made me a real wild person," he says, recalling the first few months back home. "I would go to biker bars and hang out and not take sass from anyone with the explicit mission of getting in a hairy fight. And I'd always get the shit beat out of me. But that wasn't the thing. I was physically addicted to my own adrenaline. They never bothered to tell me that. They never debriefed me. They just took me out of the jungle and put me on a plane to the States."

Sarge, by nature an outgoing, engaging person, shut down. Closed up. He became a recluse, spending much of the first decade of his marriage cooped up inside a trailer or a tent or a rental. He strung barbed wire around one home. Sometimes he'd step out the front door and fire a gun into the dirt. Anything to purge the demons.

The VA hospital gave him Thorazine. Turned him into a zombie. But a light still flickered inside.

"Even during Sarge's darkest hour," Leslie says, "I always saw him as one of the most special beings that would be on this earth. I guess that's what other people didn't see. I always saw that in him."

Says Colt, "Even when I was too young to understand, there was always a stress level in the household, a tangible edge, so to speak. As I grew up, I learned more and more details of what Dad had been through. In a lot of ways it was good to know and made a lot of sense. It put the pieces of the puzzle together, as far as explaining the bizarre depressions he would go through. The period where my mom was working to get him on disability was a really tough time. They had to fight tooth and nail with the VA to get him listed as disabled.

"I'm extremely proud of where my dad's at today because I saw a lot of the lows he had to go through along the way. He went through an antisocial period where he wanted himself and his family to be secluded. He didn't really want to interact with people. He wouldn't talk with other veterans or even about Viet Nam. The progression to where we are today, even though I've seen it every step of the way, is really unbelievable. If I were to describe my dad in one word, I would just say *perseverance.*

"My dad's never gone into detail with me about what he did in Viet Nam. But he was with the 101st Airborne. They weren't there to do anything but . . . they were aggressive ground troops. I know for a fact that he had to do a lot of unspeakable things. He has such a respect for life. He won't even kill an insect because he knows how quickly it can be taken away. Even though he can't make up for what he did at the time, I know his heart was pure and he was doing what he thought was right at the time. All the regrets he has and will always have in his heart he's turning around. He's *saving* lives now."

#

When Sarge was just three years old, his father died.

"My mom and my grandma raised us," he says. "My grandma died when I was in Viet Nam. At the time, I was so out of it with malaria they put a toe tag on me. They ended up sending me to the wrong field hospital, and I didn't get any mail for thirty days. I hitchhiked to another hospital to get my mail and found out my grandmother, my second parent, had died. I had been granted a thirty-day leave to go to the funeral, but she had already been buried. So I couldn't go. That clerical error cost me."

Nearly ten years later, in 1975, Sarge took Leslie, Colt, and Brandy to Kansas, where his father's parents had just been put in a nursing home. Sarge took his grandparents back to their home, where they would live with them for a year.

"I called my mom and told her we were starting our own old folks home," Sarge remembers, "and she was to pack and we would bring her to Kansas and we would take care of her. She died that night."

#

Sarge Lintecum delivers *Viet Nam Blues: Combat Tested Blues* with a throaty, gritty vibrato, conjuring up the vocal stylings of old bluesmen long gone. On the title track, he reads poetry over the sounds of helicopters hovering above the jungle.

"His music," says Max, his 15-year-old son and youngest child, "is like medicine."

After the flood in 1983, two things happened for Sarge that would change his family's fortunes forever. First, he gradually qualified for a full disability check from the U.S. government. Money, though by no means in ample supply, was now no longer a pressing need. Secondly, and perhaps more importantly, Sarge discovered music and poetry.

"I actually started playing harmonica early on after I met this guy named Colt, who I named my first son after," Sarge says. "He was this wild person. He really latched onto me because it's hard to find people as wild as we were. He would be on the scene in Tempe, and then he would disappear. And then maybe a year later he'd come back. It wasn't until years later that I found out every time he returned he had just escaped from San Quentin. He taught me how to play harmonica, and he played it in a wild way. So he affected my style. I always had a natural affinity with the blues. Seemed from the very start I could play blues harmonica."

Something Sarge gave little thought to in his early adulthood slowly grew into a passion that, by the '90s, had become his profession. He released his album, *Viet Nam Blues: Combat Tested Blues…for Peace,* and performed locally, regionally, and even nationally. He also tried his hand at poetry, eventually joining the Phoenix Slam Poetry Team and publishing a book of poetry. He organized benefits for several organizations, including Saint Mary's Food Bank, which had, many years ago, helped feed his own family. He became a featured speaker at high schools, colleges, conferences, and workshops.

In essence, Sarge became an entertainer, something his family already knew he was. The barbed wire was just a façade.

"He's curious, always youthful," Brandy explains. "He's an intellect and a genius musician. He's seen the most horrible things that you could possibly see, and he still has the most optimistic outlook. That's what makes him forever young."

He eventually caught the attention of Lee Oskar, owner of the Lee Oskar Harmonica Company and a former member of the famous '60s band, War. Lee joined him onstage at a benefit for St. Mary's Food Bank, and a relationship of mutual admiration was born.

"I was impressed and intrigued by his story, his songs, and the hardships the guy had been through," Lee says of Sarge. "I sent him a harmonica. And then I finally met him when I came to Phoenix.

"I said, of course, I'll do whatever I can for his cause. He has something real to talk about. And it seems like he's very good for other people who've been traumatized by Viet Nam. He's managed to survive and turn it into good things. He's amazing – both he and Leslie. They survived. Not only did they handle it well, but somehow through it all they found a niche."

As for Sarge's music, Lee refuses to play the role of critic, a role that seems dwarfed, made irrelevant even, by Sarge's message.

"He's like a homemade guy," Lee insists. "He's not trying to be stylized at all. It's so homemade and simple. He's not a harmonica player or a singer. He's Sarge. He uses poetry and music and whatever it takes to deliver a message from the heart. And his message is more important than the playing. That is not to be misunderstood that the playing isn't important. The message comes *through* the playing. Whatever he's gotta do, the important thing is he's trying to deliver the message. Does he deliver it well? I would say, yes!"

As his career blossomed, Leslie became his manager, booking agent, and publicist, organizing Sarge's appearances and orchestrating his busy schedule. And Sarge did what he does best: entertain.

The Lintecums, meanwhile, became a living resource for other vets, especially those in trouble. Sarge and Leslie literally saved lives, talking vets out of suicide over the phone, donating their time and money when possible, and generally going out of their way to give the kind of help they so desperately needed decades earlier.

Leslie went back to school, taking advantage of benefits from the VA, and earned a pair of Associate of Arts degrees, one in science and one in the arts, at Phoenix College. Sarge, too, attended Phoenix College, where he took all the art classes he could and "majored in recess."

#

These days, Sarge and Leslie rent a comfortable house in Tempe not far from Colt, who is married and has two kids of his own.

"My mom and dad have found some success," Colt says thoughtfully, "but they never forget that they want to help people. They've never gotten self-absorbed, where they just want to make money and get ahead. That means a lot to the veterans they deal with. When a veteran calls and asks, 'Can you help us?' their first response is always, 'Yes,' not, 'Is this a paying gig?'"

Max echoes his older brother, saying, "My dad doesn't sell out. He could probably be real big if he was a flag-waiving, patriotic guy, but he sticks to his guns and tells what's real, no matter what the cost."

Fortunately for Carrie and Max, childhood has been a little more stable – and a little more comfortable – than the kind their older siblings knew. Of course, there has been somewhat of a tradeoff. Colt and Brandy saw more of their parents, even if some of the time spent together was tense and the stakes were dire. Ultimately, all four kids have had a fairly unorthodox upbringing. All four have been home schooled, at least initially. And all four enjoyed plenty of time on the road, either between homes or, as in the younger kids' case, between gigs.

"I hear a lot of stories from my older brother and sister about my parents and how they used to be," Max says. "They kind of calmed down by the time they had me. We lived in Patagonia, but I was too young to remember any of that. I only remember three homes, including this one. There hasn't been that much jumping around. In my younger days, we used to go on a lot of road trips for my dad's performances. We once drove to Maine, just loaded everything up. It took us three weeks to get there because we had a bunch of shows on the way. I just remember having a lot of fun with Carrie in the back seat as we drove to places."

Adds Max, "Just the other day, we were riding in the car, going to get some movies. I told Dad he makes the best role model that I can think of. He can teach me so much stuff that's morally right. It's hard to understand how my dad can do what he's done and hold down such a nice family. We all get along together so well. It's very rare when me and my siblings fight or my parents fight. That's not something you'll find in families, period, much less in one with a dad who went through such horrible stuff. Just seeing a happy family every day for him probably heals stuff."

The Lintecum kids agree that both parents, despite or perhaps *because of* their unconventional lifestyle, are excellent teachers. Over the years, Leslie and Sarge tailored their lessons to each child. And they played different roles – confidante or drill sergeant – when needed.

Mostly, they taught through example.

"What's impressed me most is their undivided love for each other every day," Carrie, nineteen, says. "I feel really blessed that they're able to still love each other. Every day they seem to love each other more. They grow together, not apart."

Brandy, though, is quick to point out the nuances that exist – both in the present and in the past.

"My father has always had that communication with his children and his wife and his close friends," she says. "The difference is that, during those dark moments, he's just remembering the horrific things he's seen. Those incidents of depression or upset have just decreased in frequency. As a younger person, he was just like any young person; he was more active, and more apt to react. For the decade of the '70s, maybe all veterans were pretty much living in Viet Nam still. In the '80s, it seems as though you could go one way or another. My dad found music as an outlet. By the '90s he was a hundred times more sociable. But he was always teaching something – he taught my friends growing up how to play guitar. And he still battles bad times.

"It wasn't that bad early on. And it isn't perfect now."

#

When they talk about their generation, both Leslie and Sarge evince a painful sense of loss. Viet Nam vets are still taking their lives, consciously or unconsciously, overtly or covertly. Countless abuse drugs or alcohol – or both. And many are still searching for someplace to call home.

The statistics, whether focused on homelessness or suicide or PTSD, are nebulous at best. There are varying degrees, varying levels of suffering. But the war rages on.

"It was the war we lost," Professor Moise explains, "and America is not supposed to lose wars. Most wars are fought badly in one way or another. Warfare in general is the least well conducted of all human activities. If you win, this helps gloss over the memory of how badly it was done. If you don't win, then the memory is likely to stick in people's craws."

Professor Moise draws his own conclusions for how and why we lost the war. But he's quick to point out that there is no predominant school of thought on the issue.

"I'm not sure I'm eager for consensus," he says. "There is virtue in lack of consensus. We thought we learned from World War I, and our suppositions brought us into World War II. We thought we learned from that war, and our suppositions brought us into Viet Nam."

Says Leslie, "I don't know where it ends with Viet Nam. I know our grandchildren will be dealing with it to some extent. Even the wives. Sometimes I feel like *I* have PTSD. It's a legacy."

What can be done to finally put the war to rest?

"Nothing that comes to mind," Professor Moise says. "There are some particular individuals for whom something can happen that will help put it to rest. But for the vets as a general group, I don't think there's a recipe."

#

Every Sunday afternoon, Sarge, Colt, and Uncle Dave (Sarge's brother) get together for a game of dice at Sarge and Leslie's place. It's a 20-year-old tradition that started in Patagonia and traveled with the family to Tempe. The men play for hours until, eventually, they call it quits for the night and go their separate ways.

Afterward, Sarge reconnects with Leslie and basks in the glow of his family.

"Every day we're more in love than the day before," he says of Leslie. "It's unbelievable to me. My family – this is my reward for doing Nam. I've never bought a lottery ticket. I feel like it would be redundant."

Chapter 10: Career Moves
The Rudow Family

Talking with a Viet Nam vet is like peeling an onion.

Slowly, subtly, the layers fall away. Reticence becomes effusion. The unspeakable . . . catharsis. The vet's voice rises on a tremor. And the past becomes the present. Immediate. Percussive. Enough to shake the earth beneath your feet. Somewhere a dam breaks. And the moment, as clear as it was three decades ago, comes pouring free.

"It was a typical day, really," the vet says. "We were out walking all day. It was really muddy. I fell into this river in over my head, and my friend took a picture. I still have the picture. My hair's all plastered down. My clothes are stuck to my body. Right after that, we got fire from a nearby village.

"We brought fire down on them. It wasn't really a village. Just a collection of hootches. Kids. Women. Old people. Blown to shit. They were all screaming and crying."

His voice cracks, and the vet pauses, searching for control.

"There's this little Viet Namese girl," he continues. "She looks like a little China doll. She's staring at her hand. It was blown in half.

"She's just beautiful."

The vet is Martin Rudow, a 59-year-old editor and publisher who makes his home in Seattle, Washington. He's driving the winding coast to California, where his mother-in-law is dying of cancer. Beside him sits his youngest son Matt, a history major at the University of Washington who dreams of studying law. Martin's on his cell phone, reliving a moment that he has spent the better part of his adult life trying to, if not forget, at least transcend.

Like so many other Viet Nam vets, Martin came home from the war and threw himself into the business of moving on with his life. And like so many other Viet Nam vets, he has done an admirable job of building something normal from the ashes of man's most ludicrous pastime: war.

A husband. A father. A career man. Martin throws himself at his work with the same kind of zeal the ghosts of his past call upon while doggedly chasing him. He works. He concentrates. He outruns the past. But still it comes.

"Another medic and I and a couple other foot soldiers went in to help," he says later. "That's when our helicopters came in and just let us have it. I was pretty lucky, actually. My elbow was laid open. I could see the joint. My knuckles, too, so I could see the tendons and the bones in my hand. I just felt numb all over, and there's this ringing in your ears. When I relaxed, blood was squirting about six inches out of my chest. I thought I hit an artery. My lung was punctured. My face had so many pieces of shrapnel in it – I put my hand up to it and just felt gore. It wasn't a pleasant day.

"I have these cuts in my chest you can still see. But it missed my heart, my eyes, my teeth. If I had just collapsed right there and lost consciousness, I would have died. My lungs would have filled with blood. But the other medic put the plastic wrapper from a bandage over my chest. That seals it. A regular bandage would get full of blood. Then you'd breathe through the blood and pull blood into your lungs.

"Once I knew I was gonna live, there was an exhilaration. I didn't feel any pain. They don't give you morphine for a chest wound anyway. I was hurting, but there's this huge adrenaline rush. If you're an athlete, your adrenal gland is quite developed anyway. And I always had a great finishing sprint. It really kicked in."

#

Martin Louis Rudow was born in Seattle on June 2, 1943, the first of three children. His father Harold worked for a scientific supplies company but should have been a stand-up comedian. Or a writer. At times bordering on manic-depressive, he was a crazy character, bright but not exactly affectionate. Martin's mother Kay also had difficulty showing warmth. A Phi Beta Kappa and public health nurse turned career housewife, she nevertheless imbued her children with liberal idealism. Both parents had high expectations for their children. They taught them how to laugh, and how to think for themselves.

Martin attended venerable Franklin High on the west side of Seattle's Mount Baker neighborhood, where he ran cross country and track. From there he went east of the Cascade Mountains to Ellensburg, home of Central Washington University and back then a tiny cow town. At Central, he was a self-described "mediocre" distance runner, covering two miles in nine minutes and forty-two seconds. He didn't distinguish himself until he discovered racewalking, at the time only an AAU (American Athletic Union) event and not one he could race at the collegiate level.

He spent a lot of his time on the road, either logging miles or driving back to Seattle for weekend races. By his junior year, he was one of the nation's top ten racewalkers. He showed up at the '64 U.S. Olympic Trials relatively untested on the national level, but hopeful.

"I got blown out," says Martin, who finished twenty-fourth out of seventy competitors in the twenty-kilometer race. "I was never in it. It was just nerves."

Undeterred, he continued to race – and win – on the local and regional levels. He graduated from Central in December 1965, earning a bachelor's degree in sociology. The following spring, he set the national record for fifty kilometers.

As Viet Nam continued to heat up, he applied for grad school at the University of Washington and was accepted. Before graduating from Central, he had also applied for a deferment at the local draft board, detailing when he would start grad school.

"I wrote the present year [1965] instead of next year," Martin says with equal parts amusement and bitterness.

The mistake cost him. He was drafted a few months later in May.

"I walked in the door [of the induction center] on May 10, 1966," he recalls. "I was very excited, actually. I wasn't happy, but I was excited. It was going to be an adventure. I didn't have a girlfriend or anything like that I left behind. I was twenty-two at the time – much older than most of the kids getting drafted."

As for the war, he didn't think twice.

"I basically thought we should be there and that we were doing the right thing," he remembers. "I wasn't a super patriot about it, but I would have said yes, we should be there. I really thought we were such a great country and we were invincible and could beat anybody. It was a carryover from World War II. I feel so different about the whole thing now. I felt different before my two years were up."

#

In the prime of his youth and ready to take the racewalking world by storm, Martin instead reported to boot camp in Fort

Riley, Kansas, a miserable dustbowl far removed from the temperate environs of Seattle.

"Christ," he says, "it was in the middle of summer. I had never been in weather like that before. It was just an oven, a blast furnace. There was no attraction to this place at all. It was ugly, flat, brown."

Martin quickly found out that, although easy going and not exactly the prototypical American GI, he was far better prepared for the training than most of his fellow soldiers. For him, boot camp was, in fact, a joke.

"I was in such good shape," he says. "A whole bunch of guys in my unit were from Brooklyn. They were tough guys but so out of shape. We'd go on these forced marches, and I'd be eating and talking, and they'd just be dying."

His only shortcoming: he couldn't throw a hand grenade to save his life. So Martin aced four of the five physical proficiency tests used to measure the new soldiers.

As often happens in the military, Martin befriended someone who happened to be standing next to him in line when the troops were organized alphabetically. He actually met Bob Reedy in Seattle before the two went to Fort Ord, where they were issued their fatigues. From there, they went to Fort Riley and then Fort Sam Houston to train as medics.

Bob, a native of Eastern Washington, busts a gut whenever he rehashes those first few weeks together.

At six feet three inches, Martin stood above the rest of his fellow soldiers. So he was often singled out for the worst duties. Bob, seven inches shorter, made a habit of standing next to him in formation, knowing that officers never picked two soldiers in a row and that the looming Martin would always be the first to go.

"They made Martin a platoon leader," Bob recalls. "He hated that. He'd say, 'Please, guys . . . march!' And nobody listened to him."

Bob's favorite story from boot camp is Martin's, as well. While running a mile time trial on the track, Martin found himself being "encouraged" by a young upstart lieutenant on the final lap.

"He tried to chase me on the last lap," Martin says. "He was tapping me on the butt with a stick, trying to be all macho. I just burned him. He didn't last a hundred yards. The guy was such a jerk."

"You had to be able to run a mile in six minutes in your gear," Bob explains. "Marty could do that with his eyes closed and not even break a sweat. He was just loping along, and he was just gonna do it in six minutes. This lieutenant comes out to pace him on his last lap. And Marty just opened up." Bob chuckles. "He's almost finished, and here comes the lieutenant walking across the field from the other side of the track. He hadn't even lasted half a lap with him. Martin could walk as fast as most people could run."

Martin ended up stopping the watches at five minutes, twelve seconds. Not exactly jogging.

He wanted to join the Army track team. Unfortunately, he had been drafted in the Ninth Division, which was already slated to go en masse to Viet Nam.

"I knew the Army track coach," Martin says. "He said he'd love to have me, but there was nothing he could do."

#

The Ninth Division was the last group in U.S. history to be deployed by a troop ship. The men left the U.S. shore on January 4, 1967, and arrived in Viet Nam on the first of February.

The trip was nauseating. Tiny bunks. Huge waves.

"To get to the deck, you had to walk up several flights of steep stairs," Martin says. "I got to the top and got out, and all I could see were the asses of these guys who were all bent over the rail vomiting. A solid row of khaki butts lined up."

The men spent most of their time in the bowels of the ship, living in cramped quarters and eating gruel while the officers dined and slept in relative luxury above. Despite the conditions, Martin discovered a bond with his fellow grunts and relished the fact that he was an enlisted man.

As they came ashore at Vung Tau, the men were greeted by a band, and donuts and coffee for the officers. They boarded trucks and followed a convoy through the rice paddies and into the jungle. It was blistering hot.

"There were all these little kids yelling good things to us and at the same time giving us obscene gestures as we drove by," he says. "I remember seeing these huge black spiders sitting on webs – more like strands – between the telephone poles."

Martin and Bob parted ways initially, with Bob's unit going into the field and Martin's staying behind to fortify the base camp.

"We started sandbagging the thing like there was no tomorrow," he says. "It was really hard work in the hot sun. The first day we dug ourselves in and sandbagged around ourselves. Then we just started sandbagging everything. One guy had a record player and one 45 with two songs in it: *Sugar Town* and *These Boots Were Made for Walking* by Nancy Sinatra. I could sing both songs from start to finish by the time we were finished, and I still can."

The weeks went by at base camp, with only an occasional round of artillery to puncture the calm. The men would do roll call, followed by sick call. Martin would treat ingrown toenails, change bandages – the basics.

Half the time he was assigned to the hospital unit, where he gave VD shots until his thumb felt like it was going to fall off. He also treated civilians and saw more puss and oozing infections than he'd care to remember.

Life got more interesting – and dangerous – when he and his unit were rotated into the field, which for them meant the Mekong Delta. Their principle enemy, other than snakes, spiders, scorpions, heat, rot, and disease, was the Vietcong.

"It was so wet you couldn't stay out long," he says. "Terribly wet. Hot and humid. A miserable fucking place. If you stayed out too long, your feet would get rot. Every chance I got I'd take my shoes and socks off, wring out my socks, and hang 'em up to dry. I didn't want to ruin my racewalking career."

The missions typically lasted one to seven days. The men would wake up at sunrise, stand to, and then march into the jungle on a search-and-destroy mission. Hours of boredom were spliced by minutes of terror. Mines, booby traps, and snipers all took their toll.

"Sometimes we were transported by helicopter into hot LZ's [landing zones]," he says. "The grass would be blowing from the helicopter blades, and we'd land in muck. We'd be taking fire, but we'd be afraid to get too close to the dikes, which were usually mined. Sometimes you'd just stay in the middle of this shit and stay low. Unfortunately, somebody would get hit. Then you'd have to go out and get 'em."

Martin and his fellow medics would treat the wounded soldiers where they fell. Typically, a sniper would shoot the lead man on a patrol and then wait for the medic to come to his aid before opening up on him, too. While everyone else sat around waiting for an air strike, the medic had to go to anyone who hollered, "Medic!"

"Most days, though, nothing would happen," Martin says. "We'd just walk around all day, find booby traps, walk in water up to our necks. Every so often someone would step on a booby trap or a trip wire, which would trigger a bamboo tube full of explosives, rocks, nails, and shit. They just go up and blow your face off. They were often set to blow up crotch high."

As was the case on both sides, it made more strategic sense to maim someone than kill them outright. A wounded soldier required medical help and at least a couple of soldiers to carry him out.

Martin passed his days as best he could, all the while reading running magazines and keeping tabs on all his competitors back home. He trained at base camp, always with a firearm handy, and inspired awe and perhaps a little incredulity in his fellow soldiers, who typically crashed – or grabbed a bottle and a pack of smokes – as soon as the day's duties were completed.

A big fan of Joseph Heller's classic novel *Catch 22*, Martin saw examples of black comedy and dark humor all around him.

As his wife Judy would recall decades later, "He's always been able to find humor in things, which doesn't mean he takes things lightly. He just has an ability to see their absurdity."

He had a writer's eye for detail, as well as the compassion that goes along with it. He did carry a rifle, and even fired it a few times into the tree line. But to this day he hopes he never hit anyone.

Before Martin got wounded and was awarded the Purple Heart, Bob Reedy earned his own Purple Heart while coming to the aid of someone in a minefield. He remembers the painful aftermath, when Martin was instructed to use a nylon brush to help keep the wound open so the shrapnel could work itself out.

"Marty was too gentle," Bob recalls. "It seemed to hurt him as much as it did me when he was brushing it. He was such a gentle, caring person. He was like a brother to me."

Later, a doctor took the brush and finished the job.

"Oh, did that hurt," Bob says.

On the day the small village was essentially massacred, Martin had no idea what was coming until he himself was bleeding. In retrospect, the moments between watching the artillery flatten the hootches and then taking fire himself are easy to discern. Images, sounds, his body's reaction – all intertwine with the rhythm of sequence and linear causation. Sensation is heightened. And memory becomes more vivid than the present.

But at the time, the episode unfolded rapidly and unpredictably. Shrapnel splintered and found its way into Martin's body. Before he could assess the situation, he had been patched up and was himself attending to the wounded.

Eventually, the endorphin and adrenaline high faded, and he came down.

"The medevac helicopter was so overloaded it was scary," he remembers. "I thought it was gonna crash. It was just loaded with dead and wounded. There was a medic on board, and he was so scared he just stared at us. I was going around putting bandages on people. It had to be done. People were dying. The guy didn't do anything. Finally, I said, 'Hand me some bandages.' There was so much blood in the helicopter that it would sway one way and the blood would run out that way. Then it would sway the other way, and the blood would run out that way.

"The kids still stick with me. And I wasn't even a parent at that time. Now it would be so much worse. They were lining us up at the hospital. We just stood in line. Boy, there was some butchery going on there."

The doctors patched Martin up, taking one hundred pieces of American-made metal from his body in the process. He spent ten days in the hospital before he was sent to a hospital ship to recoup for a month. He spent the remainder of his tour back at Camp Bear Cat.

#

While recouping from his own wounds, Martin went to Tokyo for some much-needed R&R. He had managed to train some on the base, despite wearing a cast. In Tokyo, the weather turned cool the second night after he arrived.

He went for a run at an officer training school, its grounds beautifully manicured with ornamental trees and a sprawling green lawn.

Twilight. A cool breeze. Lights twinkling on in the surrounding buildings. The enchanted scene afforded him an epiphany of sorts, a triumphant release from the horror of combat.

"I had the ultimate runner's high," he says. "I've never had a feeling like that in all my life. There are no words to describe the feeling I had. It was just pure elation. Ecstasy. It went on for thirty minutes . . . peace."

A few weeks later, Martin came close to recapturing, if not the same feeling, at least something equally intense. He was going home. As his plane lifted off the runway in Saigon on January 10, 1968, he looked down at a world that would follow him the rest of his life.

"It was just an unbelievable sensation," he says. "I've never had anything like it since. It was kind of like the last day of school, but you're not a little kid anymore. And you know the future isn't going to be rosy."

\#

What does a vet do when he comes home from war?

Like everyone around him, Martin had been trained how to dress a wound, keep his head down, and fire an M-16 at phantom muzzle bursts in the tree line.

What now?

What . . . now?

Martin landed first in Oakland, where he endured several agonizingly long hours of waiting around, standing in lines, and getting his orders punched.

"There was no deprogramming killers," he remembers. "Cripes, that's a joke."

An officer told Martin and the others gathered around, "You're gonna see some old friend and say, 'Hey, Pete, you motherfucker!' But that's not how people talk."

That was it. The men had been debriefed.

Martin went home to Seattle. His parents threw him a party, and several old friends of the family came to show their support. One couple even told Martin they had prayed for him every night while he was in Viet Nam.

"Nobody knew quite how to talk to me," Martin remembers. "But I think my dad was pretty proud of me because he was 4F in World War II."

The party was as close to a hero's welcome as any vet would receive after coming home from Viet Nam. Martin quickly assessed the volatile mood on the home front and found his own feelings about the war ambivalent as well. One of his own sisters, Margaret, then a student at UW, was a vociferous anti-war demonstrator.

Martin's tour, of course, was not over. He still had some time left on his two-year stint, the remainder of which he spent at Fort Campbell, Kentucky. The lieutenant in charge knew about Martin's racewalking goals and was supportive of them. He let Martin go out and train every day. And he looked the other way when Martin fudged the rules.

"We had to give a phone number of where we would be at all times in case we were called in because of potential riot control duty," Martin says. "This was 1968. There were race riots going on nearby. In the evening, you could only get out to go to the beer hall. You had to give the number of the beer hall – there were several on base – so they could call you and get you back quick. If you went anywhere else, you would get in big trouble. This certainly included going out to train.

"So I came up with the idea of giving them the number of the office at the track. I put on my shorts and T-shirt under my uniform and carried my shoes stuck down my pants leg. I went to the track and slid under a fence – which was locked up for some reason – changed by taking off my uniform, and did my workout, reversing the process to return. It was real quiet at the track, so if I heard the phone ring, I would hightail it back to the barracks. This worked. I did it about ten to twelve times. One time the phone did ring in the middle of a training session. I immediately changed and took off for the barracks, but it must have been a wrong number."

What had sustained him in the Mekong Delta now took center stage in Martin's life. He was almost giddy with anticipation, and he attacked his training with unparalleled focus and discipline. At weaker moments, he wondered if he was good enough, if he could rise to the occasion, if he could make good on the passion that had burned so fiercely while he waited out his tour in Viet Nam.

His moment came in May at the U.S. National Racewalking Championships in Sacramento, three weeks after he had finally finished his two-year tour in the Army. A dark horse who had disappeared from radar the last two years, Martin finished fifth, surprising the field and earning a trip to the Olympic Trials, which were to be staged in two races. The top ten from the first race would train together at high altitude in South Lake Tahoe, Colorado. Martin grabbed seventh, and took his place on the ten-man training squad. At the final race, he earned first runner-up, just missing a bid to the 1968 Olympics.

"I was training seventy miles a week at the time," Martin remembers. "Lake Tahoe . . . that was my reward."

Though he didn't make the Olympic team, Martin kept the pressure on. He was only twenty-six, and the next Olympics were still a distinct possibility. He moved to Pomona, California, to train with the nation's best racewalkers. He also took classes at the University of California, Riverside. He planned on moving on to UCLA, where he had been accepted into the master's program for sociology.

But something didn't click. Something felt wrong.

"One day I saw this guy I had known in the Army, a complete idiot," Martin recalls. "He was speaking at an anti-war rally on campus. That was like the last straw. I dropped out of UC, Riverside. I had people asking me to participate in the protests. It wasn't that I didn't agree with them. I just thought they didn't know what they were talking about. Like they didn't have the right. *They weren't there.* You wanted to justify what you did. You felt like such a fool for what you went through and what your friends went through if that was just a big mistake."

The protestors, however inarticulate or misinformed, had struck a nerve. Years later, Martin would, for the most part, agree with them. Even then, he knew instinctively that the war was wrong, that a "credibility gap" existed in the White House and the Pentagon. But at the time, he couldn't handle the hypocrisy from either faction. He had served his country. He had done his time. To question the war was to cast a shadow over his own sacrifice.

Unfocused but searching, Martin floundered for the next few months. He suffered a string of short-term relationships. And before 1969 was two months old, he blew out his knee.

"That was it," he said of his racewalking career.

#

Though perhaps a pariah to some in the anti-war movement, Martin had little difficulty in finding a job. He got a break when he needed one most.

"I was a salesman for Kraft Food Company," he recalls. "The guy hired me with zero experience. But I had fought in Viet Nam. A lot of people supported the war in Viet Nam, and those were the people who were hiring."

Martin made deliveries to stores, stocked the shelves, and put up displays. Initially, he struggled. He was unsupervised and wholly inexperienced. Sales intimidated him. But he kept at it until he was more than competent at his work.

"I used to think sometimes after what I went through in Viet Nam, how could I be nervous about these things?" he says. "But I still was. Hearing someone call 'Medic!' two hundred yards away in a rice paddy with bullets flying by – and then I'd be nervous about going in to talk to some grocer about putting up a display! It used to really frustrate me about myself."

Adds Martin, "It's real simple in combat. You go straight ahead, and you do what you have to do. It's like sports heroes who can't do anything else. Middle-aged parents trying to raise their kids and hold onto jobs – that's heroism."

Martin would find that out soon enough.

#

Despite being unable to train or compete because of his knee, Martin kept in touch with his passion. He had made several friends in the racewalking community, and he stayed close to them by keeping involved with his sport. He manned a stopwatch, put on races – even judged races.

Then he met his future wife Judy.

Martin found in her a wellspring of compassion and tenderness. They were different in many ways. His experiences in Viet Nam would, in future years, sometimes drive a wedge between them. But there was something there. Something worth building on.

"I was dating a friend of his," Judy recalls. "A friend of mine called me up and asked if I could get a date for Martin. But my friends all said, 'Well, if he can't get a date for Saturday night ....' So the three of us went out. And I was very attracted to him. I thought he was very handsome."

At the time, Judy was working as a photo lab technician at Pomona's daily paper, *The Progress Bulletin*. One of Martin's housemates happened to work there, too. Judy mentioned to him that she found Martin handsome. The housemate passed the news on to Martin, who called Judy on the phone and asked her out on a date.

A little over a year later, the two were married.

"Martin didn't talk about the war that much," Judy says of their early years together. "But when he did, those were incredibly intimate moments. It was obviously an extremely emotional time for him. So what he shared was really powerful stuff. It wasn't just off the cuff. It took a while for him to trust me.

"Even though Martin wasn't a whiner or a complainer, I thought the war had hurt him and scarred him deeply. And he would talk about these experiences. Often the first stories were hysterically funny, just unbelievably funny. But when we went beyond those stories, they were things that I don't think people should have to experience."

Had the war changed him?

"It's hard for me to answer that because I didn't know him before he went," Judy says, "so I don't know what kind of a person he was before. But by the time I met him, the war certainly was a big part of who he was. He was trying to find out what he wanted to do. Maybe because of the way the Viet Nam vets were looked at and not appreciated, I think he didn't have a lot of confidence. He was still treading and trying to find out what he should do with his life – and certainly recovering."

Martin never lost his focus – racewalking – while in Viet Nam. He rejoined his quest as soon as his feet touched American soil. But to go on without acknowledging the war and his experiences in Viet Nam would have been difficult at best. Injuring his knee – and subsequently losing that primal outlet of training and racing – made such a feat impossible.

\#

The young couple moved around for a few years before having their first son, Kurt, in San Jose in 1973. Martin, meanwhile, had been at Kraft for five years when he came to a crossroads: he was up for a big promotion, a career move really, and to take it would mean moving to Chicago.

"I don't think when Martin came back from Viet Nam that he ever imagined doing what he's doing now," Judy says. "I think he imagined himself doing something very different. But I also think that Martin really did learn somewhere along the line to honor your passion. Perhaps that did come from Viet Nam – that life is short, and if you love something, pursue it."

Instead of taking the promotion at Kraft, Martin got in on the ground floor as a marketing director at *Runner's World*, then run out of a small office in Palo Alto. Now it's the nation's most popular running magazine. He didn't stay long; the guy who ran it was, in Martin's estimation, an utter jerk. But the move signaled a lifelong commitment to the magazine business.

A year later, Martin, Judy, and little Kurt returned to Martin's childhood haunt, Seattle, where Martin caught on with *Fishing and Hunting News*. After that he and Judy both went to work for another startup publication that would eventually succeed enormously: *The Seattle Weekly*.

"It was a wonderful, incredible ride," Martin recalls, "and I was real active in racewalking by then, as well. There was no money in either. But I sure was challenged. This is why I like doing what I'm doing now so much. I have to do things that let me use all my talents. Even if it's something I'm not very good at. Just something that lets me use everything."

While Martin was flourishing, Judy had had enough. She left the magazine, and the couple briefly separated.

"She said she'd never come back if I stayed at *The Seattle Weekly*," Martin remembers.

"Things have been a bit of struggle," Judy explains, "particularly early on. I think Martin felt rather than go out and earn a lot of money, he had to give back to the world somehow. Maybe Martin in all of this lost part of his sense of value. He wasn't sure what he was worth. He spent a number of years, particularly in the 1980s, giving back, and I'm not sure to what. He did a lot of volunteering for racewalking. Took a small paycheck in order to launch *The Seattle Weekly*.

"I think he lost a bit of his soul in Viet Nam. A part of Martin was left there – a sense of who he was – because maybe he was doing something that he didn't feel right about doing but that he had to do. So when he came home, he felt kind of hollow. He tried to fill that up by doing good deeds to make sure people loved him and appreciated him. Not just his family and friends, but the country. I think a lot of vets were looking for that from the country. And they never got it."

Their marriage survived, while Martin's career continued to evolve. He helped launch *Washington Magazine*, another upper-echelon publication, before eventually working for Group Health as the editor of *View* magazine.

At *View*, he ran into a problem common among vets with combat experience.

"I was having a hard time managing a department," he explains. "We did an evaluation, and they wrote down their complaints against me. I thought it was a bunch of meaningless bullshit. How could they get worked up about this? It's just nothing. My job counselor told me that's a typical response by someone who's been in combat. For those people, this was the biggest thing they'd faced."

Not so for Martin. Still, he gamely hung on despite a lack of support from upper management.

"I stayed there for three or four years," he says. "The pay and benefits were so good that, even though I hated it, I would have stayed. I'd still be there. I remember thinking, I've done all these great things, now I'm gonna hunker down and stick with it. But I couldn't kiss ass. I paid the price; I got laid off."

Despite losing the job, Martin continued to cultivate his standing in the racewalking community. In 1988, he had coached the U.S. Olympic squad in Seoul, capping off four years of international travel and coaching. His career reached its zenith in 1996 in Atlanta, where he served as chief judge for the men's 20-kilometer race.

Money, though, was still an issue. Martin passed on a couple of lucrative job offers so that he could officiate in the '96 Olympics. Afterward, he put himself and his family in a financial hole when he made a walking instruction video and wrote a book to support it. He toured the country, doing clinics while hoping to cash in on the walking boom. After a strong start, the business fizzled, and Martin was still in the red.

It was 1998. For many his age, retirement wasn't that far around the corner, and Martin was still trying to make ends meet. Once again, opportunity presented itself when needed most, this time in the form of the editor position at *Northwest Runner*.

"I had reached what I thought was the absolute lowest ebb," he says. "I had applied to a daily newspaper for a sales job, and I couldn't even get that. That scared me. And the whole walking thing was going to pot."

The editing job wasn't exactly lucrative, though a huge amount of work. But it, combined with cranking out *Vintage Drift*, a quarterly magazine dedicated to vintage sportscar racing, and Reno's *Hot August Nights* program, helped Martin pay the bills. It continues to do so today, which gives Martin the luxury of thinking about the future.

"My dream is to have a publishing company."

#

Perspective. Perhaps when he came home from Viet Nam, a scarred young man determined to go on with his life, Martin lacked a little. He didn't know exactly where he was going. But he found a road out, and he followed it as best he could. Of course, though he dodged the pitfalls common to many who returned from the war, he couldn't escape the war itself. Nor could he escape life back home. Or himself.

He'll be the first to tell you that, in the end, that's all a soldier has.

"I didn't expect anything from the government when I got back," he says resolutely. "Look at what the people from World War II got. They got nothing. I had a better perspective than a lot of people had, I guess. When you come back, it's your life now."

Martin has some empathy for those from the war who came home addicted to heroin, or disabled by Post-Traumatic Stress Disorder, or reduced to an empty shell of their former selves. But his empathy knows limits.

"If you went in fucked up," he says, "you came home fucked up."

An oversimplification, perhaps. A generalization, certainly. But Martin's dogged refusal to give in to the war on any level is essentially what separates him from those still mired in the horrors of Viet Nam. And it's precisely what inspires and informs his two sons to this day.

"I think he spent a lot of time trying to reshape himself after Viet Nam and not allowing those experiences to shape him," Kurt explains. "A lot of people who went to Viet Nam let it destroy them. What impresses me most about my dad is that he came back and raised a family and led a normal life. I know there's a lot he could have done personally had it not been for Viet Nam. I think he's had to spend a lot of time focusing on not reliving the war or letting those experiences shape who he is."

Adds Kurt, "He had pretty good support with his family when he came back. He had a loving family, his mother especially. That helps. A lot of people came back to nothing."

Neither son knows much about their father's war. He rarely talks about it, and when he does, he ruminates over the lighter moments, slapstick humor merging with dark comedy. When a war movie comes on the TV, he leaves the room, quietly and without a fuss.

Instead of the war, their father talks about the future. The lessons are multidimensional, with as much nuance as grit. Work hard and focus as best you can. But don't take life – or yourself – too seriously.

"He's one of the greatest men I've ever known, if not *the* greatest man," Kurt maintains. "I think that sometimes he feels as though those experiences might have hindered him in being a man later on. Sometimes he wants to completely escape them. And of course there's no way he can. But he's done a hell of a job."

Martin, meanwhile, would be the first to say that he hasn't come this far alone. His career entices him. His sons inspire him. And his wife steadies him, especially when the war comes back from the past to haunt him.

"I have a recurring dream that people are wounded and screaming," he says. "And I can't find my bag. It's a horrible feeling."

Early on, those dreams were violent, shocking nightmares from which he awoke in a cold sweat. Judy was there to talk him through each one.

Judy's father, a World War II vet, spent years trying to shake off the war in his sleep. On the other side of the wall, she listened. And learned.

"I remember watching my mom deal with my dad," she says, "particularly his bad dreams and nightmares. She was such a great role model for me. I could hear them at night, and I could hear her console him. When Martin had those dreams early on, it didn't frighten me. I remember hearing my mother's soothing voice. And I would try to do that for Martin.

"I know that was what I was supposed to do. My mom had given me those skills unknowingly. She didn't know I had lain in bed and listened to her talk Dad through the nightmares."

Unbeknownst to them, John and Janer Rowbottom had given their daughter a firsthand education in coping with war's heart-wrenching aftermath.

#

In the play *Streamers*, a group of men have been drafted together, and they're waiting for their assignments.

"They're afraid that the war will sweep them off their feet," Martin says, "and they'll be plunged into it. That's how we felt. It sounds corny, but the best way to put it was like you were sliding off a cliff."

When a parachute doesn't open, its streamers dangle free in the breeze. Martin often thinks about what life would have been like had he not been called upon by his country to go to war, or had he not answered the call.

The adventure taught him at least one thing about himself.

"I'll do what I have to do," he says. "I'll do what's required of me."

What of the little Viet Namese girl, bloodied and in shock yet somehow radiating innocence and beauty, who still haunts him today?

Maybe he sees her in his own two sons, now grown but still his little boys. Maybe he sees her in the faces of the many men who never came home from the war. Maybe he sees her in the dumb, plodding futility of the war; the savage beauty of Viet Nam and its recalcitrant warrior citizens; his own old soul, forever scarred by a war he helped fight but never believed in. Maybe.

"You can never be a civilian again. Whether that means you hate the military and would never pay taxes to the military-industrial complex, or you're a knee-jerk patriot. You can never be a civilian again."

Chapter 11: Honor Restored
The Gray Family

The drive from Collingswood, New Jersey, to Sumner, Illinois, is a long one. I began the 830-mile journey alone on March 12, 1969, arriving fifteen hours later at an old Sumner farmhouse just past three o'clock in the morning. I had left my family in Collingswood so my daughter and youngest son could finish out the school year while I made our new home habitable.

Local boy Michael Seibert was already in Viet Nam. So was my oldest son. So, too, was Kenny Hayes. Within a few hours I would meet Kenny's father, a great man who could work as hard as anyone I knew.

It was cold as hell outside – 13 degrees above zero – and spring was nowhere in sight. I sat in my big truck, which was piled high with personal possessions, household goods, and shop tools, and studied my new home. The old farmhouse sat on the ground. No running water. No toilet.

Huddled under a couple of blankets, my breath freezing as it escaped my lips, I finally fell asleep in the frigid cab. When the sun came up, I awoke to see my new neighbor John Gray (no relation) walking toward me. He welcomed me, and his wife Phyllis graciously offered to fix breakfast for me.

Before I could get started on the farmhouse, I had another more pressing chore to tackle: sowing clover seed on twenty-five acres of wheat that the prior owner had planted. I had to sow the clover – by hand – now because it was the last dark-of-the-moon day fit for sowing seed. So after breakfast with my new neighbors, I started up a tractor I had bought a year earlier. By this time, it was about eight in the morning. As I rumbled toward the back of the property, the tractor hesitated, and I found myself stuck in deep silt at the north end of the pond. I had thought it was solid ground.

I checked with Phyllis, and she called Raymond Hayes, who lived one mile due west. Raymond arrived with his own tractor and pulled me free. Thus began a loyal friendship that would endure three decades, until Raymond passed away a few years ago. As the years went by, two of Raymond's sons would work for me on the farm, baling hay and toiling without complaint. One of his daughters would work alongside my wife at the hospital. Raymond fathered ten children in all, raising them alone after his wife passed away at an early age.

He and I would both lose a son – one to the bottom of Olney Lake, and one to a fractured relationship. A few country miles away, Stanley Seibert, another father and close friend of mine, would lose his son to a fiery helicopter crash in the jungles of Viet Nam. Three fathers and their sons. All of us casualties of a war no one won.

#

Southeastern Illinois has always been home. Its fertile soil has nurtured the maternal side of the Gray family for more than 160 years. Timothy, corn, wheat, oats, rye, barley, and sorghum cane. Beef and dairy cows. Hogs. Chickens. Geese. By the time I was born on November 22, 1923, my parents, like my maternal grandparents before them, were successful, hard-working farmers who gave as much to the land as they took from it.

Several months earlier, Jesse and Ethel were sitting on the front porch one evening, resting in the pause before another hard day's work, when my mother told my father she was pregnant. He chewed on the fact a while before finally uttering, "I hope it's a boy."

Indeed, he already had three daughters – three mouths to feed. The idea of having another helping hand, though, was an attractive one. But less than a week after I was born, one of those prospective helpers was lost to diphtheria. Verna Irene Gray, the youngest of my three older sisters, died at age four.

As for me, I did my best to contribute. By the time I was old enough to go to school – a one-room schoolhouse in nearby Shady Grove – I was old enough to gather eggs, feed and milk the livestock, and work in the fields.

At Shady Grove – also called Hog Heaven because years ago pigs used to rest under the floor after eating nuts and acorns from the surrounding fields – I sat in an oversized, uncomfortable wooden desk and soaked in my first grammar lessons. The Great Depression – and its offspring, World War II – waited for me.

#

Growing up in southeastern Illinois, I learned how to raise a calf and how, a few years later, to sell a heifer. During one stretch, I stayed up late many nights to nurse a sickly litter of pigs. Later, when a local citizen in the dairy milking business knowingly sold me a self-nursing purebred cow, I recognized for the first time my own vulnerability – and the limits of some people's morality. How could I know that 33 years later, this professed religious citizen would chastise me on how to raise children?

As a young man in the U.S. Army a few years later, I learned those same lessons again, first in the Italian Theater during WW II, and then stateside at Fort Dix, New Jersey. I also found an angel of hope when I met Mary Antoinette Hanaka at a Service Club dance in 1946. We courted for three years before exchanging wedding vows in January 1949. By September, Mary had given birth to our first child: a son, Gordon Thomas Gray, or Tommy, as we would always call him.

Mary, two years my senior, was born on September 4, 1921, in Syracuse, New York, the daughter of recently arrived Polish immigrants. Not long after, her family moved to Camden, New Jersey, where all roads led to the Campbell's Soup factory. Five blocks away was the National Radio Corporation of America (RCA). The tomato harvest, tidy adjoined brick homes with compact but bountiful back gardens, St. Joseph's Catholic Church, the inscrutable mystery that was the Polish language – the forces that shaped her life added up to nothing less than the classic American experience.

After graduating from nursing school in the summer of 1943, she accepted a commission as an Army nurse that August. Basic and advanced training was followed by orders for England, where her stay in buzz-bombed London paled in comparison to her next assignment: joining the field hospital of General George S. Patton's Third Army, which eventually took her to Austria. After suffering serious injuries there, she endured hospitalization and a long series of treatments before finally retiring from active duty a major in January 1947.

Three years later, I took her – and our young son – back to Europe after re-enlisting in June 1950. Our own adventure was about to begin.

#

Roots and routine – the comfort we find in the predictable, in recognizing our own bed, the same ceiling above us each morning – you can't miss what you don't know. You can't miss what you've never tasted. It was only later in my life that I recognized the upheaval my family endured while I chased the phantom of a military career.

West Germany was, at the birth of the Cold War, a fascinating, if tense, place to call home. The Nazi Empire had only just crumbled. But the Soviet Union already menaced, its tentacles propping up satellite governments in nearby East Germany, Poland, and Czechoslovakia. My family lived in Bad Mergentheim while I worked as an instructor at the Adjutant General's School several miles away in Darmstadt. When the school was relocated to the once famous Nazi spa town of Garmisch, still more geography stood between my family and me. Six months went by before I took a new assignment as Sgt Major of the Hanau Military Post near the Fulda Gap, the theoretical launching pad for a Soviet invasion. Finally, I was reunited with my family, albeit on an intermittent basis.

My outfit was constantly on alert, regularly moving in the field so that opposing forces could not guess our actual location. Periodic returns to base amounted to little time with the family because we were typically preoccupied with making preparations for the next excursion. Nevertheless, Mary gave birth to our second child, Mary Catherine (Mary C.), here on June 23, 1951.

After three years on this precipice, I was transferred stateside to the Virginia Military District in Richmond. On March 15, 1956, Mary gave birth to William Stephen Gray. Though I was busy with diplomatic and administrative duties, I saw my family daily, and we spent as much time together as possible. For a brief period, the family almost felt like . . . a family.

But, as so often happens in the military, such bliss was short-lived. In the fall of 1957, I was given orders to proceed to Iceland for a one-year hardship tour of duty on the Arctic Circle. In order to hold onto at least some form of continuity,

Mary and the children stayed in Virginia, refusing for the moment to pull up the few stakes – friends and school – we had.

But after six months, the family joined me for what turned out to be a brief but exciting period of growth and discovery. Mary C. and Tommy learned to read, speak, and sing songs in Icelandic. We all absorbed as much as we could from this highly literate, staunchly independent culture.

The adventure didn't come cheaply. We had to pay our own transportation to Iceland, live off base, and use two separate guard posts on entering and exiting the base. Our food and clothing were purchased on the local market. The mess hall was available to us three times a day, but I didn't subject my family to military meals 24/7. Off base, we ate pork and fish, usually flounder, which was in abundance. And we ate plenty of "beef" – dry but otherwise wholesome and palatable whale meat.

The American presence there was highly regulated, many of the details kept top secret. Absolutely nothing could be done except by agreement – on a weekly basis – between the Icelandic government and the Icelandic Defense Force (IDF), a joint operation between the U.S. Army, Navy, and Air Force. As Chief Clerk, J4 Section, I attended many or most of these meetings and tallied the minutes. I knew the Prime Minister well.

Then it was back to the States, this time Fort Knox, Kentucky. Again, the family lived off base, fifteen miles away in Elizabethtown (E-town). Despite our nomadic lifestyle, Tommy discovered the Cub Scouts and happily embraced a meaningful extracurricular activity. He managed to explore the Cub Scouts and all they had to offer for just twenty-one months. As first sergeant of Headquarters and Headquarters Company, 2nd Medium Tank Battalion, 37th Armor, I – along with my family – was shipped to Kirch Goens, West Germany, as first sergeant of Headquarters and Headquarters Company,

1st Cavalry near Butzback. Once again we were thrown into the highly charged atmosphere of the Fulda Gap.

Finally, at age forty-one, I could see the proverbial writing on the wall. With only a high school diploma, plus a few highly specialized skills valuable to no one but the U.S. Army, and with no military pay raise in over five years, I realized that the so-called payoff for living a life without roots wasn't worth sacrificing my family or our future. We had done our time. Twenty-years' worth. It was time to "get a life."

#

Life, though, rarely lends itself to such tidy transitions. I discovered an interesting wrinkle in the GI educational benefits I thought I had earned: they were awarded on a descending basis, and I had only twenty-seven days still due me. Twenty years for twenty-seven days.

We moved to Collingswood, New Jersey, which was near my wife's hometown. I borrowed money so I could buy some property and go back to school. Now we were in deep debt. Tommy and Mary C., meanwhile, finished high school in one setting, and the traveling road show finally came to an end. For his part, Tommy made several friends, one of which he would reunite with years later on a mountain top in Cambodia during the Viet Nam War.

"Dad," Tommy would say afterward, "when you were in the Army, all we ever ate was beans and hot dogs."

Determined to break free of the military lifestyle, I earned a degree in automotive repairs. For three years, I worked on the White Horse Turnpike leading to Atlantic City. The money was good, and business was booming. But one thing hadn't changed: I was still spending the bulk of my hours on the clock, as opposed to being with my wife and children. By that time, Tommy had already shipped to Viet Nam.

After much deliberation and discussion, we bought a modest farm near Sumner, not far from my family's ancestral home in southeastern Illinois where I had grown up and which I now owned. Free of military red tape, free of the never-ending bustle of commerce, we were determined to live on our own terms, to live by the seasons.

So I traveled to Sumner to make our house livable while the children finished out the school year. I met John and Phyllis and then Raymond Hayes. I worked around the clock, connecting water to the house, installing a bathroom, and planting crops.

I finished in time to watch my daughter graduate from high school back in Collingswood. On June 22, 1969, the family loaded up my big truck and our Ford Galaxy sedan. With Bill in the passenger's seat, I drove in the lead. Only seventeen years old but a skilled driver, Mary C. followed in the Galaxy with her mother.

We stopped around eight o'clock in the evening in Bedford, Indiana, where, after eating and taking a short break, we called ahead to the neighbors.

"Things are in fine shape," they said. "We'll have the lights on in your house before you arrive."

What none of us knew was that a vicious storm was closing in on them from the west and moving rapidly toward the east – and right at us. We found out soon enough, finishing the last leg of the journey in wind and driving rain. By the time we reached the road leading to our property, we found a dizzying trail of downed trees and limbs, a path cut through the middle of them by John Gray and other neighbors who pitched in to help.

They couldn't do much for our house, though. A tornado had touched down on our property, obliterating electric poles and wiring, leaving our house in the dark. We spent the remainder of the night with John and Phyllis, who insisted on feeding us breakfast the next morning. It was my daughter's eighteenth birthday.

My wife had already landed a job at the hospital and went to work almost immediately upon our arrival. Mary C. applied for work at a bicycle factory and for school at the local community college. Bill, due to start his freshman year in high school that fall, went to work with me on restoring the house. It was due for a complete renovation. A full basement had to be dug, and central heating had to be installed. Before we could do any of that, though, we had to clear downed trees and restore electricity.

Weeks later, we would learn of the loss of Michael Seibert, county citizen, to Viet Nam. Our son Tommy had been in that hellhole for more than a year. His letters had grown dark with misgivings and disappointments, and he wrote contemptuously of "lifers." Something was happening.

#

Tommy had signed up for a three-year enlistment in September 1967. In April 1968, after infantry basic training followed by 12 weeks of medical training at Brook Army Medical Center (BAMC), his leave was abruptly cut short by a Western Union telegram delivered to our back door in New Jersey. We were to have him at the Philadelphia airport the next morning for a flight to Viet Nam.

He was given a less-than-honorable discharge during his second tour and arrived home on April 21, 1970. When he left, we knew him as Tommy. When he came home, he was Gordon: his birth name, but never something we had called him.

Prior to April 1970, the shadow of a policeman, sheriff, constable, school counselor, complaining minister or neighbor never appeared on my property. After that date, my family dreaded seeing any vehicle coming down the country road.

It would most likely be a police or sheriff's car carrying our wayward son home with an admonition to the family, "Get the boy under control," or a neighbor or citizen complaining about our son's activities. As a highs school graduate, mentally, morally, and physically sound, Tommy could not get substantial employers to invest money in any worthwhile job training. In the wake of our post-nomadic military life, we could not afford advanced schooling for him.

Before Viet Nam, Tommy was a typical Army brat. Gifted, world-wise, if a bit detached, he also chafed under the command of his vintage WW II father. I never abused him, but I was stern and exacting – two qualities which many in his generation didn't embrace. I administered physical discipline when the situation called for it on the advice of his mother. Alcohol and cigarettes played no part in our family life.

For Tommy, war promised some sort of escape, a rite of passage that would spirit him away from what he felt was an oppressive home. Unfortunately, he replaced tough love with the carnage of war.

In the years to follow, our relationship would become bitter and eventually nonexistent. In the letters he wrote home from Viet Nam, it became obvious that Tommy was identifying me with those in command of his daily activities and life. In fact, I did not read the last two months of letters until my wife presented them to me in preparation of this book. I had become his "lifer," whom he despised.

#

Tommy's downhill slide began on December 28, 1968, when his company commander promised him a promotion from E4 to E5, a choice assignment at the end of twelve months' service in the 1/35/4th Infantry Division, plus 90 days dropped off the end of his three-year commitment to the Army. All he had to do was extend his tour in Viet Nam. Without such action, he would receive a 30-day leave at the end of one year in the unit, but he would have to return to the same unit for the remainder of his enlistment.

Given the level of carnage witnessed by combat medics in the Central Highlands, few would agree to go back into that meat grinder unless something was already missing. I had suggested, through letters my wife was writing, "These promises may not materialize." I knew that promises by a unit commander often did not pan out.

At the end of twelve months, he was still an E4 picking up dead and mutilated bodies. At the end of fourteen months and fifteen days, he was going downhill. Orders were now published sending him to another meat grinder: the 71st Evacuation Hospital.

"Gray was a big-time doper," says Rodger Leffler, who served as an infantryman corporal and then a helicopter mechanic in Viet Nam. "Not that dope wasn't fairly common, but his usage was pretty on the extreme side. They didn't make anything he didn't take. He was very young – about seventeen, I think. He also drank heavily."

Though they never served in the same unit, Rodger says he crossed paths several times with Tommy. Medics, Rodger explains, floated from unit to unit and were hard to track down. He remembers my son as being a bit of a mystery man, although a memorable one at that.

"He was a guitar player," Rodger says. "He'd go off. He thought he was Jimi Hendrix. I remember him having shell cases and using them like a slide. We wound strings for him whenever he broke one. We tried everything, including commo wire."

Rodger can't remember precisely when he served alongside Tommy: perhaps August 1968. He does remember where they served, however: LZ Gene, a landing zone in the Central Highlands just a few clicks from the Cambodian border.

Dennis Cronin, a former high school buddy of Tommy's, remembers the area well. He met Tommy there around the same time period.

"There were about 150 of us," says Dennis, "with three NVA divisions – that's 45,000 – around us. Our job was to monitor them on the ground and then do combat assault."

Patrols were dicey business: a small group of men could easily get cut off from the hill and slaughtered by the numerically superior NVA forces in the valley below.

"Gordy did get a Bronze Star for going out under fire and pulling back someone shot in the neck," Dennis remembers. "He was good. But he was more or less a hippie, which puts you in disfavor with upper management, because they were mostly right-wing idiots."

Adds Dennis, "Everybody called him Gordy. In Viet Nam, it was Doc Ben Bowl." Known for his versions of Hendrix's *Foxy Lady* and *Fire*, Tommy was apparently infamous as well for his tobacco pipe, whose bowl he kept filled with marijuana. He carried it with him wherever he went.

Before the war, he and Dennis had palled around at Collingswood High. They would drive to hippie hangouts in Philadelphia and watch psychedelic bands, including Frank Zappa's bizarre underground group, The Mothers of Invention. Back home, they both worked at gas stations: Dennis at a station down the road, and Tommy at a station and automobile repair shop I ran on the White Horse Turnpike in Oaklyn. Tommy had no interest in this type of work, but he was living at home and navigating between menial jobs. Collingswood High has produced more than its share of tragic and pathetic Viet Nam stories.

"I remember one time we did something wrong," Dennis says, "and the vice principal was chasing us. We hid in the janitor's room, and we jumped into trash cans and put the lids over our heads."

Typical prep hijinks. Their reunion on a hilltop in Cambodia seemed a surreal nightmare.

"When I saw Gordy in Viet Nam, his first question was, 'What's happening at Rittenhouse Square?'" Dennis remembers. Rittenhouse Square was a hip neighborhood in Philly and a long way from the Ia Drang Valley. Both boys – now young men – hardly recognized each other.

Dennis recalls, "I'm looking at this guy, and I say, 'Gray? Gordy?' He's all red with dirt. You don't look the same after combat. And he said, 'Cronin?' And I said, 'Yeah.' And he said, 'John, I know your brother Dennis well.' And I said, 'Gordy, I *am* Dennis.' I wondered about him then."

Dennis insists that my son, though clearly struggling, was coping like everyone else on the hill.

"You have to understand," Dennis says, "there were 500,000 [American soldiers stationed in Viet Nam] that year in 1968. We lost 15,000 killed. Ninety percent of the troops were support, so that means 50,000 were actually fighting, which Gordy was one of them. So of those, we were in a bad, bad situation. People were dying."

To put this in perspective, it has been estimated that at least 80% of the U.S. soldiers in Viet Nam had what they called "a walk in the sun." A more common term used for this duty was "rear echelon motherfuckers" (REMFs) in that their service was relatively safe from enemy contact.

"You could get a pound of marijuana for one dollar," says Dennis. "You could get heroin for a can of peaches. So we were out there, sometimes without food – and ninety percent of us must have smoked herb. Maybe some officers didn't. If you didn't, something would be unusual. We didn't get beer. We were supposed to get two cans rationed a day, but we were at the far outpost, so it got stolen before it got to us.

"Of all the packages sent from home, I got maybe two out of twenty. Sometimes we'd go without water for a day, so for us listening to some music and smoking herb . . . it was no fatal flaw. Gordy – I think he got into meth-amphetamines later, which sometimes they gave to us if we were in a protracted battle. We killed 280 NVA in one three-day period. Just nasty."

A brief side note. Drug usage is not new. In my childhood days during infrequent trips to town to shop at the grocery store, I noticed an old man who would come into the store and purchase a large bottle of vanilla extract. I knew that my mother had a small bottle in the kitchen, and I asked her, "Why does that man always purchase a large bottles of vanilla?" She replied, "He gets a kick out of it."

As part of my research for this book, I attempted to get an idea of how many amphetamines were shipped to Viet Nam. I was told by purchasing agencies that they didn't know and had no way to find out.

With the purchase of many drugs at taxpayer expense and delivered to troops in Viet Nam by their leaders, and with the availability of cheap drugs on the Viet Nam market, is it any wonder that we have developed a large drug problem in America? Has America incurred a well-justified plague?

Adds Dennis, "They would drop us clothes every thirty days, and our clothes would rot off. It was 120 degrees and humid. Then it would rain for three months."

Given the stress of combat, it's not surprising that some men, including my son, did things they would later regret.

"We landed on a hill once," Rodger says, "and there were dead people everywhere. Gray was propping them up and taking pictures, saying he was sending them home to his mother."

#

Things didn't get any easier for Tommy after LZ Gene. He was transferred to the 71st Evac Hosp on June 22, 1969, before eventually finishing out his service in Viet Nam doing ambulance duty for the 51st Med Co (Amb). As Dennis Cronin suggests, his recreational drug use had become habitual. He was treating wounded and dying men, all the while in need of treatment himself.

He bottomed out with an undesirable discharge in April 1970. His early departure from the military was based on three charges: (1) violation of Article 92, ". . . having in his possession 1 ampule, more or less, of DL. Amphetamine"; (2) violation of Article 121, ". . . wrongfully appropriating a tape recorder of about $125.00"; and (3) violation of Article 134, ". . . did at Qui Nhon, Republic of Viet Nam, on or about 28, December 1969, wrongfully have in his possession 9.3 grams, more or less, of marijuana."

Ironic, I guess, that ten months after agreeing to extend his term in Viet Nam, he was busted on drug charges. Ironic, too, considering how endemic the problem had become. To send a Bronze Star Medalist home for minor theft and drug possession – indeed, to cut him off from the support of the military that had helped foster his addiction – proved a bitter pill to swallow. It stigmatized him for life, along with his family. They took his Bronze Star and reduced his rank to Pvt E1 and took many days of unused leave.

#

Back at home, without publicity or fanfare, my son's troubles made their way through the Sumner and Olney grapevines. So had my stance on the war, whose premise I didn't buy. This after the U.S. government had betrayed some 432,000 military retirees in the 1960s, including me, on the retired pay after we had completed our time for retirement. In a federal suit, the Supreme Court told us, "Congress can do what they want to do with the military." Simultaneously, the same government was in the process of taking away our earned life-long health care on attaining age 65 when no longer subject to recall to active duty.

The morning after a lively discussion in our dining room over coffee and cake with my neighbors John and Phyllis, as well as Stanley Seibert, whose son had been shot down in Viet Nam, I realized my indiscretion had cost me the goodwill of some in the community.

After finishing my morning chores, which included feeding my 150 head of cattle, I drove downtown for coffee, a rare event for me. When I arrived, the café was full of farmers and oil field roughnecks, a few of whom I knew. As I entered, the conversation abruptly dried up, and I was nearly trampled as patrons pushed by me on their way to the exit, icy stares replacing normally friendly greetings.

I took a seat at one of the many empty tables. The café's manager advised me, "Willard, it's obvious that your presence was not welcomed by those who departed."

What had happened? The manager knew. It took me a moment to realize that John, a regular early-morning visitor at the café, had evidently shared the gist of our conversation from the night before with his fellow diners. At a gathering in our house the night before, Marianne and Stanley Seibert, my wife, daughter, son, and I were told, "If you don't like America, go to the USSR." To question the war in Sumner, Illinois, was, I was finding out, nothing short of heresy.

Stunned, I meditated for a few minutes before returning home to continue my day's work. Our son was on his way home. And trouble loomed.

#

"Dad," Tommy said as he walked through the kitchen door unannounced a few days later, "you should be proud of me."

"Why?" I asked, surprised by his early homecoming.

"I didn't get syphilis or gonorrhea like all the rest of the boys did," he responded cavalierly.

Without funds, he had hitchhiked home. They had taken all of his pay.

"How are you?" I asked.

We would find out shortly. The days after his return were filled with stories, most of them grisly, of the carnage in Viet Nam. The details were luridly spelled out. The evening dinner table became his pulpit from which he launched into one bloody tale after another. He told repeatedly of being shot down three times, at which the younger children would wince. The dinner table was also the setting for many near rages.

Finally, my daughter took me aside and asked me to put a stop to the nightly horror stories. I could only assume she was speaking for her younger brother as well; Bill was too soft-spoken to make his concerns known. He appeared confused and bewildered by the stories.

Tommy, meanwhile, was drifting. I had given him a few days to recover from the war before looking for work, but he seemed disinterested, unmotivated, and detached. He was clearly relieved to have returned from the war in one piece. He volunteered to help me on the farm and in the repair business I operated, but during the first fence-building operation he vanished after a few minutes at the site. His knowledge or interest in mechanical work was nonexistent and could not be trusted.

But he wasn't ready to move on. He came and went when he pleased, often disappearing for a day or two at a time before returning with newfound friends of questionable character. And, though he professed a desire to help in any way he could, he lacked the discipline and focus to do so.

For my part, I continued to get the cold shoulder from certain neighbors and acquaintances. No doubt they were judging me for my antiwar stance and my son for his undesirable discharge. If we were in a discussion with neighbors about the war, and we made some remark about our Viet Nam problems or burden, a typical response would be, "We have problems, too." I had to remind them that we also had the leaky water faucets and flat tires, but they didn't have the extra burden of constantly having to defend themselves and their families. We had to carry this extra burden all the time.

An auctioneer named Walter, who attempted to publicly belittle me during that time, told me much later, "Willard, you have been vindicated." I politely replied, "Yes, but it has done my family and me no good."

Had the family been able to turn inward, perhaps we could have risen above the local sniping. But communication at home was difficult, and relationships were strained beyond the breaking point.

Sensing this, my daughter suggested we work to get Tommy's discharge status upgraded. The cause seemed worthwhile to me, because I knew that the stigma associated with his undesirable discharge would follow him throughout his life. Moreover, perhaps upgrading his discharge would mute community criticism while restoring my son's honor and sense of self-worth.

With an old mechanical typewriter at our disposal after a hard day's work and school, my daughter and I spent countless hours writing my congressman, senators, and various bureaucrats. Predictably, any reply was strictly perfunctory. Cordial and prompt, yes. Substantive, no. Actual visits to bureaucrats and politicians yielded the same frustrating results. Our congressman at the time was a junior highschool classmate of mine. I had known his father quite well, also. But this was not a bonus for my family.

We didn't get any further with the VA, which framed their position succinctly in one letter: "Gordon cannot even get an aspirin from the Veterans Administration." This came after an earlier communication authorizing him to obtain his GI educational benefits had been rescinded.

The futility of our cause got to Mary C. first. "Dad," she said earnestly, "I can't keep up my work and schooling and write all these letters. And I can't continue defending myself everywhere I go." Understandably, this was very hard for a teenager who had done nothing to incur the wrath of the citizens of the region.

But no one experienced it more acutely than Tommy, whose resume was worthless. Everywhere he went to apply for work, prospective employers would request a copy of his separation papers, which came complete with a Separation Program Number (SPN) code spelling out the terms of his discharge. (During the Ford and Carter administrations, the SPN code would be abandoned, only to resurface later.)

Our struggle became public fodder when it was trotted out in the letters to the editor section of the local paper. Philosophically the editor understood the family situation, but most of his staff did not. They wrote and signed a disparaging public letter directed at me.

The local veteran's commission office secretary, a woman named Mary, publicly admonished me in a 900-word letter to the editor on the need to know how to raise my children, and of the fine conduct of my son while he was in their office seeking help to obtain educational benefits – though those efforts were to no avail. Within months, her son was to die in a self-induced drug experiment.

Prior to this public outburst directed at me, she had admonished Marianne Seibert in a private letter on her efforts to clarify the loss of her son.

General James S. Sutherland, Corp Commander, admonished me about the number of KIAs and thousands of wounded who were processed through the 71st Evac Hosp while my son was assigned there. He went on to tell me, "Your children grow up just the way you raised them."

As I stopped to thank a woman named Evelyn for a favor she had done for my wife the day before, she responded with a similar unhelpful comment: "Willard, I don't know why you blame the Army for all your problems. *You* raised your children, not the Army."

Pushed beyond my breaking point, I responded, "Damn you, Evelyn, I paid your salary as a public school teacher, I'm paying you in retirement leaning against that post, and I paid you for a self-nursing heifer back in the 1930s. I'd have hoped you would have changed by now." Her only children, twin daughters, are married to men who avoided the draft by joining the National Guard.

#

I decided to shift tactics.

On a Sunday afternoon in the spring of 1972, I approached the pastor at a local church which I had attended in my childhood. I was still considered a member of the church. I presented him with several documents on the war and asked if I might address the congregation regarding a "human needs issue." I did not ask for any money, or for any specific time. The pastor seemed very open to the idea and took the manila envelope, promising to look over the documents inside and discuss them with me the following week.

When I returned the next Sunday, I found the church empty, and the parsonage occupants would not respond to a knock. Disappointed, I visited an old family friend nearby who, upon hearing my story, said, "Now I know what this morning's sermon was about!"

Eager to discover that I had perhaps struck a chord with the pastor, we both hurriedly returned to the church, where we found him exiting with the envelope I had given him the week before.

"Good!" I exclaimed as I got out of my car. "What's the word?"

"After the services this morning," he said, "they held a special deacons' meeting and decreed that you are not welcome in this church."

Apparently, he had not mentioned me by name in his sermon, but had managed to arouse the curiosity – and indignation – of several in the congregation. Upon finding out the source of the sermon, the church deacons met and wasted little time in officially banning me from the church.

I had been excommunicated. Honest debate on the war, I was finding out, was not just unpatriotic. It was heretical.

My friend was as shocked as I was. He had been a life-long member and deacon of the church, but at the time was an honorary deacon. He'd picked up his hat and headed home after the service, and had not known of the special deacons' meeting.

Two weeks later, my childhood home, which I was planning to rent out, was vandalized. Built in the 1860s, it had been where my mother, her sister, and her brothers – like my siblings and I – had been born. Now it was in pieces. Vandals had smashed the windows, shredded the plaster, and scrawled graffiti inside and out. On the front of the house at the second-story level, three-foot-high letters in all caps – and visible from the highway – read, FUCK YOU.

Friends advised me not to work the fields by my ancestral home any longer. Neighbors near the trashed house pleaded with me to remove the graffiti. I refused. "I think it represents the community well," I said.

What a memorial that still stands to this day in my name and in the community of my childhood!

#

As the months went by, our ostracism from the community grew more palpable. Some folks did business with me. And several troubled souls with a brother or son or father in Viet

Nam sought me out for advice and assistance. But most avoided my family and me like the plague. To be seen with us was to be seen with the enemy.

A visit to the local VFW (Veterans of Foreign Wars) building yielded more of the same. "I haven't got time to mess with you," growled the portly sergeant at arms, a recently retired Air Force sergeant with a beer belly. I didn't recognize the man, but he obviously knew me. My apparent lack of patriotism had preceded me.

Flabbergasted but undeterred, I set out for the American Legion building. As I entered, two men asked pleasantly, "How can we help you?" Though I did not know them, they knew me through their employment with the Norris Electric Company, formerly Rural Electrification Association (REA), that serviced the entire region. They would stop and visit or communicate regularly with my elderly father and mother while on their many line maintenance missions over the years that I had been in the service. My mother had shared many of my service experiences with them. They understood the family.

"I want to see someone in the Legion concerning help or assistance for my son," I told them.

"You couldn't have picked a better time," said one of the men. "They are installing new officers tonight, and the state commander will be here."

Finally, a glimmer of hope. I was on Cloud Nine when I headed for home to do the chores and eat supper. Perhaps someone there would talk to me. Perhaps they would grant me a sympathetic audience.

"Hell," I muttered to myself as I approached the American Legion building later that night, "I'm going to be home here." Several hometown legionnaires, classmates, and family members were standing outside the entrance. But as I approached, those who saw me, including the State Commander, turned their backs to me. It went downhill from there. One life-long legionnaire who had been a classmate offered to run interference for me, but this turned out to be a bad idea.

Taking a seat in the back of the hall, I sat through a pitiful prayer expressed by the Legion chaplain – who had been a junior classmate of mine and a post WW II veteran – the induction of new officers, and even the taking up of a collection for an American officer, William "Rusty" Calley, on trial for the massacre at My Lai.

As the night wore on, the members drank to excess, and it became exceedingly clear that I would not be granted an audience, sober or otherwise. My friend Bill also realized that I would not be seen or heard by any of the local officers or the state commander. My community, and the state Legion commander, were more interested in helping an officer who had presided over a massacre of civilians in a drainage ditch in Viet Nam than in helping one of their own sons shake off the stigma of an undesirable discharge.

After an hour of this, I departed for home.

At a restaurant some years later, I ran into Ernie, one of the legionnaires who had been my classmate. He and his wife joined me, and paid for my lunch. He said, "Willard, I want to apologize for my past actions to you." I told him he was fifteen years too late.

#

While struggling to upgrade Tommy's discharge status, we had become good friends with Stanley and Marianne Seibert, whose only son had been killed in a helicopter crash in Viet Nam. The Seiberts had fought their battle alone, with help and support only from my family. Exasperated, Marianne finally came up with the excellent idea of convening a meeting with local ministers. Stanley and I would moderate a meeting in which community support and outreach would be discussed.

The meeting was originally planned with the Richland County Ministerial Association, but that never got off the ground. Instead, it was held at the First Christian Church in Bridgeport, Lawrence County. More than one hundred people in cleric garb showed up for the meeting. Stanley and I fielded questions and tried to facilitate thoughtful discussion. Were there resources available to those of us whose lives had been damaged by the war? What could the community do to support local families devastated by Viet Nam?

As the discussion wound down, it became clear that we had caused plenty of tension but settled very little. Two ministers, as if on cue, stood up just before the meeting broke up and said, "You two should be taken out and shot!"

The meeting was over, and no apologies were offered. We were on our own.

During three full years of outreaches, I had visited or had appointments with a dozen attorneys within a 100-mile radius. The apologetic, and often arrogant, suggestion was, "Go see your son's commanding officer."

There was no way for me to find him, and in any event I knew that he could not change the discharge. One lawyer's response was essentially, "Get the hell out of here. I get my clients from citizens who respect the government."

Just when we thought we had exhausted all resources, I found a sponsor in the American Civil Liberties Union. After becoming a member, I explained the issue at hand, and the ACLU quickly appointed an attorney to represent Tommy. Taking the case to Washington, DC, the ACLU and its attorney pulled off in a few weeks what bureaucrats and legislators could not accomplish in three agonizing years: Tommy's discharge was upgraded to general. With that, he could obtain most VA benefits.

Because the court had deemed him competent, I was not able to speak in Tommy's defense. But Mary C. and I had done all the work and set the stage for his discharge upgrade.

"Dad," Tommy said afterward, "the upgrading would not have come about had it not been for the vast number of letters you wrote. They had a stack of correspondence in front of them that was a foot high."

#

Of course, restoring Tommy's honor on paper and winning back the understanding of the local community were two different things. While Mary C. and I had been toiling on Tommy's behalf, so too had his mother, albeit on a different track. Mary had helped land him a job at the local hospital, and the boy, thanks to his newfound employment as an orderly, had rediscovered the passion and self-esteem that hard work yields.

The community's self-anointed patriots and Christians, meanwhile, were in an uproar. A group of them from my childhood church organized and dispatched an emissary of two church members requesting that the county board fire my wife from the county hospital, ostensibly for helping her son find work. Their announced reason was, "To get back at the Grays in a financial way." Most of them knew that my wife was a veteran, but few knew that she had served with General George S. Patton's Third Army Field Hospital as a captain nurse in France, Germany, and Austria. Prior to that, she had been buzz-bombed in England. Mary had not sought nor gained employment by telling the hospital that she was a veteran. She had obtained employment based on her skills and credentials.

The family was now in tatters. Tommy was still viewed with disdain. His brother was guilty by association. Mary C. had left for school, no longer willing to live with the tension at home. I was a pariah, a veritable thorn in the community's side. And my wife, apparently, was guilty in the community's eyes, too.

We could handle indifference and even hostility. But the community's collective animosity had fueled a witch-hunt. And we were the heretics.

Mary sent the county board and hospital a three-page letter, doing her best to defend herself. In the end, when she had eventually had enough, she simply pulled out and took a job at the local elderly care center. The county bureaucrats, showing the same level of compassion toward her as they had shown toward our son, remained officially aloof throughout.

I was approached, separately, by two citizens and advised: "Take a gun up there and shoot the sons-of-bitches."

#

As the community ramped up its outrage against us, Tommy's relationship with the family vacillated and slowly disintegrated. He even tried to cause a rift between my wife and I. The tension that had been smoldering between us since Viet Nam finally exploded in flames on Christmas Eve, 1984.

Hoping to bring the family together and heal the wounds that had already divided us, my wife had organized a family dinner at our home. Mary C. was away at school, but both boys would be attending. Tommy, for his part, had broken the cycle of drug abuse and, though still struggling with alcohol, was living drug free. He was a graduate of Eastern Illinois University, a husband, and a father. He had, for the time being, found his way back from the abyss. Could our relationship do the same?

After having made arrangements to take Christmas Eve off from work, Mary had spent several days cleaning and decorating our home. She had just finished preparations when Bill, newly married, arrived with his wife Angie. We had scheduled the evening around Angie, who was the head of a department in a large hospital. Her busy schedule left little room for error.

As we waited for Tommy, seconds turned to hours, and Mary's heroic efforts – not to mention the festive mood of the evening – were wasted. So, too, the sumptuous feast she had prepared.

Finally, Bill and Angie had to leave.

Clearly drunk and in a foul mood, Tommy showed up moments later with his wife Linda, daughter Stephanie, and son Tim in tow. Mary and Linda went into damage control as they did their best to salvage the evening, resetting the table and warming up the dinner.

We had barely sat down to eat when Tommy, suffering alcohol's combative fog, went into a rage and began berating me. In an attempt to defuse the situation, I retired to the living room. Tommy followed, still seething in anger and intent on a physical confrontation. I defended myself and sent him to the floor with a blow to the head. Prior to that time, I had never hit or slapped Tommy on the head. But at this encounter, had his head landed two inches farther back, it would have contacted the fireplace hearth. My wife would have had a dead son and a husband bound for prison.

In a violent flash, our relationship had ended. I told him to leave, and as he did so, I hugged my granddaughter Stephanie. "Your father has a problem," I said, not understanding the full implication of what I had uttered. Bill would tell me seventeen years later that my words were still echoing in the poor girl's mind.

For that evening's dinner, I had invited a neighbor's son, who was the county's most decorated Navy veteran. Harold would later tell his uncle, "I don't know why Willard took the abuse and vile from his son as long as he did. I never saw a fight like it."

#

It still hangs in our living room today. It meant something to her years ago, even when it was on its way to the landfill. It is an early 19th-century imprint of cattle grazing in a meadow etched onto a 24x30-inch glass pane. A tiny brook meanders by the cows, and trees glisten in the background.

Mary C. noticed it, then incased in a discarded kitchen door in a pile of rubbish at the Sumner farmhouse in the summer of 1969, a few days after we arrived from New Jersey. We were restoring our new home, and she had found a gem hidden in the trash heap created by the prior owner. It is nothing short of a miracle that the pane had not been broken. She asked me, "Dad, can I have that glass in that old door?" A teenager concerned with a glass pane in a sturdy old door. How, I wondered, would little Mary remove this delicate object without damage? Years later, she would carefully transport it to New Jersey, where she would install it in a fancy frame with a professional backing and then return it to us, a fitting memento from our beloved daughter.

Mary Catherine Gray had been interested in art since the age of twelve, when she took a correspondence course focusing on the work of Norman Rockwell. By the time we arrived at Sumner, she had an artist's keen eye. She had enrolled at the local community college, the first step on her way to a liberal arts degree.

While she drank from the beauty of art, the finite world raged around her, her country at war and Viet Nam, its purported enemy, in jellied flames. Friends and neighbors tried to drag her into the war's ugly depths, exhorting Americans to kill communists for Christ.

"Dad, what's wrong with us?" she asked as our family became cut off from the community around us.

As she battled to restore her brother's honor, she got nothing but grief for her efforts: disdain from some of her peers and bellicose ingratitude from her brother who, while drunk at one party, went after his sister in a rage. Luckily, friends defended her.

When it became evident she was fighting a war she couldn't win, Mary C. got out of our home area. Art was her escape. After graduating from high school, she attended Rutgers University, where she earned a master's degree in art as a straight-A student and became a co-founder and copy editor of Rutgers' Art Review in 1980, Volume 1. From there, she went on to work as a week-end escort at the New York Metropolitan Museum of Fine Arts before eventually landing lucrative jobs at Merrill Lynch and then at First Boston of New York.

She returned and called home often, but never once asked to see her brother.

"Dad," she said during one of her visits, "I will never have children."

"Why?" I asked.

"Because I couldn't put a child through the trauma that we have had to endure."

Then tragedy struck. In October 1993, A two-year bout with a non-malignant brain tumor cut short the life of this beautiful, talented young woman. Before dying, she begged us not to tell Tommy of her terminal illness and pending death. She couldn't face the brother for whom she had lobbied so hard in her youth. A vast wellspring of empathy had given way to fear and bitterness.

#

Like Mary C., my youngest son struggled to escape the dark cloud of his brother's experiences in Viet Nam. Bill was a teenager by the time Tommy returned from the war, and classmates and others in the community made him pay for Tommy's post-war problems and for my outspoken stance against the war. As I would find out years later from two or more of his peers, Bill at some point stopped telling anyone he had a brother. It was easier just to keep mum.

After graduating from high school, he attended the local community college where he received a degree in automotive mechanics. He further honed his skills at a trade school and graduated with honors as a diesel mechanic.

Beneath the success lay potential trouble. We saw the first signs when he disappeared from home for a few months after completing high school with no explanation. Shortly after returning, he got married and started up his own repair business, the latter thanks to a financial jumpstart from his mother and me. But the business – and the marriage – failed. He moved on, slowly earning a reputation as one of the best diesel mechanics in the region.

But it didn't take long for things to fall apart. When the smoke had cleared, his trucking and repair business (also funded by us) had been shut down by the IRS. On the home front, he was now thrice divorced. And he was, like his brother, estranged from the family.

Bill has since found religion in a questionable way. The irony is not lost on me, considering our family's many run-ins with religious zealots in our community after the war.

#

What happened in Viet Nam? What happened to my son? When he left home, we called him "Tommy." An informal version of his middle name, true, but the name by which his family had known him all his life. He came home as "Gordon" – a drug abuser, a teller of grim stories, a disconnected boy none of us knew. What happened between April 14, 1968, his first day in Viet Nam, and April 21, 1970, the day he walked unannounced through our kitchen door?

We will never reconcile. The hurt runs too deep. But I reserve most of my anger for the community, society, and the

Willard D. Gray

U.S. government that drove a wedge between us. This is still my home. It always has been, and it always will be. Yet it has taken the best from me: my son, my hope, and family.

During a lengthy discussion in a restaurant relating to world and personal problems, I made the remark, "They took our hearts." My friend Steve Dickirson responded, "Willard, they also took your soul."

My wife and I don't have a family anymore.

Afterword

I wish my family's story was unique. I wish the Rigdon family and the Cantrell family and the others profiled in this book were the deviation, not the norm.

But the simple fact is this: the Viet Nam War isn't over. Not by a long shot. The men who fought and survived it are still trying to find peace. Their families and loved ones, no strangers to emotional combat, are in the trenches with them.

Living within two miles of me here in southeastern Illinois is one Anna Atkins, an 85-year-old widow whose youngest son, Jack, is serving a life sentence in Tennessee for killing his second wife ten years ago. Until poor health forced her to move into a retirement home last year, Anna maintained a neat and tidy home. I visited her there on more than one occasion, listening as she tried to come to grips with how her son, the valedictorian in his graduating class, returned from Viet Nam a loose cannon ready to rain shells down on his former hometown.

What happened to Jack, or Jackie as those close to him knew him? The answer, as so often seems to be the case when it comes to Viet Nam, is muddled.

"He was in the killing fields," says Bill Blacker, a neighbor who employed Anna for several years at his store and who entrusted the care of his lawn to Jackie before Viet Nam. "He came back tough, drank heavy, fought – he was muscled up and tough. One of the toughest guys I've ever seen. When he came back, he wasn't afraid of nothing – probably still isn't. I've never seen a person change as much as Jackie."

Jackie served with the Navy on a gunboat in the Mekong Delta in the late '60s, returning with the following decorations: National Defense Service Medal, Viet Nam Campaign Medal, Viet Nam Service Medal, Navy Unit Commendation Ribbon, and Combat Action Ribbon. He saw grisly combat, and locals can recount more than a few horror stories attributed to his foray in Viet Nam, no doubt some of them apocryphal.

Harold Fiscus, Jackie's second cousin, served in the same region, in the same time period, and in a similar capacity, even crossing paths a few times with Jackie.

"We seen each other float by," says Harold, who returned from Viet Nam in 1968 with a Purple Heart and countless pieces of shrapnel still lodged in his body. "He was on another boat, and he was just floating up and down. Twice we actually hooked up. Things would happen. One time we watched a village get mortared. That was interesting. We sat up on my boat and watched from the top. I'd say they were being shelled by the enemy, but I really don't know. It looked like the Fourth of July. There you are halfway around the world, sitting next to someone you know and watching a town getting the shit beat out of it."

Did Harold witness Jackie's transformation?

"Actually," Harold says with a laugh, "he was a nincompoop growing up. He cut off my neighbor's nose with a hoe."

According to Harold, Jackie was the classic bully, one who only respected those who could defend themselves.

"In my opinion, Viet Nam didn't change him," he says. "It just brought out what was already there. He picked his battles. When we was five or six, he was always punching somebody. I finally knocked the shit out of him, and he went home crying to his parents."

As a kid, Jackie, after being given a horse, used to race trains. As a young man back from war, he gambled, threatened more than one person with a gun, abused both his wives, and was eventually charged with murdering his second wife.

Did Viet Nam make him or simply accentuate the darker side of his soul? The question doesn't matter much to his remaining family, his mother and older brother, both of whom feel safer with him behind bars. Anna still cherishes the memories of the boy she knew. And she fears the monster he became.

#

It is likely that most of us, whether we live in rural Illinois or New York City, have a neighbor whose life was changed forever by Viet Nam. In the age of the Internet, our community is widening, and so it is easy to find others who, just a few keyboard strokes away, still suffer the war's legacy. We find their posts on bulletin boards, their agony immortalized in cyberspace. One such person is Robert McKenzie, who served ten months with the Army's 187th Assault Helicopter Company in Viet Nam in 1970.

Robert was a gunner until a few days after Christmas, when a female VIP flying alongside him fussed over how young he looked. He was demoted to the rear and, awash in his own frustration, eventually turned to heroin, then ubiquitous in Viet Nam.

It didn't take long for him to get hooked. When he realized he was a danger to his fellow soldiers, he tried to enroll in the amnesty program then being offered to drug users in the military. But his CO wasn't interested and made life difficult for the young soldier. A series of misunderstandings and bureaucratic misfires further complicated things.

When the dust finally settled, Robert was given a Chapter 10 discharge, *released for the benefit of the service as unable to adjust.* His discharge papers – the ones prospective employees and others could view – didn't show his service in Viet Nam or his awards and commendations. He had been permanently stigmatized by an impersonal bureaucracy.

Over the years, he has sought help from various officials to upgrade his discharge status. But to no avail.

"All of them seem eager at first and say my chances are good," he points out. "All of them run into something in the process and drop me without notice or comment. I know the chances of an upgrade and/or benefits are nil without [a service organization] to represent you. I don't know which way to turn. Even Social Security refuses to help, even though I've been diagnosed with PTSD and related side effects from the symptoms of PTSD and Agent Orange. They say I have to expend all possibilities of appeal with the VA first. It's a catch 22."

#

Who were we? Who did we want to become? And at what price?

Lines were drawn in the sand that still exist today. Are you an apologist or a detractor? A devout patriot or disillusioned idealist? Is it possible to love your country without loving its politics? To embrace its people without supporting the butchery?

The war in Viet Nam tore at the very fabric of our country. It pitted patriots against dissenters, hawks against doves, the status quo against uncertainty. The same failed national policy that put our youth in harm's way cast a shadow at home. The national conscience expanded and contracted and expanded again – a gut-wrenching ordeal that claimed as many victims as the war itself – as body bags arrived in Cawood, Kentucky; Acampo, California; and Sumner, Illinois.

When will the chapter on Viet Nam finally close? When will those who were maimed, scarred, or ostracized finally know redemption? What can we do to give them and their misfortunes the attention they deserve?

For those with less-than-honorable and dishonorable discharges, unfortunate victims from a lost cause that they did not create, a full and complete amnesty by the Congress and president could ameliorate a continuing cancer. Any amnesty action should look upon the dishonorable discharges with leniency. Board members should not consist of personnel who may have sat in judgment of troops of that era or have stigmatized the same youth.

But if we are to find some measure of healing, it will ultimately have to come from the family, our country's most priceless commodity. A wife will forgive the sometimes-volatile husband who sleeps beside her. A father will forgive his prodigal son. A soldier will forgive the war that robbed him of his convictions. And then, maybe, hope will take root and grow, salving the wounds that used to hobble us, engulfing the credibility gap that used to divide us.

When all is said and done, perhaps the best thing any of us can offer Viet Nam veterans and their families is to simply listen to their stories.

* End *